T0271227

Conversations with Colum McCann

Literary Conversations Series
Monika Gehlawat
General Editor

Conversations with Colum McCann

Edited by
Earl G. Ingersoll and Mary C. Ingersoll

University Press of Mississippi / Jackson

www.upress.state.ms.us

The University Press of Mississippi is a member of
the Association of American University Presses.

Copyright © 2017 by University Press of Mississippi
All rights reserved
Manufactured in the United States of America

First printing 2017

∞

Library of Congress Cataloging-in-Publication Data

Names: Ingersoll, Earl G., 1938– editor. | Ingersoll, Mary C., editor.
Title: Conversations with Colum McCann / edited by Earl G. Ingersoll, Mary C. Ingersoll.
Description: Jackson, Misssissippi : University Press of Mississippi, 2017. |
    Series: Literary conversations series | Includes bibliographical references and index. |
    Identifiers: LCCN 2017003607 (print) | LCCN 2017021173 (ebook) | ISBN
    9781496812957 (epub single) | ISBN 9781496812964 (epub institutional) |
    ISBN 9781496812971 (pdf single) | ISBN 9781496812988 (pdf institutional)
    | ISBN 9781496812940 (hardback)
Subjects: LCSH: McCann, Colum, 1965-—Interviews. | Authors, American—20th
    century—Interviews. | Fiction—Authorship. | Influence (Literary,
    artistic, etc.) | Literature and society. | BISAC: BIOGRAPHY &
    AUTOBIOGRAPHY / Literary. | LITERARY CRITICISM / European / English,
    Irish, Scottish, Welsh. | LITERARY CRITICISM / American / General.
Classification: LCC PR6063.C335 (ebook) | LCC PR6063.C335 Z567 2017 (print) |
    DDC 823/.914—dc23
LC record available at https://lccn.loc.gov/2017003607

British Library Cataloging-in-Publication Data available

Books by Colum McCann

Fishing the Sloe-Black River: Stories. London: Phoenix House, 1994; New York: Metropolitan Books, 1996.

Songdogs: A Novel. London: Phoenix House, 1995; New York: Metropolitan Books, 1995.

This Side of Brightness: A Novel. London: Phoenix House, 1998; New York: Metropolitan Books, 1998.

Everything in This Country Must: A Novella and Two Stories. New York: Metropolitan Books, 2000; London: Phoenix House, 2000.

Dancer. New York: Metropolitan Books, 2003; London: Weidenfeld & Nicholson, 2003.

Zoli: A Novel. London: Weidenfeld & Nicholson, 2006; New York: Random House, 2007.

Let the Great World Spin: A Novel. New York: Random House, 2009; London: Bloomsbury, 2009.

TransAtlantic: A Novel. New York: Random House, 2013; London: Bloomsbury, 2013.

Thirteen Ways of Looking: A Novella and Two Stories. London: Bloomsbury, 2015; New York: Random House, 2015.

Contents

Introduction

Colum McCann is that rare author who does not resist interviews. Unlike some who are suspicious of, if not overtly antagonistic toward this mode of engagement, McCann seems to enjoy being interviewed, relishing the opportunity to talk about his work, his method of writing, the state of fiction today, and an array of other topics. Indeed, at least once, he actually requested an interview; no surprise since from the beginning he has been aware that interviews bring readers to his fiction.

McCann's willingness to be interviewed says a great deal about his approach to writing and his sense of himself as a writer. This is no ivory tower recluse from the world, directing his fiction to a select few. His later novels are living proof that it is possible for authors to write serious fiction, and still find themselves on the *New York Times* bestsellers list.

In more than one of these conversations, McCann responds to the standard interview question of how he began to write. His response may surprise some because he points to his beginnings as a writer of not fiction but journalism, a legacy of his father's profession. When he later decided to write fiction, it was not because he considered journalism inferior but because he was aware his father, Sean McCann, regretted that among the two dozen or more books he had published none were fiction. From his travels in the US, McCann's father brought back the books of contemporary American writers such as Jack Kerouac, Lawrence Ferlinghetti, and Richard Brautigan for the teenaged Colum to read. Among them, Kerouac's *On the Road* was probably the most influential. After spending months in the United States trying to write and looking at the same sheet of paper in his typewriter, McCann decided that he was not writing because he had nothing to write about. The twenty-something Colum impulsively followed Jack "on the road." Being a young man of less ample means—specifically, an automobile—McCann rode a bicycle across the country, supporting himself with odd jobs and seldom staying more than a few days in one place. Quickly he discovered that everyone had a story to tell, and since these storytellers knew that Colum would be moving on down the road, they told him stories they might not have shared with family and friends. Eventually he concluded that storytelling is one of the most essentially democratic activities we can practice.

Of course, as an Irishman, McCann grew up in a culture in which men told stories in the public house, their home away from the home that was the bailiwick of Herself, who was responsible for rearing the children. Indeed, it has been argued that the Irish have probably published more fiction per capita than most other nationalities because for centuries their colonial status in the Empire reduced all of the women and most of the men to the condition of little or no upward mobility. As a result, writing poetry and fiction became one of the few legitimate outlets for the energy which had so few other means of expression.

As readers move through the collection, they will note that the conversations appear in the order they were conducted and as a result often focus upon McCann's most recent book. This chronological arrangement should enhance the reader's sense of McCann's development as a writer—what changes in his interests as well as what remains constant. In the early interviews, the still relatively unknown but increasingly well-respected McCann responded to the same interviewer—Robert Birnbaum or Declan Meade—more than once, not only because both perceptively gauged Colum's talent and accomplishments but also because there were few others interested in interviewing an Irish writer who gravitated toward being acknowledged as an American writer, eventually becoming an American citizen as well. He was writing less about Ireland and more about the United States, most tellingly in *This Side of Brightness,* a novel about interracial marriage a century ago as well as the homeless living in the New York subway tunnels in the present. From the beginning of his confrontation with America and with African American experience, McCann moved further into otherness with his novel *Dancer* (2003) and the world of Russian ballet superstar Rudolf Nureyev, like McCann an émigré, but distinguished by his ethnicity and the art of dance of which McCann confessed to know little. From that other world, McCann moved to the world of Slovakian Gypsy singer/poet Zoli, a world to which some of his readers, especially in the US were more reluctant to follow him because of their ethnic bias. That reaction in large part pushed McCann back to what had become his new home, New York, and the writing of his arguably most powerful and certainly most critically acclaimed novel, *Let the Great World Spin* (2009).

All these novels and his other fiction such as *TransAtlantic* and the recent *Thirteen Ways of Looking* are ample testimony to McCann's accomplishment in confronting the Other. Now a Distinguished Professor of Creative Writing in Hunter College's renowned Master of Fine Arts program, McCann is still sharing his approach to writing, telling students not to write about what they think they know, often themselves, but what they don't know, the Other.

McCann is in one sense the heir to traditional writers who believed that reading literature is valuable as a means of developing what he calls "radical empathy," the capacity to "walk in another's moccasins for a moon." That impulse toward cultivating empathy has led him to co-found and direct a project called Narrative 4, bringing together young people from diverse ethnic and religious backgrounds to participate in storytelling. The object is not simply to share stories but to encourage participants to invest in another's experience by retelling the stories of others as though those stories were their own. The project's guiding principle is that when a story is retold the re-teller takes on the gender or ethnicity that had once been Other to the re-teller.

As McCann will say more than once in the conversations, he lives in New York because it is the "city of elsewhere," still a mecca for immigrants, who have always been our nation's greatest natural resource, even though some have chosen to demonize these "others." He believes the writer needs to "emigrate," a trope he shapes as a wounding, a break with the Known, by which the writer seeks not to irrigate nostalgia for a lost Homeland but to grow through the encounter with Otherness. It is yet another expression of his sense of the writer as one who embraces the city's grittiness and squalor, a "darkness" within which we come to the sense of recovery and hope he powerfully represents in his 9/11 novel, *Let the Great World Spin.*

The selections in the second half of the collection reveal a Colum McCann enjoying the celebrity and acclaim that he could never have dreamed of as that young man "on the road." (Incidentally, he tells his interviewer and friend John Cusatis that he learned to show up for church on Sundays, especially in the South, because the sermon was often followed by Sunday dinner.) More often than not, these later conversations are performed before a live audience, allowing McCann to enjoy the encounter with his readers. We see in such encounters a rare openness in this author, as in his revelation, for example, of his response to a book's finally being in hand.

The work cycle begins for him with months, even years of research. This preparation for writing entails research conducted in the 42nd Street New York Public Library but also the experience of living in the subway tunnels of Manhattan; the world of ballet theaters and bathhouses Nureyev knew; the Roma, or "Gypsy," communities of Central Europe; the police departments of Manhattan as well as interviews with women who had been "on the stroll" in the seventies. That stage is followed by the months and years of writing and revising, occasionally trashing whole months of drafting to begin again—until finally the manuscript feels ready for publication.

But for McCann, as he reveals in the conversation, there are the months afterward when he awakens from nightmares of never being able to write another book. And not just *another* book but the next book in which he will set the bar higher and like an athlete compete with himself to do more than merely write the same novel again with different costumes and scenery. To stay alive creatively he must face ever greater challenges and follow the lead of his countryman W.B. Yeats in pursuing "The Fascination of What's Difficult." In this regard, he follows in the tradition of early modernists such as James Joyce and Virginia Woolf who set themselves increasingly challenging goals so that each new work aspires to transcend the accomplishments of its predecessors.

McCann's surprisingly candid expression of his fear of being unable to write his next novel parallels his confession to Danish interviewer Synne Rifbjerg that the publication of a new book brings a sense of failure. From a more calculating author, these revelations might sound like false modesty and a plea for compensatory praise. In McCann's case, however, it reveals the author's ambition to pursue ever greater accomplishments in his writing career.

This author's customary openness in these conversations makes it increasingly difficult to speak of him as "McCann" rather than "Colum." Many of the "stories" he shares with audiences with great abandon and no embarrassment are jokes he tells at his own expense, reflecting his self-assurance and risk being open with others. At one point he tells Rifbjerg he feels as though he is in a pub telling stories—though the museum where conversation took place was not serving. A happy raconteur, he professes his awareness that some in the audience may have heard, or even read the story he is telling.

In these later conversations, readers will find evidence that McCann is not only a best-selling author but also a literary master whose writing has increasingly become the subject of books and doctoral dissertations. A case in point is Cécile Maudet's pair of interviews, presumably drawn from the research for her dissertation and replete with footnotes for the reader's edification. Another case is the well-informed conversation with John Cusatis, whose book *Understanding Colum McCann* (2011) has joined several collections of essays by various hands, discussing McCann's fiction and testifying to his high regard in the academic world. Because these later conversations tend to be long, we have included a number of shorter pieces such as Alec Michod's delightful peripatetic interview, conducted on the sidewalks of Manhattan.

The editing of conversations reprinted here has generally been cosmetic or the result of an effort to achieve coherence in the collection by developing a "house style." For example, unlike some other formats for conversations using different fonts or initials to identify the interviewer and the interviewee, the format for this collection is last names in bold font. In the transcriptions of videotaped conversations, an effort has been made to find a middle ground between an obsessive attempt to supply a print equivalent of every syllable the author voiced, on the one hand, and something resembling chunks of an essay, which has lost its "conversational" tone, on the other. The John Kelly conversation especially illustrates that challenge: the videotape presents the elated author who, having successfully negotiated his way around dust clouds produced by volcanic eruptions in Iceland, was home again with the people of his native Ireland, celebrating the success of *Let the Great World Spin,* which would go on to win the National Book Award. Public interviews often have special challenges inherent in performing for an audience expecting to be not only edified by the writer's comments about writing methods and individual works but also entertained. The result can be competition for the airwaves, resulting in an interviewee's talking fast to avoid being interrupted or an interviewer's questions turning into extended statements. In transcribing a videotaped conversation, it occasionally becomes necessary to puzzle out what is actually being said when laughter covers the interviewee's words and to prune an interviewer's comments that seem irrelevant to the writer's writing.

Although these conversations don't focus explicitly on the details of his personal life, they comprise a kind of "biography" of Colum McCann the writer. They offer a portrait of the writer's energy and passion for his art, his unrestrained sense of humor, and his commitment to a clear-eyed observation of the darkness of our world and, what's more, an even greater commitment to diversity, otherness, an indomitable hope and a belief in the goodness of life.

EGI
MCI

Chronology

1994   *Fishing the Sloe-Black River* appears in England to very good reviews. Dermot Bolger publishes CM's story, "Through the Field," in his contemporary Irish fiction collection, *The Picador Book of Contemporary Irish Fiction.*

1995   Bolger republishes *The Picador Book of Contemporary Irish Fiction* in America as *The Vintage Book of Contemporary Irish Fiction,* and positions "Through the Field" last, implying that Irish fiction is going global.[1] The McCanns settle in New York City. CM's first novel, *Songdogs,* appears in the United States and receives the nomination for the International IMPAC Dublin Literary Award.

1996   *Fishing the Sloe-Black River* appears in the United States.

1997   The short story "As Kingfishers Catch Fire" receives a Pushcart Prize.

1998   *This Side of Brightness* appears in the United States, and becomes CM's first international best seller.

2000   *Everything in This Country Must,* CM's novella and two short stories set in Northern Ireland, appear. In her *New York Review of Books* review, Joyce Carol Oates writes: "No more beautifully cadenced and moving collection of short fiction is likely to appear this year . . ."

2001   CM goes to Russia to teach and to research his novel *Dancer,* based on the life of Russian dancer Rudolf Nureyev.

2002   CM receives the first Ireland Fund of Monaco Princess Grace Memorial Literary Award.

2003   *Dancer,* CM's second international best seller, is published.

2005   *Zoli* is published in England. CM begins to teach fiction writing at Hunter College, where he continues as Distinguished Professor. The film adaptation of *Everything in This Country Must* is nominated for Best Live-Action Short Film.

2006   *Zoli* is published in the United States by CM's new publisher Random House.

2009   *Let the Great World Spin* is published by Random House to extremely positive response. Two months after the novel's publication, it appears on the *New York Times* best-seller list. *Let the Great World Spin* receives the National Book Award, making CM the first author born in Ireland to receive an award reserved for major American writers. Amazon.com ranks *Let the Great World Spin* #1 on its list of the most important novels. CM is inducted into Aosdána, acknowledging his contributions to the arts in Ireland.

2010   Random House agrees to publish CM's next two novels. CM receives a Guggenheim Fellowship, the Ambassador Book Award, the Deauville Festival Literary Prize, Medici Book Club prize, and the Grinzane Award in Italy. *Let the Great World Spin* is named Best Foreign Novel in China.

2011   CM wins the lucrative International IMPAC Dublin Literary Award as well as a literary award by the American Academy of Arts and Letters for *Let the Great World Spin*.

2012   CM receives an honorary degree from the Dublin Institute of Technology. CM co-founds Narrative 4, an effort to bring together young people from literally around the world to share their stories, each listening to another's story and then retelling it to the group, the outcome being the generation of empathy each gains through the experience of otherness

2013   CM publishes *TransAtlantic* and it immediately appears on the *New York Times* best-seller list. CM receives an honorary degree from Queen's University, Belfast.

2014   CM receives the Distinguished Author Award of the University of Scranton's Friends of the Weinberg Library.

2015   CM publishes *Thirteen Ways of Looking*, a novella and three short stories, to very strong response from critics. CM receives a Pushcart Prize and inclusion in the Best American Short Stories of 2015.

Notes

1. My introduction to Colum McCann two decades ago was thanks to Dermot Bolger's inclusion of "Through the Field" in his *Vintage Book of Contemporary Irish Fiction* which I included in the syllabus for my course "Modern Irish Writers" because I was unusually impressed by the story's power. From there I went on to read each of his books as it appeared, kept up with the critical response to his fiction, presented papers, and published articles on his writing.

Conversations with Colum McCann

Interview with Colum McCann

Stephen V. Camelio / 1994

From *Nua: Studies in Contemporary Irish Writing*. 3.1–2, 89 –100. Reprinted with permission of Stephen V. Camelio.

Stephen Camelio interviewed Colum McCann in 1994, shortly after McCann's collection of short stories *Fishing the Sloe-Black River* appeared. At McCann's request, the conversation took place in St. Dymphna's Bar on the Lower East Side of Manhattan.

Stephen V. Camelio: Countless reviewers have called your work "poetic" or "lyrical." *Publisher's Weekly* said your prose has "poetic logic." Also, you have a penchant for quoting or referring to poets—Yeats, Kavanagh, Wilfred Owen, Gerard Manley Hopkins—to mention some. Have you tried to write verse? Are you influenced by poets or do you think that being described as "poetic" is just par-for-the-course for the "Irish" writer?

Colum McCann: I read loads of poetry, perhaps as much as I read fiction. I have attempted to write poems but they are all dreadful. The sound is wrong, the lines are wrong, the whole feeling is off-kilter. I really don't have the discipline that is necessary for poetry. Still, I don't mind being called poetic, though it's often a kind of a curse word for fiction writers, isn't it? *Songdogs* was based on a poem I wrote. This was when I was in a writer's workshop in Texas, and it was probably the only halfway decent poem I ever came up with. My poets would be Heaney, Muldoon, Mahon, Carson, Ní Dhomhnaill—perhaps it's dangerous to start naming names because it becomes like a sort of literary Olympics. But I read a lot of the North American poets too. James Galvin, Wendell Berry, Jim Harrison, Anne Michaels. Strangely enough all of these four have written fiction as well. But they're braver than I am. There's often a gulf created between "poetry" and fiction as if they're forms completely foreign to each other. But in the best work I think the two forms meet each other gently. It boils down to using language in the freshest and most innovative way possible. When I write something, I read it aloud to myself to get the rhythm right. I read it over and over again. I find myself becoming more laconic as I get older—cutting back on the high language, hopefully becoming more disciplined and pared down. *This Side of Brightness* was less overtly poetic than, say, *Songdogs*, which at times was a little infatuated with itself. You have to hate your work in a certain way when you're finished. You have to have failed in some manner. The Beckett quote: "No matter. Try again. Fail again. Fail better." So in many ways you have to be disturbed a bit by your work in order that you can go forward and take on the next challenge. The other challenge is to try and avoid a high self-consciousness. Dostoyevsky says, "To be too acutely conscious is to be diseased." If you are too aware of what's going on, if you are too aware of yourself as a writer, if you're not prepared to embrace the mystery, then it carts a sickness to the work.

Camelio: One of the poets you mentioned is Seamus Heaney. Heaney says it is a necessity for Irish poetry to bring together the antithetical views of Kavanagh and Yeats. You, like Heaney, bring together both sides of Ireland: Kavanagh's detailed portraits of the common man and the everyday, and Yeats's mythology and vision. Do you purposefully try to work both these elements into your fiction?
McCann: Kavanagh and Yeats are two of the big bookends of Irish poetry this century. I think Heaney negotiates the spaces between them incredibly successfully. I don't know where my own work lies in relation to these poets—I didn't start reading them, really, until I was in my mid-twenties. I had studied them in school. But they began to mean something different to me once I had left the country, once I was trying to form my own style, create my own myths, however small they were. But I don't think I purposefully invoke them. I think they are deep within me, but I don't consciously call on them.

Camelio: After interning for UP in New York, they offered you a job as photojournalist. Are you an experienced photographer and, if so, how do you think it affected your writing, especially in *Songdogs?*
McCann: I'm not an experienced photographer. I'm not even a good photographer. But I would like to be. The Germans and the French talk about "making" photographs, whereas in English we "take" photographs. I think I have a certain tendency to make photographs with words. In some ways my style as a writer is both about stills photography and a certain cinematic sweep.

Camelio: After interviewing you, Eileen Battersby wrote, "Facts, facts, facts run through his conversation."

McCann: That came about as a misunderstanding. She's a well-known interviewer in Ireland. The night before the interview, a "friend" of mine informed me that Eileen Battersby didn't like my work. So I went into the interview nervous. I kept trying to pull it back into some sort of manageable shape. As it turned out, she actually did like my work, and she wrote a very good review, but it was an awkward moment.

Sometimes a writer gets asked about the specific themes, metaphors, concerns of their work. What does this mean? What does that mean? But writers aren't always fully in control of their work. They aren't always fully aware of what they are saying. This is the "mystery" we were talking about earlier. It's not a refusal to confront the demons, it's an acknowledgment of the angels.

Camelio: You wrote *This Side of Brightness* while living in New York City. In previous interviews you have said, "Things are in a constant flux . . . nothing ever solidifies" and "I will write an Irish book . . . I would like to write an Irish book." To capture a changing Ireland, would you have to return to Ireland to write about it and, if so, is this one of the things that will possibly attract you to such an undertaking? You said your new collection is about the North. Did you go back there at all?

McCann: I originally set out to write a book about the hunger strike because I felt it hadn't been done before and that it was time to confront it, twenty years on. I spent the best part of a year writing a novel that just didn't work. It was a really difficult thing to do. I was trying to go into the mind and body of a hunger striker. I ended up despairing. Sometimes I thought to myself that the Northern Irish novel, for instance, should be written by someone completely outside the sphere. Like someone from Portugal or China or Bosnia. As if a writer like José Saramago could go along and write a great Northern Irish novel because they're not lumbered down with all the facts and figures. They can come to it and interpret it creatively. On the other hand, I wondered if it should be just reserved for the Northern writers. Was I stepping in on somebody else's territory? I had spent my summers there as a kid—my mother is from a small town in County Derry—but still I wasn't sure if it was "mine." In the end I went ahead and wrote a couple of stories and a novella which I'm very proud of. In fact, John Hume, the leader of the SDLP [Social Democratic and Labour Party], the Nobel Peace Prize winner, said that the collection should be compulsory reading for all politicians in the North. It's about the glancing blows that kids get from political situations they don't entirely understand, yet the self-same situations determine the outcomes of their lives.

You ask about "going back" in order to write. Yes, I go back very often. But Ireland is, in Mary Robinson's famous words, beyond its borders now. It's here. It's in Paris, it's in Prague, it's in Sydney. This notion of Irishness is an interesting question, and I'm enamored of this idea of the sort of mongrel generation, the international mongrels, where you are fatherless in terms of a country, or you're motherless in terms of a country so you make your country elsewhere. The best practitioner of that in contemporary literature is Michael Ondaatje. Born in Sri Lanka, educated in England, lived in Canada, wrote his first novel about a turn-of-the-century jazz musician in New Orleans. So he broke all sorts of borders, geographical, metaphorical, and spiritual, and did so comfortably. So I think it is possible to do that. I also think it possible to write an Irish novel without writing a word about Ireland as well. I was acutely aware when I was writing *Brightness* that it wasn't on the surface an Irish novel, but the opening scene begins in 1916 and there is sort of a resurrection scene. But then the main Irish character gets locked in a tunnel underground and does so for the rest of his life, he's dead. His Irish body becomes trapped in American soil.

James Joyce also famously said that he had lived so long outside of Ireland that he could all at once hear the music of it everywhere.

When I was writing *Brightness*, I was so acutely aware of my Irishness that I shoved it under as much as I possibly could. So when I finished the novel I went to an actor here in the city, Arthur French, and asked him to read the novel for me. He said sure, but what I meant was that I wanted him to *read* the novel *to* me. He read it out loud to me for certain cadences for the black sections in particular. He's from southern Georgia and lived a long time in Harlem, and trying to get all that dialect right was very important to me so that I didn't have some sort of weird Irish phrase cropping up in the middle of it. So in some ways being conscious of not wanting to write something too Irish, there's a flip side to that as well.

Camelio: Staying with the Irish subject, in a review of *Phoenix Irish Short Stories*, a collection in which you have a short story, Colin Lacy states:

> One wonders what a reader coming to this nation's literature for the first time since, say, the 1960s would make of us. Emigration looms large. Over the sixteen stories included here, so does the Catholic Church, sex, alcohol, and various forms of physical and cultural displacement—hardy perennials all. . . . [This]

collection suggests that the themes that have teased Irish writers since the days when the Celtic Tiger was a malnourished cub are still the themes that bind.

Furthermore, Desmond Fennell contends that Irish writers continually overlook "contemporary adult theme[s]" to instead focus on the "subadult, subliterate, offbeat, weird, [and] poor" (Fennell, *Eire-Ireland* 1977). Do you think that some of your more Irish short stories sometimes wander into stereotypical themes and, if so, is that one of the reasons you chose to set much of *Songdogs* and all of *This Side of Brightness* outside of Ireland?

McCann: I'm just trying to get all of that together. Is Fennell suggesting that we are mired down by the same old topics? If so, he's being ridiculous. Ultimately what literature comes down to is what Faulkner says in his 1950 Nobel Prize address, that you confront the elements of the human spirit and you do so as honestly as you possibly can. Those are stories about family, about love and pride, pity, compassion, honesty, violence. All these things that go to making up the human spirit.

The interesting question is, I suppose, what constitutes an Irish novel? Does it have to be concerned with Ireland?

When I wrote *Fishing the Sloe-Black River* and that particular story, I wrote it at a time when Irish emigration was really at its peak and now it has come down, and as an issue emigration does not really exist anymore. We don't emigrate really anymore. We go places, we commute, we go back and forth. But when I was writing that particular story, I really wanted to write a story that was about emigration. When I started writing, I was aware and maybe scared that so much good writing had come from Ireland and even contemporary stuff. McGahern, Neil Jordan's collection *Night in Tunisia*, Des Hogan, Edna O'Brien. People like that. Not to mention the great big heavy ghost of the early part of the century. I knew that, I think I knew, again it wasn't conscious, that I had to get out in order to have something to say and what I wanted to do was go to other places and talk about other places in an Irish context. But, yeah, maybe I was scared by the fact that so much great literature was coming out of Ireland. I wasn't quite sure if I was able to confront that. I confronted it in some stories.

"Cathal's Lake," which is to this day probably, apart from my new stories, still my favorite story. It is all based on mythology, of course. It is a confrontation of a very Irish theme with a very Irish myth at its core. *Songdogs* has a very Irish myth at its core. You know, the myth of the salmon of knowledge. The poet waiting by the river, and Finn [McCool] comes along and tastes the salmon of knowledge. That's what the whole book is based on, the same way

"Cathal's Lake" is based on the myth of the Children of Lir. But it is also based on a Jewish myth that involves the thirty-six hidden saints. There are supposedly thirty-six hidden saints in the world and they are generally men and they are generally working men. They work on farms, they're shoemakers, they're carpenters, and what they have to do is bear the sorrows of the world. For me, Cathal in that story is bearing the sorrows of Northern Ireland. There is one of these thirty-six hidden saints who is forgotten by God and has no communication with God. Cathal was just cursed, cursed to do this thing, cursed to bare the sorrows of what was happening in the North.

So those were specifically Irish themes, but then having lived the way I have done, having been *lucky* enough to live the way I've done—taking a bicycle across the United States for a couple of years, living in southern Texas, spending a lot of time in northern Mexico, living in Japan, traveling quite a bit around Asia and so on—it just seemed to me there were newer things for writing.

I would love to see Fennell attribute his quote to something beautiful and powerful like Seamus Deane's *Reading in the Dark*.

Camelio: Actually he talks about *Reading in the Dark* in the postscript of that article. He says, "In Rome where I'm living, the two latest Irish books to appear in translation are Frank McCourt's *Angela's Ashes* and Seamus Deane's prize-winning novel, *Reading in the Dark*. On the cover of the former is a little girl, on the latter a little boy" (Fennell 203).

McCann: What this seems to be is a case of outside critics putting their own interpretations of what Irish literature should be upon the book rather than letting the book guide and inform some of those opinions. This happens particularly in England, people wanting Irish writing to be of a certain type. They want the alcoholic father, they want the brutal poverty, they want this sort of image that confirms every other stereotype that they've had for how many years. But I really don't know how Fennell could apply that to *Reading in the Dark*, which is an incredible novel. Also a lot of critics like Fennell enjoy taking a whack at Frank McCourt—basically because he's successful and wrote a wonderful book. If *Angela's Ashes* had not been a successful book, every critic and academic person would be saluting this great novel that was forgotten, that should be a slice of Irish history.

Camelio: Recently I saw an interview with Sean Penn, and he said he thought that making films only for entertainment is a misuse of the power of film. *This Side of Brightness* seems to have a sort of social commentary running through it. Do you think fiction should have a political or social point to make?

McCann: Yeah, I think it should be important. I don't think it should be like knocking you over the head . . . I'm not a sociologist . . . I'm not a political candidate . . . but it should have power and meaning. It is quite an arrogant act to write in some ways, to believe that you have something to say. That people are going to pay twenty-five bucks for a book, or fifteen pounds for a book, and then to have nothing really to say. I mean, there is a place for entertainment, yeah, sure there's a place for entertainment. But as a writer you got to have some substance behind it. If even you are only reacting sort of viscerally to your material, you don't know why you are doing this. Like I didn't set out at the beginning to write a novel that was about homelessness, that was about race, and about . . . it's about religion in a lot of ways. But they became part of the book. You have to try to keep the writing as honest as possible to your material and to your ideas. But if you start writing tracts, political tracts, then write a political tract, you know, rather than writing fiction. There should be spaces in the work, moments, where people go in and bring their own things to it. Creative reading. Like, for instance, *Brightness* ends ambiguously. I've been criticized because it was supposedly too upbeat an ending.

Camelio: You were also criticized for *Songdogs* because it wasn't upbeat enough . . .

McCann: Well, you see, I think the whole *Songdogs* leads to a moment of triumph. I think the son learns how to love. That's pretty upbeat I think! Some of the book, of course, is dark and dirty. It certainly doesn't smell of lavender or air freshener. But what it moves towards is hope. I believe in hope. And then there's this note, as far as I was concerned, this note of triumph at the end where the son tastes the salmon of knowledge and understands something about his father and kisses him, and he walks away, and he sees this fish which represents the mother and finally understands everything. That this father's obsessive fishing in the river was an act of love. That's what he's been doing for all those years since she disappeared. That he's been fishing for the mother. The son *finally* understands that. So to me I was sort of trying to downplay it because I thought, well, they're going to criticize me for being too upbeat. Then in *Brightness* it's very ambiguous. I mean, he's walking through these shafts of light and he's on his way, he has burned everything, but he's left in the tunnel in the end. He never gets out. If a reader wants to take him out and bring him to Chicago to meet his wife and daughter, all very well. If a reader wants to leave him in the tunnel, all very well. If the reader wants him to get out and get himself a job and maybe in a few years be able to explain something to his daughter, then that's all very well. I know what *I want him* to do, but that's all right; we'll leave that out of the equation.

Camelio: You are involved with Redeemable Features, a film production company.
McCann: Absolutely, the greatest guys on earth.

Camelio: How did you get involved with them and has writing screenplays had any effect on how you write fiction?
McCann: I don't know yet whether it has had any effect. I know it's dangerous and I know it's seductive, but if you're aware it's dangerous and seductive then I think you can handle both at once. Basically what happened was my American publisher Michael Naumann, who is now the German Minister for Culture, was at Paul Auster's house and this producer Peter Newman from Redeemable Features was there. Michael started telling the story of my novel *Songdogs.* Peter said this sounds like a great idea for a film. Peter came to me, and I started writing the film a couple of years ago now. It's almost gone through loads of different times. That's the thing about the film business. You can't rely on it entirely. If you wait for a film to be made you are going to be waiting for a while. Screenwriting is an interesting world, but not one I want to overtake my fiction by any manner or means. But it is a way to make a living. I mean, novelists teach or they write journalism or they do some other job or they do films. It just so happens I got involved in films. Do too much of it now. That's just the function of having family and trying to get it all squared away. I'm heading into a novel that is going probably to take me about four years. A lot of traveling and a lot of things I don't know about . . . yet. Try to squirrel away enough to work on that project for a few years, that's a hard thing to do. I'm very excited by the whole idea of it. So film is a password, an economic password into my fiction.

Camelio: You talked about teaching. A lot of writers teach. Over the Internet I have seen various university-level literature course syllabuses that include your work. You have worked as a teacher and have a BA in English Literature. What do you think of your work being studied as "literature" at this level? Is that something you strive for?
McCann: No, I think it's great, though. Really, as a writer, what I would like is to be read in fifty years, to write a book that is read in fifty years. That would be the ultimate goal, not to be studied in university. But it's flattering. Yeah,

I'd be lying to you to say, Oh, I don't want that to happen or something like that. I kind of enjoy it. The biggest kick I got was hearing that *Fishing the Sloe-Black River* is on the Leaving Certificate in the Republic. So that was a big kick for me. I'm actually very lucky because I'm only, how many years, seventeen years out of the Leaving Cert. myself so . . . I've also seen some university critiques of *Songdogs* . . . I had them sent to me and read them. They're a bit embarrassing but it's like, that's a good idea, I never thought of that, yeah . . . yeah that's what I was doing. Because again, a lot of this stuff is emotional rather than analytical for me. I'm a very different writer than, say, John Banville. He's very cool and detached, and writes beautiful crafted sentences, artifacts, really. I'm much more ragged and emotional the way someone like Des Hogan is much more ragged and emotional. Or Edna O'Brien as well. So to discover certain things about your fiction that you didn't necessarily think of is interesting. I mean sometimes you don't realize until years after you've written a story or years after you've written a book what you truly were writing. For me, I never really realized why I was writing *Songdogs* until about two years afterward. In some ways, I suppose I was writing about myself because you have this artist who destroys his family for the sake of what he considers his great art. He publishes these pictures of Juanita because it is all he can do, it is all he can cling on to. He ends up the rest of his life regretting this act. In some ways I was sort of living out that fear myself because writers wound a lot of other people with fiction or writing. They forget about the ones who are around them and get completely involved in their art. There is this whole idea of the baby carriage being an anathema to art. That's bullshit. It's the artist who destroys him- or herself, not his or her children.

Camelio: Have you found a new pulse since becoming a father?
McCann: I mean, obviously, it's changed my writing in lots of ways, and I adore being a father. My kids are the scaffold to my heart. Of course my time is more limited than it used to be, so I've got less time to write, but I'm not sure, though, how they have changed the actual tone and direction of the writing.

Camelio: You'll find out ten years from now?
McCann: Find out in fifty years, I don't know. I still don't entirely know what *Brightness* was about apart from the obvious stuff it was about. But I don't know what it was about for me. Except I had a great time writing it.

Camelio: Sounds like it. Sounds like you met some characters along the way.
McCann: Absolutely. I learned an awful lot. I was lucky, when I started researching, that I didn't have any kids. I don't know if I'd do it now. It was

so dangerous. I was lucky in a lot of respects. It was great fun and a laugh to research it. But also really eye-opening to me about what I felt about history, about our own histories, about what we do to other people, about homelessness, about race, about all those things. I get loads of letters from mixed-race kids now. It's really nice. I was sort of hoping there would be a to-do about the book in some ways in that it is culturally arrogant and economically arrogant for white writers to write about black families or even black people in general. That is a really interesting argument to me. To say that white people can't write about black people. Can you make the equivalent jump that black people can't write about white people? It seems to be that the consciousness of race should become the consciousness of class instead—but that's a whole other ball of wax. Anyway, *This Side of Brightness* is on a list taught by an African American teacher at the New School for contemporary black novels. He uses it as a sort of model, and he really likes the novel. He wrote to me and said this works in all sorts of unusual ways. He said he was pissed off at first that I didn't have any black connection or even any American connection whatsoever. So that's real nice. He uses it as a sort of catalyst to talk about these issues in his class.

Interview with Colum McCann

Declan Meade / 2001

From *The Stinging Fly*, 1.9 (Spring/Summer 2001). Reprinted with the permission of Declan Meade.

Declan Meade: Maybe you could begin by talking about your first experiences of writing, how all this began for you.

Colum McCann: I think most of it goes back to my father. He was Features Editor with the *Evening Press* so the house was filled with books. He wrote twenty-eight books himself: *The Irish in Love*, *The Wit of Oscar Wilde*, *The Wit of Brendan Behan*, a history of the Abbey Theatre, a book on roses. He also wrote wonderful children's fiction. He'd bring books to me by Dylan Thomas, and he had recordings of Dylan Thomas from the BBC. We would sit out in his little shed—he had a shed out the back where he did his writing—and we'd listen to these. When I was fifteen or sixteen he showed me Ben [Benedict] Kiely's stuff, and that revolutionized my whole idea of what contemporary Irish fiction could be. At the same time, he was going to the States and bringing back Kerouac and Burroughs, Ferlinghetti, people like that. I wanted to be a journalist, and my father said to me, "Don't," so, of course, I went ahead and I did. I went to Rathmines and started out with the *Irish Independent*, then moved over to the *Irish Press*. Then, at the age of twenty-one, I just decided I was going to travel, and I ended up riding a bicycle across the United States for the best part of two years. And that's when I think I became a fiction writer, during that time, making that journey.

Meade: And how was it happening at that time?

McCann: I sat down to write a novel when I was twenty-one. I'd bought a typewriter in Cape Cod. It didn't work very well. By the end of the summer, I had two or three pages with half-characters that I couldn't even read. And I knew that, essentially, I didn't have anything to write about. I had this fairly traditional, suburban Dublin, middle-class background—not really the stuff of fiction. I didn't make a conscious decision to go out and learn about other people's souls or stories; it just happened that way. Now I think it was vital in that I needed to go out and get myself into different skins. It was a fantastic trip. And dangerous too. I did about twelve thousand miles. I worked loads of different jobs: bartender, waiter; I dug ditches, worked in a school for juvenile delinquents.

Meade: At what point did the short stories start coming together?

McCann: While I was on the road, I wrote a travelog for the *Evening Press.* I started in Massachusetts, went down to Florida, across to New Orleans, into Mexico, finished up in San Francisco. Then I went back to Texas where I worked with these youngsters, and while I was there I wrote my first short stories. I also wrote a novel at that stage which never got published— thankfully. In 1990 I got my first story in the *Sunday Tribune,* a story called "Tresses." I never published it again. I think now it was very much a first short story, but I was very lucky because I won the Hennessy Award for that. Then I floundered around again for about two years—which seemed like an awfully long time at that stage, but now seems like no time whatsoever.

Meade: And how did the publication of your first book come about?

McCann: I was extraordinarily lucky, even though I didn't think so at the time. I had about two years of rejection slips from various publishers and agents. I wallpapered the bathroom, the old story. What happened was that David Marcus heard that I'd had a short story published in a very tiny literary magazine in Texas. He picked it up, he really liked it, he wanted it for an anthology he was doing. He gave it to his agent the very next day and within a week that same story was included in the *Best British Short Stories 1993.* Giles Gordon became my agent then. It happened tremendously quickly, but I felt that it didn't happen so quickly. I was almost at the stage where I said, "Well, I'm just going to write anyway because this is what I felt destined to do." Goethe says: "Such a price the gods exact for song, to become what we sing." At various stages I thought that this was the price that I had to pay: I was going to keep on writing and probably never get published.

Meade: Did you have all the stories in your first collection written by this time?

McCann: No. I only had three or four. When this one story was picked up, they asked to see all my other work. At this stage I was in the University of Texas working to get my BA. Within a year I wrote the rest of the stories.

My father encouraged me all along. I'm honestly very grateful for everything that has happened. I've been very lucky, especially in the sense that I've been able to write full-time.

Meade: At what point did that happen?

McCann: About four years ago, after I wrote *This Side of Brightness*. It wasn't just from writing novels and short stories, though. I started writing films as well. A well-paid horror.

Meade: How do you differentiate between the different forms: novels, short stories, screenplays?

McCann: I don't see myself as a better short story writer or better novelist. I don't differentiate between the two that much, although they are, of course, wildly different animals. I can't juggle the two. I can't write a novel while I'm writing short stories. I try to give myself fully to whatever I'm working on. The only thing I can do while I'm writing fiction is write screen plays, because it's so completely different. I love the beautiful, tense singularity that you get in short stories. With about ten or so pages you can learn—or at least intuit—so much about a character's life. I love that intensity. Every word counts. And I don't think you can afford to make much of a mistake in a short story. The novel is very different. It's much more loose and diverse and less secretive, I suppose. In the one I'm working on now, there's a whole orchestra of voices. It's an interesting experiment for me. The characters all have different geographies, different backgrounds. It's a fictionalization of the life of a famous dancer.

Meade: Where did the idea for this new novel begin?

McCann: A friend of mine told me this story of his father bringing home the family's first television set to their flat in Ballymun. This was the 1970s. The family was desperately poor. After fiddling with the rabbit's ears, the first image that appeared on the screen was that of Rudolf Nureyev dancing. And my friend from Ballymun fell in love with him, both literally and figuratively. He became haunted by the image. And I thought it was an extraordinary story—that a Russian dancer could reach into the living room of a Dublin teenager. I would tell others this story, and it just so happened that a lot of them also had a story about Nureyev. He's emblematic of all sorts of things in the latter half of the twentieth century: of exile, of the Cold War, of celebrity, of the power and function of art. I didn't realize what a huge monster of a book it was going to be, and still is, for me. It won't be out until at least late 2002. The novel isn't really about ballet; it's not about ballet at all. It's more about stories, lies, fabrications, who owns stories and who has the right to tell these stories.

Meade: How important is research to your work?
McCann: It's important to my novels, very important. *This Side of Brightness* took a huge amount of research. My present novel is snowing me under. I don't want it to show in the novel—it doesn't need to be telegraphed—but I generally research incessantly while working on a long book. But short stories I often never research.

One exception is when I went to write a novella, "Hunger Strike," in my last book and I did a huge amount of reading on what happens to bodies in the act of starving oneself. I got all this tabulation from Italian hunger artists, French hunger artists in the nineteenth century, all this work the doctors had done, measuring the fat in their bodies, all that sort of stuff. I ended up not using much of it whatsoever. I read all about the blanket protest too, but it struck me more and more that it was a story that had to be told from outside the physical reality of the hunger strike. It had to happen within an imagination that was on the outside. It would have been extraordinarily difficult to get inside the head of a hunger striker, and I kept coming back to this little kid in Galway and I started working on that. Then I wrote the story very quickly, but I had done all this research beforehand. I think with a lot of writing, you have to write through what it is you think you want to do until you get to the point where the work itself takes off.

I remember with *This Side of Brightness* I tried to write from the point of view of an old Irish man who goes down into the tunnels to look after the homeless people. I wrote like that for nine months. Basically what I was doing was writing myself out of the novel. One morning I woke up and I realized that this old man was me and I didn't need him anymore. Very Freudian this! Murdering the father, the self, the consciousness, and all that! Anyway, I literally took the ninety or a hundred pages of work and threw them in the bin and started again. I work very long and hard to get through something. I wish I could say it comes to me just like that. Oh yeah, I'm going to write about the hunger strike so I'm going to have a boy meeting an old Jewish Lithuanian couple, obviously Holocaust survivors, living in the west of Ireland, bingo, there it is. It doesn't work that way.

As a writer I have to struggle. I have to go out to meet the story. The story seldom comes to meet me unbidden. With both short stories and novels, I work from the starting point of images. I have a first image and a last image, but I generally have no idea what is going to operate in between. Some novelists map the story out very carefully, but the way I work is that I start with one image and I try to move towards another. It's a sort of journey, a process of discovery the whole time. Later when I've finished a first draft, I start to lay more structure on it. Or I begin to interpret it in a more mannered, intellectual way.

Meade: And the act of throwing all that work away? Is that liberating or just depressing?

McCann: Boring, really. I do throw it all away, but it's not as if it hasn't filled me with all that it was supposed to fill me with. It's not as if I'm starting all over again, tabula rasa. I've worked so long and hard with it, and I've lived with it for long enough, that I've forced myself to discover all these things that I didn't necessarily know before. Most of my work, rather than coming from an intellectual place, tends to come from a deeper, unacknowledged emotional place. I can't really talk to you about what I'm writing or why I'm writing it at any one time. I can tell you afterwards because it becomes clearer to me then. The new novel has been like a constant series of this all along because of the different narrators. I've never had to work so hard on anything. You should ask my wife Allison. To interview a writer, you really should talk to his wife and kids, the people around him who see him when he's down and depressed, when he's being a pain in the arse, when he just wants to curl up into a ball.

Meade: What is your writing routine then?

McCann: I get up early in the morning. Often I'm with the kids now early in the morning, but I still get in here to this room as soon as possible. I'll put on an album. Right now it's David Gray, but it's often Van Morrison. So I'll have the kids out that way and the traffic of New York out that way, and I want to be in Caracas or in Paris or St. Petersburg. The music creates an alterior reality. I tend to put in a lot of hours, often working until late at night. But the best time is the morning.

Meade: Do you write every day?

McCann: I try to but I don't. Some days I'll get minus ten words or minus one hundred words and some days I'll get three thousand words.

Meade: I wanted to ask you about how important living in New York has been for you and for your work.

McCann: Very, I would think. I'll probably only be able to tell you the truth of that by being away from New York now again for a little while. I've been more or less here for the last six years, and we intend to get away to Italy for a year or two next year. But it's been wonderful. A few things like having the New York Public Library—that's like having all the libraries of the world right there. And there's lots of stuff going on, writers moving through and having the chance to meet them. I just enjoy it here. The fact that you can go to somewhere like Astoria in Queens and hear twenty different languages being spoken. That one quarter of the population of New York is immigrant. All the wanderers arriving and colliding. And the sheer energy of the city. And the fact that I can make my own little village out of it.

Meade: Dublin does not appear to be as important to your writing.
McCann: I've only ever set one short story in Dublin ["Along the Riverwall"]. When I talk about Dublin, I still talk about it as home, going home. As a spiritual or literary place, no, I don't see it like that. I don't imagine, for instance, that I am able or willing—and really I mean the word *able*—to write a novel about Dublin. That's not to say I'm not Irish, or not of Dublin. Dublin is important to me. It just doesn't fire my imagination in the same way as other places do.

Meade: In the short story "Breakfast for Enrique," you clearly made the choice to have the narrator come from a suburb in Cork, rather than Dublin.
McCann: I'm much more at home outside of Dublin. If I was to write an Irish novel, I'd definitely set it in Mayo-Castlebar or Louisburgh. I spent a year there working for the *Connaught Telegraph*. I have much more of an affinity with those places.

Meade: A lot of your stories have rural settings.
McCann: Yes. I don't know why that is. Here I am living in the least rural place. I just feel much more at home there. I have spent a lot of time in rural areas, particularly in the States. When I go home I tend to put on a backpack and head out walking. I've walked from Dublin to Galway, from Derry to Kerry. But this thing with Dublin, it's nobody's fault but my own. It's not as if I'm saying something happened to me in Dublin. With "Breakfast for Enrique," I don't know why I wanted him to be from the countryside. He just seemed a very gentle, loving spirit and if he came from Dublin he would be a slightly different person. I think our geography affects us in very specific and peculiar ways. A lot of it too is about the act of imagining things outside

of myself, so that I'm not on the surface writing about myself. I haven't written about growing up in Dublin, cycling around the States, my time with the delinquents in Texas, my time in Japan, or life now with my own children. The five big facets of my own life and I haven't written about them. And yet they inform everything I do. So maybe that's it, maybe that's the answer, maybe there's all of Dublin in my stories.

Meade: In the same way that New York is not like the rest of the United States, do you feel that Dublin is set apart from the rest of Ireland?
McCann: Right. I'm not enamored with Dublin really when I go back.

Meade: Have you witnessed the changes in Dublin? The old Celtic Tiger?
McCann: Well, that's the other thing. I go back very often. Last year I was back six times. The previous year I was back twelve times. I'm back for at least a couple of months each year. And so much has changed. Even small things. The whole notion of being able to tell a story in a pub, for instance, is completely fractured by mobile phones. Five fellas walk in, four phones go down, and suddenly everybody's talking about where they want to be, rather than where they are. The whole notion is not to be static in a place and enjoy a particular time. It's all about where everyone else is and where you should be going to next. That didn't happen ten years ago. The art of conversation has changed. The language has changed. People hail cabs in Dublin now. They don't shout for taxis.

Meade: We have talked about it before, but let's go back to your most recent book, *Everything in This Country Must*. What has the reaction to that book been like?
McCann: I was very happy with the reaction to it. I was a bit scared. I had an Irish novelist who will remain nameless tell me I was "an effing eejit" to write about the North. As if the North was a foreign country and nothing to do with the whole experience of being Irish, nothing to do with us whatsoever. As if our consciousness is not affected by it at all. As if the very intimate physicality of the place doesn't affect us. How can this be said on a political level, let alone a human level? So while I don't think it's a necessity for an Irish writer to write about Northern Ireland, I wasn't going to shy away from it. I don't think the book makes overt political statements; it tries to make statements about the human spirit. The book is not glaringly political. Just like other great writing about the North—Seamus Deane's *Reading in the Dark*, for example—does not make political statements. I'm very happy the

book got such a good reception, particularly in the North. I was particularly concerned about the reaction to the novella on the hunger strike.

Meade: That was the first time I'd read about the hunger strike in fiction. Were you the first to write about it?
McCann: That I know of, yes. I may be wrong. I looked for it but I couldn't find it. It might be in some political thrillers or potboilers. Beresford's non-fiction book *Ten Men Dead* is a classic. The poets, of course, have written about it: Montague, Heaney, Muldoon, Mahon, the whole lot of them. The oblique approach of poetry makes it easier to talk about something like the hunger strike. But I haven't seen much about it in prose. It's almost twenty years since it took place and it's time for fiction writers to take it on. I actually end up reading more poetry than fiction.

Meade: So what are you reading at the moment?
McCann: I'm judging an award [as a judge for the IMPAC Prize], but apart from that I'm having this great time because I'm reading all this stuff that I've never read before: Pasternak, Yesenin, Mandelstam, Ahkmatova, Tolstoy, all the Russian greats. It's such a great thing about writing and researching and going beyond your supposed immediate experience. You get into all sorts of different worlds and you're continually learning. It's like constantly going to University. I'm also reading a lot about the theory of dance.

Meade: Have you taken any dance classes?
McCann: I've been at dance classes, but I haven't taken any. I don't think I'd be the proper person to get into a pair of tights. But it's a fascinating world. The thing I've become interested in is the sort of violence this art does to you. It does a violence to your psyche and to your soul, but it also does a violence to your body. The first thirty pages of the novel are war scenes. It's supposed to be about a ballet dancer, but all it is, is war.

Meade: What is your motivation as a writer?
McCann: I have two motivations as a writer. A friend of mine, Jim Harrison, writes in a poem "Letters to Yesenin": "Children pry up our rotting bodies with cries of 'earn, earn, earn.'" So to some extent my ambition as a writer is to make it okay for my two kids and to look after them. That would be something very new. Do you see that nasty calendar on the wall there? I wrote the text for that. That's a bullshit job, a complete bullshit job, but I took it. They asked me: "Will you write the text for an American calendar about Ireland?" "No way." "We'll pay you this amount of money." "Well, you know, maybe."

My other motivation sounds very high-minded and snobby and pretentious and ridiculous. I honestly would like just one thing to remain in fifty years, whether it be one short story or one novel to be still around after I'm gone.

Meade: With what work have you come closest to that so far?
McCann: The short stories, I'd say. So far. I wrote a story called "Cathal's Lake" about Northern Ireland, about a man digging up a swan. And maybe this weird little hunger strike novella. It's very simple and maybe could have done with some chopping down. Oh, I don't think that will last. Who knows? But I'd rather believe that I haven't done it yet anyway. I think you have to fail. It's the old quote from the boy on the wall (points to a photo of Beckett): "No matter, try again, fail again, fail better." That's what you do. I have to acknowledge that everything I've done so far has to some extent been a failure. Because if you think you've done the right thing, then why bother going on?

Meade: What role does fiction play in the world?
McCann: I don't believe in the death of the novel or that the novel is not important any more. Other things come along, cinema for instance, which change the role of fiction, and change fiction itself, but I still think it's important. I would have to think that. To some extent, it's an act of arrogance: "Oh, listen to this, I have something to say." At other times writers come along and they give you a gift. John Berger is one of those novelists, Ben Kiely, Edna O'Brien, Michael Ondaatje, Roddy Doyle. Sometimes I read a book by people like that and I say: "Wow, that's why I'm around, that's why I read." It just affects you so much and it can change you.

Meade: What would your advice be to writers starting off?
McCann: Write through things. If at first you do succeed, well, don't be too astonished. But if at first you don't succeed, work through it. I think we all have to work very hard. And don't be too impatient either. I always wanted to get published when I was twenty-one because I wanted to go to all these publishing parties in my torn black overcoat and tell everyone to eff off. Now I realize it doesn't matter whatsoever. I was always saying I have to be published before I'm twenty-five, or before I'm thirty. That's a very important driving force, but it's the quality of the work that matters. It's not so much the writer, it's the writing—that's what it's about.

Meade: Do you teach writing?
McCann: Sometimes. And when I do, one of the first things I bring up is that notion that you should write about what you know about. I tell them you

should write about what you don't know about. Then we have this massive argument, and basically it comes around to saying that when you write about what you don't know about, like say, when you start imagining a heroin addict in Bangkok, and you're in Dublin or in New York, you start writing into this character and you start learning things about yourself that you didn't necessarily acknowledge before. Ultimately, you can only write about what you know about. But if you move out of that little box for a little while, just in your imagination, I think you can learn beyond what you think you know.

Meade: You also act as fiction editor for a journal. What has been your experience with that?

McCann: I'm fiction editor with *The Recorder*, which is the journal of the American-Irish Historical Society. It's a good publication. They've published [Seamus] Heaney, [Benedict "Ben"] Kiely, [Paul] Muldoon; Martin Scorsese has written an essay on film; and young writers too, Claire Keegan, Michael Collins, and Molly McCloskey. Some really good new writing. We don't get inundated with stuff, thankfully. Sometimes we get a lot of shit, as you know—an awful lot.

Meade: Where does that shit come from?

McCann: I don't know. I'm sure it's always been that way. People think it's hip and cool now to be a writer. They think that all they have to do is go out to the right pub, wear the right leather jacket, have the right look. To come from the right country means that, suddenly, your stuff is going to be good. It's not really getting beyond the surface. I don't think people concentrate so much on the writing as on the supposed life of the writer. The truth is, I have a great life. I am very, very lucky. I get to travel, I get to go to universities, I get to go to parties. But most of my time is spent sitting on my arse in an office, staring at a blank wall, saying: "Oh Jesus, what am I doing, how am I going to get around this today?" Most of it is about hard graft.

This Side of Brightness Interview

Robert Birnbaum / 2003

From colummccann.com. Reprinted with permission of Robert Birnbaum.

Robert Birnbaum: What kind of role did "research" (everyday materials, files . . .) play in *This Side of Brightness?* How much did it affect the final result?

Colum McCann: At the beginning of the novel, or when I was researching it, I used to go down to the tunnels four or five times a week. I'd hang out, outside the tunnels, chatting with whoever came along. I got to know quite a few people who lived underground and eventually they sheltered me, took me under their wing. Word went along the tunnels to leave me alone. Of course, I never pretended to be homeless—homelessness is in one's eyes, you cannot fake it. I often brought down candles, food, money. My favorite times, though, were when I spent hours and hours with a homeless person, and they would ask for nothing—simply the time spent with them was enough. It's about dignity. Sometimes we would sit in silence for a while. A woman named Doreen, a former crack addict, used to await my visits. She had her underground shack cleaned up when I came. She would hug me and kiss me on the cheek. Another woman, Brooklyn (who still lives underground) was terribly embarrassed about the mess that her fifty cats left in the tunnels, but she needed the cats to take care of the rats. I met all sorts of people—junkies, war veterans, people who'd recently been let out of mental asylums, others who had just lost their jobs. I was put in all sorts of different situations. Being Irish helped me—I was never seen as part of the established order, the system. I was outside. And they were outsiders too. So often I felt aligned with the people who were living underground. I was only in danger a couple of times—once a homeless man tried to accost me and another time someone wanted me to smoke crack with them. I was able to get out of each situation safely enough, by talking, keeping an even keel, not forcing anyone, least of all myself, into a corner. It's dark down there, scary.

You can have hallucinations. The darkness seems to hold things. But to be honest the tunnels of New York are less dangerous than the streets. We are all scared of the darkness. Even the darkness sometimes seems scared of itself. Try going to a shelter, though. They are horrific. I slept in a shelter in the Bronx one night. That's when I was most scared.

Then there was a whole other order of research as well: finding out what life was like for a black man in the early part of the century. What clothes people wore. What hats. What sort of cars might drive by. There are issues here—is it culturally arrogant, economically arrogant, socially arrogant for a young, white Irishman to write about a black American underclass? I dealt with this the only way I knew how—I said that I would write the novel as honestly as I could, and after that I could stand proudly against any criticism. To get the language right, I worked with black actors. Arthur French was amazing—he read the book aloud to me. Also, I scoured the history books. In the end (when the book was published), it was embraced by black critics and writers, it was even put on university courses in multi-culturalism, which surprised me, but pleased me greatly, of course. Who expects that sort of affirmation? Another part of me wanted it to be controversial. Controversy sells books after all.

I didn't want the research to overwhelm the book, since I'm a novelist, not a sociologist. So I buried as much of the research as I could—which, I hope, gives it authenticity. In other words, I knew what sort of hats men were wearing in Harlem in 1924, but I didn't put them in the novel, I didn't want to flag them. I wanted the novel to have the sway and heft of a constant present tense.

Birnbaum: Where did you get the inspiration for the underground explosion? Is there a sort of metaphorical purpose, considering its position at the beginning of the novel?

McCann: I was standing in a dark corner of the tunnels one afternoon—hiding from Amtrak police, in fact, out of the way, in the corner—when I looked up and saw a plaque on the tunnel wall, saying, "1913." And so I thought to myself: Who built these tunnels? Who died here? What sort of ghosts live here? And so I went to the New York Public Library down on 42nd Street to research the lives of the "sandhogs." Deep in the files I found mention of the accident where (on two different occasions in New York history) men got literally blown from the tunnels. I knew immediately that I wanted that image. In fact I knew immediately that in some ways it would become a focal point in the novel, since I was aware that I wanted to write about resurrection in some way.

Dostoyevsky says somewhere that "to be too acutely conscious is to be diseased." He is talking, I think, of the necessity of mystery. Talking about one's metaphors is bound to remove that mystery. I tend to leave it to the reader to decide the metaphorical intent. I believe in creative reading as much as I believe in creative writing.

Birnbaum: You describe an underground and dark New York, which apparently remains unchanged in time. Why? Is it a sort of contrast with the "open air" NYC, or is it a world completely apart?

McCann: I saw the tunnels really as the subconscious or unconscious mind of New York City. It contains all that the city aboveground chooses not to think about. It is a world apart and yet it is also the root.

It always surprised me that American writers had not used the tunnels as a setting in fiction. Of course, Pynchon did it with alligators in the tunnels, but that's another form of storytelling, and it wasn't like he was using the landscape in its real sense—not a criticism, just an observation. I'm talking about the real people living underground. It seemed like such an American thing—to lay claim to a patch of land, to take on another frontier, only this one was a nightmare frontier, where people were taking their wagons (their shopping carts) across a whole different sort of landscape; they barter (for cigarettes) and they lay a piece of cardboard box (a flag) onto their very own patch of land.

Birnbaum: Where did Treefrog come from?

McCann: Treefrog is an amalgamation of many different characters that I met underground. He's also a sort of everyman. The novel concentrates on forty days and forty nights in Treefrog's life. Interpret from that what you will.

Birnbaum: Your work often reminds reviewers of the social novelists of previous decades—Zola, Steinbeck, Orwell.

McCann: I'm flattered to be even considered in this company. The writer must work with a conscience, yes. The reader creates their own conscience out from the work. If this is social fiction then I'm a happy practitioner. I'm not really interested in navel-gazing. Eventually we finally realize that there is only lint in there anyway.

Birnbaum: Both in *This Side of Brightness* and *Songdogs* you describe the lives of different generations, their encounters and their struggles. Do you have a particular interest in the generational gap, and in particular for the relationship between fathers and sons?

McCann: Whatever we were is whatever we are, I suppose. I have an interest in generations, yes. But not in an historical manner—more their effect in the present. Certainly it seems from my fiction so far that I am (like many Irish writers) deeply haunted by family and the place of mothers and fathers. I wish I could explain more about this. I don't truly understand it. I don't think I want to understand. Perhaps then I would lose it as a theme. I am very close to my family—my folks in Ireland, my family here in New York. There's nothing more important to me.

Birnbaum: The river (and the lives connected to it) seems to be a recurrent theme in your writings. Is it an autobiographical element or a particular personal interest?

McCann: Who knows where these things come from? I seem to be interested in rivers, in maps, in the act/art of fishing. And yet I do not own a fishing rod and because I live in New York I don't think I'll go swimming in the rivers anytime soon! I do, however, have a deep connection with the outdoors—I have walked across Ireland numerous times, and I have taken a bicycle across America (eighteen thousand kilometers). I think I am interested in rivers and maps as symbols more than anything else. They reverberate deeply with me. What they "mean" is still a mystery to me.

Birnbaum: Could you please talk about yourself and your life? How and when did you start writing?

McCann: I'm afraid I don't have the requisite dysfunctional childhood that many writers seem to have lived or desired. I grew up in a lower middle-class family in Dublin. My parents were (and still are, of course) extraordinarily good people. My father is a former soccer player and journalist. My mother is a homemaker. They're both retired now. I grew up in a family of five and I never once moved house. It's not exactly the stuff of fiction!

But my father as a journalist and writer used to give me all sorts of books: Kerouac, Ginsberg, Burroughs. It put a certain wanderlust in my blood. For some reason I was also considered by my family to be the sort of child who could access anyone—even at the age of five, six, my sister would bring me into pubs, and I would immediately start talking to the "strange people." Perhaps even at that age I was attracted to the outsiders. I had a relatively normal schooling with the Christian Brothers in Ireland and then took a course in journalism.

After four years in journalism in Dublin I went abroad. I took a bicycle across the States for two years. I literally flung myself at the road and embraced as much difficulty as I could. I found myself in numerous extraordinary situations—I lived with Amish families, poor black families, rich Southerners, worked in bars, was a bicycle mechanic, ranch hand, swimming-pool attendant. I devoured everything around me, but mostly as an observer. And I began to realize the value of stories. Everybody seemed to want to tell me their story. I understood then the crux of what writing would be about for me—there is a deep need for things to be told all over again.

I ran a wilderness education program for a while, went to university, married Allison in 1992, moved to Japan for eighteen months, returned to Ireland, and then moved to New York, where we now have kids. That's the censored version of my life! What is a life anyway? It's impossible to distill. When we talk about our lives they often seem irrelevant and untrue—even when the facts are right, the mood is wrong. I would like to find an image to give voice to my life . . . but not until I die.

Birnbaum: Which authors did inspire you most?

McCann: A dangerous question. Of the contemporaries: John Berger, Michael Ondaatje, Gabriel Garcia Marquez, Toni Morrison, Cormac McCarthy, Jim Harrison, Benedict Kiely, John McGahern, Edna O'Brien, Jim Crace, Peter Carey, John Michael [J. M.] Coetzee, Louise Erdrich, Seamus Heaney. The list is endless, and it's a dangerous pastime. I'm afraid I'll leave people out and kick myself tomorrow for forgetting them. My reading habits are constantly changing. Of the gone and the great: [James] Joyce, of course. [Samuel] Beckett, [William Butler] Yeats, [Vladimir] Nabokov. I like the Russian poets too: [Boris] Pasternak, [Anna] Akhmatova, [Osip] Mandelstam, etc. It's crazy to start making lists. People turn it into a sort of literary Olympics. I hate the shit where people start trying to make lists of the "Twenty-Five Best Young Irish Writers under Forty who just had Cornflakes for Breakfast." That sort of stuff is ridiculous. Even good newspapers are guilty of it. It turns everything into a competition. How facile. And judgmental.

I like hanging out around writers. I like having good friends who also just happen to write. I also happen to admire them—people like Tom Kelly, or Nathan Englander, or Sasha Hemon. I also love discovering a new book and feeling that I've known this person for a long time.

Birnbaum: Is it possible to define the position of the Irish writer in contemporary literature?

McCann: The Irish writer has always had a peculiar home in the world. By a combination of strategies—going into exile, subverting the language, twisting the fictional form—he or she has, in general, remained provocative, at the edge. Being an artist of a colonized nation always helped. We took the language foisted upon us and twisted it into our own form of joyful Hiberno-English. Our writers have always reveled in a willed linguistic ambiguity. The English language was a weapon our colonizers gave us and then we turned it around. Of course we're not the only country to do this. The Indians, for example, have been tremendously successful at using language as a weapon.

Some British critics still tend to see the Irish as either torturously poetic or insufferably comic—but they simply didn't have Joyce or Beckett or Wilde or Yeats or Flann O'Brien. My favorite British-born writer of all time—the great John Berger—happens to have an Irish soul and lives in the south of France.

The times they are changing for the Irish, of course, of course. The question is, can Irish writing survive the brave new economy? Has our sense of language changed? With a prominent internationalism, is it possible, or even necessary, that there is an "abroad" in the soul of the Irish writer? Being Irish, of course, we don't have the answers; we just keep changing the questions.

Terry Eagleton, in his hilarious thorn of a book *The Truth About the Irish* says Ireland "is a modern nation but was modernized only recently, and at the moment is behaving rather like a lavatory attendant who has just won the lottery." So much of the west of Ireland, for instance, is in the process of being destroyed.

Birnbaum: Both in *This Side of Brightness* and *Songdogs,* landscape, even if different, is a fundamental feature. Why?

McCann: We are in many ways made by our weather. Even our bodies have adapted to the land we grew up in. I am inordinately interested in landscape and how we are shaped by it. Also, of course, by how we choose to shape it. If pushed, I would say that, in my fiction, a sense of place comes quite naturally to me. I tend to write in cinematographic strokes. In other words, I create pictures. From these pictures, people emerge. The landscape gives birth to the people, and gradually the people take over. Whether or not I do this successfully is up to other people to decide.

Birnbaum: How do you juggle New York and Ireland?

McCann: New York is the city of exiles—everyone comes from somewhere else. Ireland has been for years a country of exiles—everyone wanting to be somewhere else. I adore New York for its anonymity too—something difficult to find at home. See, I still call Ireland "home," even though I've been gone for fifteen years or more. But I'm at home here, too, I mean in New York. This is my city. The Irish writer Brian Moore talked about knowing where he was from when he finally knew where he wanted to be buried. He lived in Canada and California, but ultimately wanted to return to a small cliff-face in Northern Ireland, where he's now buried. I'm not ready to answer the question, but I'd be very happy to end up well-scattered.

Interview with Colum McCann

Declan Meade / 2003

From *The Stinging Fly*, 1.15 (Summer 2003). Reprinted with the permission of Declan Meade.

The following conversation between Colum McCann and Declan Meade was conducted via e-mail in January 2003 to mark the appearance of *Dancer.*

Declan Meade: This is ostensibly the story of the life of Rudolf Nureyev and the lives of the people around him. What inspired you to write this novel?
Colum McCann: "Ostensibly" is a good word. This is not a biography. It's a story, a novel, a tale. For a long time I toyed with the idea of calling it "a false portrait."

Recently I have begun to have doubts about the word "fiction." Everyone is a storyteller, whether their stories are "true" or not. I suppose the job of telling stories is to probe the small, anonymous corners of the human experience that are sometimes beyond what we would normally term non-fiction or history. But then, lurking over your shoulder, there's the inescapable force of public events and the moments of history. As a writer you want to see inside the dark corners in order to make sense of the room that has already been swept clean (or clean-ish) by historians, critics, and journalists. The story-writer has to follow a sort of reckless inner need in order to go on a journey into an unreliable or perhaps previously undocumented area of the human experience. Poets do this also of course. So too do historians, but in a different way.

But to get to the story of inspiration, well, it's an Irish inspiration of sorts. A few years ago I heard a story from an acquaintance of mine about how, as a seven-year-old who lived in Ballymun in the early 1970s, his father used to come home almost every night and, well, beat up his family. But then one night the father came home, sober—carrying a television set. The whole family gathered around the television. At first they couldn't get any reception, there was just snow, but then, later that night, when the boy carried the TV around the room, the first image finally appeared. It was Rudolf Nureyev dancing . . . dancing in his arms essentially. And my friend sort of, fell in love with Rudi, or at least the idea of Rudi. So much so that now, thirty years later, living in Brooklyn, he is still obsessed by Nureyev.

I thought it was an extraordinary image, and I began to wonder what it is about our world that allows a Russian dancer to penetrate the consciousness of a working-class Dublin boy. The story seemed to reflect how simultaneously large and small our world has become. Living in New York, away from Dublin, meant that I could connect and dis-connect with that particular story (which is not in the novel, by the way, it was the inspiration towards the novel). And so perhaps I could connect and disconnect with all the other stories, or rumors, or facts also. In the end, I felt driven to write a novel that might try to cross all sorts of international boundaries and intersect, perhaps, with forgotten lives.

I was, naturally, led to the biographies of Nureyev. I was immediately enthralled by his life—the charm of it, the recklessness, the beauty, the ruin. And I was struck by the fact that Nureyev's very first public dance (at the age of six) was in a hospital for soldiers home from the Russian front. It was a fact largely glossed over in most of the biographies. I wanted to know more. And so, from that moment, I decided to try to write about him . . . or rather write about him by writing about others. The problem was that I'd never been to Russia and I knew next-to-nothing about dance. And so I began reading everything I could lay my hands on. And traveling. And becoming more and more curious.

Meade: Tell us a bit about the amount and nature of research involved. How do you move from accumulating all these facts to writing a work of fiction?

McCann: First of all I consciously avoided anyone who knew him well. That left my imagination open to go where I might push it. I read the biographies, including Diane Solway's *Nureyev*, which is a great book. And then I started reading, as they say, "outside the box." I would have been lost without the libraries, in particular the New York Public Library on 42nd Street, which is one of the greatest in the world. There, I was able to find Red Army booklets from 1941, dance dictionaries, biographies, photographs, films, slides, depictions of the gay world in the 1970s, articles about Nureyev, celebrity quotes, weather reports from the southern parts of the Soviet Union in 1983—you name it.

I began watching dance classes, and then I went to Russia during the summer of 2001. In Russia, I didn't do the traditional sort of research.

Rather, I walked a lot and talked with what might be called "ordinary" people. Of course ordinary people are always the most extraordinary—they live outside the confines of accepted history. I put myself in strange situations in order to try and understand that particular history and culture. I hung out in cafes in St. Petersburg, sat for hours on end in the stairwells of apartment buildings, went to steam baths, sat in the grounds of military hospitals, walked the graveyards. I went to Nureyev's hometown in Ufa. Amazingly, very few people there knew him. He was sort of like a rumor. That, in itself, helped contribute to the novel.

One night, in St. Petersburg, I ended up drinking with local mafia bosses. In fact we ended up dancing on the tables with some of the artists from the Kirov. It's a long story, but these things happen. All these experiences helped form a mosaic through which I tried to understand Russia, both contemporary and past. It was much the same with ballet. I'd never even been to a ballet before I started this book. Then I started to go, in New York first, and then in St. Petersburg, and suddenly I was captivated. I attended performances, watched classes, talked with dancers. I was struck by the grace and beauty and violence of it all at the same time. And my daughter, Isabella, began dancing too, at the same time, totally independent of my project. Watching her dance gave me a whole new appreciation for it and a strange link with Nureyev's youth.

There was a lot of political discovery for me also. In the research I was looking for the dust that settles between left and right, the contradictions between the absolutes. But the conflicting ideologies are always there in the human stories—the story of Yulia, for instance. Ideology is unavoidable, of course. But being too aware of it can "disease" a book. It struck me, after writing the book, that Rudolf Nureyev's life could be taken and interpreted as a metaphor for the life of the Soviet Union. It could be said that he lived the life of his country in advance, right down to the physical disintegration of the body and then, indeed, the curious ongoing "resurrection," whereby his reputation is being rehabilitated now in the former Soviet Union. One hopes that the Russia we see today will not be a country without a theory.

Meade: You employ a wide range of styles and storytelling techniques throughout the novel. I'm thinking here of first-, second- and third-person narratives, straight narration, journal entries, letters, flight reports, etc. Was that part of a challenge you set yourself? How did that evolve?

McCann: At one stage, early on in the process of writing the novel, I wanted to tell the story from the point of view of hundreds of different characters—it seems crazy now—each one different and never repeating. In the end I couldn't sustain this. I began to feel like it was just a literary exercise. It didn't have the heart that I wanted. And I missed some of the characters I had created—I wanted Yulia, the dance teacher's daughter, to come back, for instance. I missed her. I missed her voice. In the end she finishes the novel for me. That's a strange way to put it, but in some ways I felt like a ventriloquist: these voices, imagined or not, had a duty to be heard. The other thing is that I just had a great time writing the novel . . . I was learning all sorts of things from all sorts of different angles.

All the time I was aware of John Dos Passos and how he had dealt with multiple narrative viewpoints and the camera-eye technique that he used in his novel *U.S.A.* I wanted to see what might happen to a story if it became a chorus, even a dissonant one, where everyone gets up and sings in different voices. It seemed an interesting way to tell a life—the big and the small moments shouldering up against one another. The shoemaker and the hustler and the soldier and the nurse could tell their sides of the story, while Warhol and Fonteyn and even Jimi Hendrix could be included also.

I ended up approaching it in a more-or-less chronological manner, so it blended a certain amount of experimentation with quite traditional methods. But its construction was unique for me: all the time I felt that I was writing something new. Now that I'm finished I'm not so sure it's new at all. Other writers create new things: Berger, DeLillo, Edna O'Brien, Doctorow. I realize that now. I'm still learning. I hope always to learn and someday write something, well, new. It goes back to the notion that you always fail. If you don't fail in some way, then you're in difficulty: the difficulty of sameness. I want to tack that Beckett quote up on every wall I work in front of: No matter. Try again. Fail again. Fail better.

Some sections were easier to write than others. The major problem was trying to make it all seem simple. But that's the art of dance as well . . . making all that violence that you impose upon the body seem simple and, God save us, organic. What I mean is, I was just trying to tell a good story and attempting to use the proper language to tell it. I don't see it so much as Nureyev's story per se, but as an embrace of many different worlds. I wanted to talk about the international aspect of where we all currently are.

The primary advantage to having so many different narrators is that you can hold the story up like a prism—the light shining through will give different beams every time you shake it, or turn it, or distort it. And that seemed to me particularly apt for a story about the reflections of a star, an international celebrity, in the lives of ordinary people.

In some ways the novel is a progressive history of dance. It becomes a dance—both in terms of the way the language is structured and also how the narrators take center stage for a while and then move off to allow other narrator/dancers to appear.

Meade: There is a very large cast of characters involved, including some very famous cameo appearances. I'd love to know which, if any, of the main characters were either entirely fictional or composite characters?

McCann: Basically everyone in the novel is "fictional" or "dreamt," apart from the very obvious ones. For example, Rudi had three sisters. In the novel, he has one. She's an imaginative composite. She shoulders quite a lot of the narrative. His dance teacher, Anna, is based on a character who taught him how to dance at age eleven. Victor, who carries much of the New York narrative, is based upon a rumor I heard about a gay character living in New York in the 1970's . . . I have no idea whatsoever if Victor and Rudi knew each other or not, but I made them best friends. So Victor is essentially made up from scratch.

The only bit of absolute poaching I did for the book was to take Andy Warhol's diary entry and reproduce it verbatim. Curiously enough it was one of the things people pulled me up on. "That can't be true," they said.

Ingmar Bergman at one stage in his life said: "Sometimes I must console myself with the fact that he who tells a lie, loves the truth." Same goes for plot developments, if we can avoid giving too much away.

I wanted to be fairly true to Nureyev himself. I didn't want him fathering some child in Paris, or living in China, or something ridiculous where the accepted facts become farce. No. The basis of the facts are there. The story-line is largely true to his life. On the broad canvas it's fair . . . but it's an abstract fairness, if you will. It's an abstract portrait, concentrating on lines and brush-strokes and traditionally neglected parts of the canvas. The darker reaches that the eye doesn't necessarily go to. Is it factual? No. He wasn't in Caracas in the early 1980s, as far as I know. But facts are mercenary things: they can be used and exploited in so many ways. I wanted to create a texture that was true. I also wanted to question the idea of storytelling. Who owns a story? Who has the right to tell a story? Who and what legislates what becomes a supposed fact? If the historian pushes the storyteller aside, shouting No, No, No, then, fuck it, the story teller should shout back and say, Why not? Why not? Why not?

Imagine you were at the bar last night. Who is going to tell the story of that night? The bartender? The waitress? Your friends? Or you? Or maybe a composite of everyone who was there? Maybe even the ones who didn't see you. After all, the ones who didn't see you might have an insight also: they might create an atmosphere or might, indeed, have noticed something about the bartender who claims a truth. It's six degrees of separation and preparation and instigation.

And so, for me, Rudolf Nureyev's first public dance is governed as much by the soldiers he danced for—and what they fought for—as by Nureyev himself.

I don't think readers share those doubts, nor do they need to. What readers want is a good story, well told; and that's what I want when I read. I really don't care whether it's fiction or non-fiction. It's about language. Hugo Hamilton just wrote what he's calling a memoir, *The Speckled People*. I couldn't give a shit whether it's real or not. All I know is that it's brilliant and it moved me to tears. If that's not enough, I don't know what is.

Meade: What are you going to work on now? How will the experience of writing *Dancer* influence what comes next?

McCann: I'm over the point of exhaustion that one gets after finishing the equivalent of a marathon and how I'm opening up to new ideas. I like the idea of a novel in New York, something beyond the edge of what's normally written about in this city. I don't want a novel about townhouses or antiseptic parties or divorce. Something edgier, I think. But who knows where I'll go? I'm generally led by images. I'm not sure how much the experience of writing *Dancer* will influence me—hopefully not too much. I generally see stories as distinct entities: they find their own language and form and length.

Of course it can be dangerous to talk about these things. The famous phrase is that the unexamined life is not worth living, but the over-examined life mightn't be too much fun either.

Meade: You wrote an account of the immediate aftermath of September 11 that was published here in the *Irish Independent*. Eighteen months on, how is New York now? When I talked to you two years ago, you talked of perhaps moving to Italy. Has that been postponed?

McCann: Really, I'd love to pack up and head for somewhere like Lucca, or Florence. But I've postponed moving to Italy for all the wrong reasons: I'm lazy, I've got kids going to school now, I renovated an old apartment built originally in 1896. One day soon, I hope.

As for New York, this city is well recovered. I recently went marching against the war, or the idea of the war. That was one of the healthiest days that this city has had, in terms of showcasing its recovery. The past doesn't matter here all that much, never has. It's not as if everyone's out running around, trying to buy gas masks. It doesn't work that way and never has, despite what some of the European media would want you to believe. Also, I think there's a healthy skepticism and raging doubt here—again, something that hasn't become part of the wider American image. People are not as thick or as pliable as the *Daily Mail* might have us believe.

Meade: I also wonder about how novels that are based on factual people or events are received differently. I'm thinking of the reaction, particularly here, to Edna O'Brien's last novel. Was that just a case of lots of different people here believing they owned the story in some way because it was so recent?

McCann: Well, I thought that was a great book. And a brave book. And I applaud what Edna has done and how she stood up against the onslaught. She has such dignity. The fact of the matter is that a "documentary" crew could have gone in and made a "factual account" of the same incident and they would never have been assaulted the way Edna was. It's about our perception of facts. It's about how they are manipulated.

Using historical material as a backdrop or indeed foreground for stories, which in some way sheds light on what it means to be human, is a way of connecting experience with politics.

I'd rather not leave my sense of history, and certainly politics, to the talking heads on the six o'clock news, thank you very much. There is a point— and a valid point—where writers can step in and recreate another logic, or another angle, or another question. Why not? There has to be a point where we, as writers, enter what people call "history." Not necessarily to legislate it, but certainly to witness it at its stranger, darker, quieter angles.

Colum McCann

Robert Birnbaum / 2003

From *The Morning News,* February 25, 2003. www.themorningnews.org. Reprinted with the permission of Robert Birnbaum.

Robert Birnbaum: Is there really no Russian word for "privacy"?

Colum McCann: No, there's not. There is nothing that accurately reflects what we believe of as privacy.

Birnbaum: That's peculiar, isn't it?

McCann: There might be now. Certainly not in the forties, fifties and sixties. Right now there might be a developing word for privacy. That's a country, right now, without a theory, looking for a theory. An interesting place for a writer to be. A lot of interesting young writers coming out of there too. I would go there if I wasn't here with kids. I think it would be a really interesting place for a writer to go. You walk down Nevsky Prospect in St. Petersburg, and there's twenty different groups vying for your attention, and some are National Bolsheviks, and others are pro-Stalinists. Others are pure Communists, others are what they call benevolent Communists. Fascists.

Birnbaum: How can anybody still be a Stalinist?

McCann: Lots of the old people in the hospitals. I went to the military hospital in Ufa, and a lot of the old people wanted the bedrock feeling of Stalin back. Because it gave them security. Now they are sixty, seventy, eighty years old, and they are thinking all the sands have shifted. Everything is new, and they can't deal with it. And they look back fondly, as people do.

Birnbaum: Is this with the full awareness of what Stalin did?

McCann: They grew up through it. I talked to toothless old men, one in particular who I will never forget. In June of 2001 he sat down and talked to me through a translator for a half an hour about how his father had been murdered by Stalin and dumped in a barrel. Shot in the head and dumped in a barrel. And other family members taken out. And how he wished that there were people around like Stalin these days in order to institute an order over these crazy young people who were running rampant over the country. Seriously. It's absurd, but it's so absurd that it has to be true. I found it to be a fascinating place. In America, as in most Western countries, the writer is not really feared anymore. Nobody fears your bite. So you have to work from a reckless inner need. That ability to go in because you need to do it. You just need to do it yourself. But whereas you are not muzzled in any way—I'm not favoring censorship—but I was talking to my friend Alexander Hemon, one of the great young writers in America, who was saying that at least the Nazis hated books, George Bush and his cronies don't even like books.

Birnbaum: Laura Bush seems to.

McCann: Somebody said that to me that she really liked books. I asked if he would go to one of her readings, he said "Absolutely not!"

Birnbaum: I don't understand. You have a sense of a view that writers are effete in the USA. Why would being in Russia today make writing more vital and meaningful? Do writers mean something in Russia?

McCann: Writers have always meant something in Russia. As writers have always meant something in Ireland. And the language is revered and cherished. Being a writer over there you can help create a consciousness. In the same way rock bands over here are more prone to create ideas or consciousness—or to stab at an idea.

Birnbaum: Are books expensive in Russia?

McCann: Yeah, they are, but a lot of these magazines are still around. Although Russian art doesn't sell all that well apparently. A lot of people are embracing Western art. But it would just be an interesting place to be a writer in—and you can rail against the system and things like that, yeah.

Birnbaum: Their gangsters are crazier than ours (if you believe the movies), aren't they?

McCann: I spent a night with mafiosi there. They were funny. I knew exactly what they did. But I asked them, "What do you do?" And they said (in a deep accented voice), "We are babysitters."

Birnbaum: I'm still trying to make sense of the image of the ineffectiveness of writers in this country, as against other places?

McCann: It's not necessarily always a bad thing. One of the things about American writing is that it's so provocative and fine. And working outside systems is a really healthy thing to do. Look at the number of great writers that are in this country right now in comparison to say Britain or Ireland. I find it wonderful. You start naming names, and what happens is you leave out your best friend. And then they are not your best friend anymore.

Birnbaum: I have a guilty pleasure of looking at web sites that cover literary matters, and a number recently gave publicity to the Underground Literary Alliance's attendance at a reading where among other things they criticized writer Ben Greenlee because his story about a tree was not sufficiently transgressive.
McCann: Wow. They took a shot at Rick Moody, didn't they? It's all bullshit. It doesn't matter. It's all about people's social lives, and the literary artist is part of it.

Birnbaum: Why are you living in New York City? It strikes me that it might be the last place a writer would want to live.
McCann: First of all, my wife is from New York.

Birnbaum: Okay, say no more.
McCann: I love it there too. I'm really happy there. It's a good thing to be there. I get to see my editor—I have wonderful editor. If I wasn't there I would be in the boondocks, you know.

Birnbaum: Let's talk about *Dancer.* It strikes me that there might be a couple of reasons to base a novel on a real person. One, to use that figure as some kind of conveyance for a big idea. Or to somehow embellish the sense of or the reputation of that person. What was it that you were doing in writing a novel with a character named Rudolf Nureyev?
McCann: Not the second. More so the first. If number two happened accidentally, if I was trying to bolster up or shore up or scaffold up his identity in the world—I mean, why would someone like me do it anyway? If it happened accidentally, great, fine. I'm very happy. Why should someone like me who was never really interested in dance and didn't know all that much about Russia prior to trying to research it? So that wasn't my intention.

My vague intention was to try to write a novel that was completely without boundary and without border. And so one of the first intentions was almost to write a novel with every country that you could possibly imagine. That obviously fell by the wayside. The second intention was to write a novel or stories around which there was a centrifugal force, but none of them would ever collide and none of them would repeat. John Dos Passos was an ideal for me. Both of those vague ideas were turned on their head and didn't happen for me and became this.

I started creating hundreds of characters, and then I started missing them, and I wanted to go back to them, and I enjoyed them and wanted to know what happened to them. And it's just far too pretentious to do every single country in the world. So I was looking for a figure for whom that would happen. I was also thinking a lot about stories and how stories get told and why they get told and how we create stories. Who owns a story and legislates it? What right do journalists have to make a figure iconic, and historians can, but novelists can't make a figure iconic? Or go into the iconic life styles?

So, in terms of brute reality what happened was, I heard a story from a friend of mine in Dublin who, this kid who carried this image—basically, his father came home with a television set, and when he plugged it in later on, the image of Rudolf Nureyev came on, and he was carrying the image around in his arms. It's a pretty extraordinary thing for a seven-year-old, working-class boy in Dublin to be inhabited by this Russian dancer in the early seventies—grown up in Bashkiria, trained in Leningrad, defected to Paris. He was probably being beamed in from somewhere like Germany. The beam itself was probably coming from the British Broadcasting Company, and all these things collide in this tiny little apartment in the flats in Dublin, a working-class apartment. That would never become part of the official Rudolf Nureyev story. But it seems to me to say as much about someone like Nureyev as it does about Dublin at the time, as it does about fame at the time, as it does about the guy Jimmy at the time and what has happened to him. He fell in love with Rudolf Nureyev or at least fell in love with the idea of this figure. Years later he is dealing with his bisexuality and moves to Brooklyn as an actor. He used Nureyev as this idea for himself. That was a great story. I think that is a really fantastic story.

When I heard it I said, "Oh fuck, yes." I went straight to the biographies and then I got another "Oh fuck, yes," by seeing apparently he danced for the soldiers home from the Second World War, all the injured coming back from the front—twenty-three million Russians died—all that pure horror. Around the corner from that I began to think, Well, this is a six-year-old boy dancing for soldiers who have no arms and legs—it's only a half a line in the biography. So surely the experience of those soldiers is equally important to the dance that he creates, as it is to the dancer he becomes, as it is to the air that he breathes around him in the hospital on that very day. As just saying, "Well, Rudolf Nureyev's first public dance was at the age of six for

the soldiers home from the war. Let's move on because we are only interested in Rudy." That's like a camera making a film about somebody and only
following that person.

I started to think about the larger ramifications of where that goes. Of
course you could go on forever. It could become ridiculous. You could
unravel it way beyond the front and go back generations. It seemed to me
the experience of that war must have affected Nureyev in some profound
unconscious way. So that's why I wrote the start of the novel the way I did,
as this outer canvas moving in, in, in, and in, and down on him and out
again to some other washerwoman who goes out, out, out and then in, on
and then going in on him close and then coming out again and then moving
around. John Berger says, "Never again will a story be told as if it were the
only one." That great quote. I admired him tremendously. He's one of my
great heroes. I think that's part of the writer's function right now—to call
into question story and storytelling.

Birnbaum: At what point in the story and its construction did you decide to
use the William Maxwell epigram?
McCann: Pretty early on.

Birnbaum: To use a cliché, does it inform this narrative?
McCann: Yeah, it was probably about a quarter of the way through the book
that I remembered it. I loved that book, and I knew he had written something
along those lines. That definitely informed the work. Although I tried not to
disease myself by thinking about it too consciously, all the time. Now that I'm
finished and away from it, it makes more sense to me, what I was doing.

Birnbaum: You are speaking about the construction of the narrative in cinematic terms. One of the things I was stuck by was this monologue by the
character Victor, in which I don't think there were any periods.
McCann: Right, there are none.

Birnbaum: The intense focus was like a tight headshot of the character. You
get that close to Rudolf in that way. Why Victor?
McCann: Victor is almost like the shadow image of Rudy. Victor was everything. I could go through Victor and deal with all the issues of sex. All of the
things, if you take him as the main character of the book and you put him
through all of that directly, people would pull away and say, "Oh no, don't do
that." In some ways, it was a way to glance off and come at Rudy by glancing off. But in other ways I began to fall in love with him. It was like, "God,

who is this character and where the hell is he coming from?" From me. Yes, thirty-five pages without a full stop. I knew that I wanted to do that because I wanted to capture the energy of the seventies and I wanted it to feel like you had gotten a couple of blasts of coke up your nose and you were like, "Whoa, okay." And where am I going to go next? So it shifts and turns and shifts and turns. But also to embrace how wonderful it was for people, it seems. I talked to a lot of people who were around in the early seventies, and they are a little bit tired of all the moralizing now, that goes on about it. At the time, they were having great fun. It was like taking a Coca-Cola. The way we take a cola was just like having a line of coke. People didn't see that it was going to damage you. People didn't see that ultimately that all of this stuff is going to collapse, and we are going to get this dreadful disease that's going to plow us under. None of that was there. There was just this, "Hah," that we embraced the world. I loved doing that character of Victor. He is sort of based on this character Victor Hugo who was around in the early seventies, who my agent had told me about. He told me one quick story about him and he was a friend of Halston's. I changed him and made him be from Venezuela.

Birnbaum: Your agent is Andrew Wylie?

McCann: Yeah. So he was telling me some stories about the seventies. Wylie was a pretty wild man in the seventies too. So I was there and I was telling them—Andrew and Sara Chalfant, his right-hand woman—and I'm like stuck in the fucking thing. I need some character to take me into that wild place. And he just did it like that, "Well, let me tell you about this Victor." After that lunch I went home—I read a lot of stuff about the baths and all that sort of stuff and the early seventies, but I knew I wanted to capture the energy of that in prose. Also, I wanted to come to that last sentence, "Here comes loneliness applauding itself all the way down the street." Because that was very much about Rudy. So by not being about Rudy, people find it very instructive about what Rudy went through in the seventies. I would have loved to be around in those particular times and try and make sense. I can't make sense of anywhere where people are politically now. Fucking boggles my mind. Who are these people who are out shouting for war? Where are people of my generation?

Birnbaum: Well, the opposition seems fractured, and the administration's message is a combination of a beer commercial and a televangelist's pitch.

McCann: It's horrific isn't it? I don't know who is speaking out. Obviously, there is [Noam] Chomsky and all those writers or thinkers who took out an ad recently.

Birnbaum: I commend you on the way in which you captured the utter dreariness of Soviet life, and still there was a spark of life in the people.

McCann: I'm very glad you said that. The fact that they could fight and divorce and laugh and walk down the street and get drunk . . . a couple of Russian historians came to me and said that they haven't seen in recent fiction, apart from Don DeLillo's *Libra,* a capturing of the Russian spirit and the Russian ideas. By not shirking, by not making it all gray, doom and gloom and piss stains on the stairwells and cabbage leaves on everybody's teeth and soaked in vodka. By having that and whatever that meant and those sorts of feelings, but also trying to have people who laughed and loved each other and had these grand human feelings and contradictions. Rudy, he doesn't defect because he wants to embrace some vast political idea. He just does it because he's a dancer. And he just wants to dance more and in less classically structured situations. But he was used as a political icon. This is what's interesting. I think he lived the life of his country in advance in some ways. If you take Rudolf Nureyev as a loose metaphor for the Soviet Union and then the breakdown of the Soviet Union itself—it's shift to democracy—he being its greatest leading capitalist for quite a while. His embracing of art, his reaching for great heights and then this sickness that invades him. This cultural sickness which happens to be called fame in his case, but in the Soviet Union it could be called something else. And then eventually succumbing to this disease. I'm not trying to impose an exact map. But in a very curious way we could talk about Rudolf Nureyev as having lived the life of his country.

Birnbaum: In terms of fame, he defected in '61. In the USA, ballet was a marginal art form, then by the seventies he ended up in the Warholian clique.

McCann: In '63 he was on the cover of *Time* and *Newsweek* in the very same week.

Birnbaum: What I am trying to get at is that I don't think celebrity meant as much in the sixties as in the seventies and after.

McCann: You are absolutely right.

Birnbaum: Did Nureyev get on this moving train of celebrity or did he propel it?

McCann: He got on the start of the train. He got on the very first carriage. As far as I can see, he was perhaps one of the most truly international celebrities of the century. Perhaps more famous at one stage than John Lennon. Of course, Lennon said he was more famous than Jesus Christ.

Birnbaum: More famous than Muhammad Ali?

McCann: Yes, Nureyev was as famous as Jagger and Ali and the Beatles and maybe even Marilyn Monroe and so on. He's a truly international figure, comes from the East, really, and takes over the West. He's used by all sorts of people for all sorts of things. Like Ali was used as a political symbol, yes. Ali was a symbol of sports, of fame. Rudy was all of that and a sex symbol and then a gay icon. So he was a poster boy for all sorts of things, but the only thing he wanted to do was dance. But all these things would intrude upon him. So he was on the front of that train, I think. So if he did know what he was doing, then there would be photographers waiting at the stage door. He would get on and say he was doing *Giselle.* First of all, he would wait fifteen or twenty minutes to make the crowd impatient and say, "Fuck them, fuck them, I don't care about them. I just want the Angel of Dance." He'd get on and dance and take all the oxygen from the air. And they would all love him. He'd get off, "The fuckers." And run down to public toilets, slam away, for however long he wants to, and then saunter back with an overcoat on, go into the wings, and dance again. Imagine what would happen if someone went cottaging today? With ABC News and CBC News, *People* magazine and all these others, outside. Celebrity has been ruined for the poor celebrities. At that stage it was something so new that they didn't know what they were really getting themselves into and they just embraced it all. I think it must have become really horrendous for them. I know it must be really horrendous to be a celebrity nowadays. It's quite awful.

Birnbaum: It's a little difficult to feel sympathy. So much of fame is what these people have worked for . . . maybe the accidental celebrity might be a sympathetic figure.

McCann: Say, someone like Sean Penn. Sean Penn is a great fucking actor. He's a great director. He has a great eye. He has something to say about the human spirit. This is the best way he knows how. And some fucking photographer comes to the restaurant and starts snapping pictures of him and his kids. That's not very fair. Enough then. We blame the celebrities because we want the celebrities to fall. Because that's always really nice, because instead of us falling we watch them fall.

Birnbaum: You're right about the intrusiveness of the media and the rabid need for this private information. There are no boundaries, which is bad.

McCann: Someone like Daniel Day Lewis, one of the few who has the absolute honesty to say, "Fuck you all, I'm going to Italy and I'm going to hang out with a shoemaker for a couple of years. If a great project comes along, then I'll go and do it. I'll shave off all my hair so I won't have the screaming hordes." It's like a real fuck-you. A real, powerful person, but it's very hard to be that sort of person.

Birnbaum: There's a collage of styles in *Dancer.* What did you mean to do in the end of the book by presenting a list of possessions sold from Nureyev's estate?

McCann: What do you think?

Birnbaum: Well, what I got out of that list was that almost everything was sold at a greater value than it was offered at. Also, that he was an uninhibited consumer.

McCann: Ahm, there's an item in there. Most of these lots are absolutely true, all right. They are ripped off from the Christie's auction. But lot 1274 pre-revolutionary Russian china dish in oak box, box damaged, is the dish that Yulia gave to him at the end, that was given to her by her father and so on. The buyer is Nikolai . . . the suggestion here is that . . . perhaps the suggestion is, I don't even know, if someone wants to take it up that way . . . is that the boy who gets adopted because it's an adopted name . . . the suggestion is that the boy buys the dish back. It takes place in 1995 when it's possible he could have bought it back that he could have been one of these new Russians who embraced things in all sorts of ways. In other words, the stories go on and on and on and on and on. So really, the story could go on in all sorts of ways, hundreds of pages afterwards. The other thing that it's trying to say is that our stories are important. That no matter who you are—if you are a rent boy, if you are a housekeeper, if you are a soldier or a washerwoman, if you are a translator—no matter how much you are seen on the periphery, your stories matter.

One of the things that has never come out about this book is that it's vaguely social. But it's—I don't want to sound like an idiot—it's not a proletarian book, but it's a fairly angry book. But because it's called *Dancer* and because people hear it's about a ballet dancer named Rudolf Nureyev, people expect something else. If you think about it, there is a lot of war there and a lot of comments on what wealth does to people and so on. People are sort of surprised that I have gone from—I did a book called *This Side of Brightness*, which was about homeless people in the subway tunnels and the people who built the tunnels—to writing about a gay Russian ballet dancer. And it does sound like an enormous leap, but in truth it's not all that huge. I'm still talking about people who are on the periphery.

Birnbaum: It's not huge if one recognizes the centrality to you of the large reservoir of stories that are available even when you are telling one person's story. I don't know if Americans see it that way these days. Maybe they do.
McCann: Do you think they might?

Birnbaum: I keeping wondering. Writers do favor using words like "stories" and "narratives," and that they are found everywhere.
McCann: That's more a European thing. I don't like the word "fiction" anymore. "Fiction" and "non-fiction" are categories set up so that we make it easy on ourselves. The fact that his old lovers came to me in London and embraced me and said that they had for the first time since Rudy died found Rudy again, was really extraordinary. That they could look at photographs of him and they could feel objects in the room, but for the first time they found him in these pages. They could read into the text in whatever way they wanted to. It was extraordinary to me.

Birnbaum: On the other hand, you weren't writing a biography.
McCann: No, and it goes back to your very first question, your original question. This is not a book about Rudolf . . . certainly not a biography of Rudolf Nureyev. It's a book in which a character by the name of Rudolf Nureyev appears as a shadow unto other things that are being talked about. Like stories and storytelling, their value. Like fame, like all these little human moments that operate around . . .

Birnbaum: You mention that Julie Kavanagh has a biography of Nureyev forthcoming. Is that something you intend to read?
McCann: Fucking right. She was one of the ones—I thought she was going to have the knives out for me, like chop me up and feed me to the pigeons in Covent Gardens because I was over in London and she asked to meet me. "Oh Jesus, what am I gonna do now?" I was really worried. I met her and she said I had captured both the angel and the devil about him. She's been working on him for ten years. She was so gracious. She's a gorgeous woman, too.

She's a dancer and she understands dance. She wrote a great book about [choreographer] Frederick Ashton, so I read that. I have no doubt she will do a great book. If she had written her book before mine I would have been dead in the water. Hers is about two years down the line. But facts, here's the other thing. We were talking about fiction, facts, non-fiction, and facts can be . . . we all know we just have to listen to the newspapers what they can do with facts. Osama bin Laden's tape today. "The fact that he mentioned the word 'Iraq.'" Which is a fact, yes, he mentioned Iraq but it can be shipped off and used in all sorts of ways and be very mercenary things. Whereas fiction is more about texture and trying to get into the heart of something.

Birnbaum: Not to mention memory and recollection, which is a whole other realm.

McCann: Exactly. It's something that interests me . . . even back in *Songdogs*, which is my first novel written about ten years ago. I had a line in it, "That memory is three quarters imagination and all the rest is lies." I think I am still riffing on that in some sort of way.

Birnbaum: Isn't that the beauty of what we call fiction? You get to say things that people will and ought to take more seriously than if they read it in some literary theory exposition.

McCann: The thing is you have to make it real. And that's why I call this character in the book Rudolf Nureyev, rather than Dmitri Garasamov, or whatever. Because if it's Dmitri Garasamov, who gives a shit? First of all, I don't want to write a book about Dmitri, that's not what I'm trying to get at.

Birnbaum: Right, what would the frame of reference be?

McCann: I'd much prefer to go into a steel works and write about a steelworker in Bethlehem, Maryland or wherever he happens to be. That would be much more important to me.

Birnbaum: What is next for you?

McCann: I'm on the cusp of a number of different things. A hundred different things. The funny thing is to wait around waiting for the . . .

Birnbaum: A message?

McCann: Nah, it's like somebody says something to you, accidentally. Most of my novels have arrived accidentally. I've had some sort of general idea that I wanted to do. This had the general idea I wanted to an international boundary-less novel. For example, *Everything in This Country Must.* I definitely, definitely wanted to write about Northern Ireland. It was really important to me. Because people in Ireland had said I had become an American author. So I wanted to turn around and say "Fuck you." And with *This Side*, this happened when I was at a party in New York, somebody just mentioned to me there are homeless people living in the subway tunnels of New York. "Did you know that?" I'd been in NYC six months. But I was down there the very next day.

Birnbaum: Have you seen Margaret Morton's book [*The Tunnel* Yale, 1995] on people in the tunnels?
McCann: Good photographs. Really good photographs. She's got a nice eye. She has a social conscience. I like that. And she's brave. That's the other thing. Think about the writers that you like. The brave writers that are doing things right now. There aren't all that many around, really.

Birnbaum: We are afflicted by a high comfort level. Even the poorest among us are better off than the poor in the rest of the world.
McCann: Sure, sure.

Birnbaum: Give me a sense of where you rank *Dancer.* How do you feel about this book?
McCann: There's a couple of things. I'm very happy. I'm very surprised how people received it. I thought it was much more obscure than what people are perceiving. I thought my brother wouldn't read it. Or my wife's parents wouldn't read it. Or might find parts of it offensive or tough-going. It gratifies me that they don't find it tough-going. I thought it was going to be ripped a little more than what it was. I'm a little disappointed that it seems to go to dance critics and people who write biographies. Because it's a novel. But that's just the ways and means of the way they ship out the books to people in newspapers. I read through it now and then. The one thing, I have a mistake in there and nobody has come across yet. I'm sure you put it on the web site, and people will say there are fifteen hundred mistakes in this thing.

Birnbaum: I read that when you first came here to the US you rode a bicycle for eight thousand miles around the country.
McCann: Actually twelve thousand miles. That translates to eighteen thousand kilometers. The things that people get wrong and they become fact.

Oh, I forgot to tell you this earlier. Rudy had invented the fact that he danced for the soldiers, home from the war. He told that [story] to a reporter. Right. This reporter printed it as fact. A biographer, not Diane Solway, who did very well, but a peripheral biographer had taken it as fact and written it down. Right. I said, "Oh, what an interesting fact. I'd love to spin a fiction out of that, right." Then I come up with this fiction. I only recently learned that he was the one who created the fiction, and I spun the fiction out of it afterwards.

Birnbaum: You are talking about the incident in the beginning of the book?
McCann: He said when he was six years old he danced for the soldiers, home from the war. Apparently, that's a lie. He said this to a reporter, "Yes, when I was six years old I was a beautiful boy and I danced for the soldiers who came back from the front." Julie Kavanagh is convinced it's a fiction. So I spun this fiction out of fiction. Which I think is really nice. And gives me the spiritual connection with Nureyev.

Birnbaum: And other professional liars.
McCann: What were we talking about? Oh, the bicycle journey. That's where I learned to grow up, actually. I bought a typewriter in Cape Cod, worked as a taxi driver and motel clerk. I said I was going to write the great Irish-American novel. Twenty-one years old. I still had the same page of paper in the typewriter at the end of six months. I realized, "You're a middle-class, white, suburban, well-treated Dublin kid who didn't have any traumatic upbringing. You have fuck-all to write about. So get out and do something." So I took off on a bicycle, went from Massachusetts to Florida, Florida across to New Orleans. Stayed in New Orleans for a while, into Texas and into Mexico. Back up through Texas. Worked there with juvenile delinquents for a while. Back up through New Mexico, Colorado. Worked there as a bicycle mechanic for a while. Into Utah where I was digging ditches for some of the forest fires. Wyoming, Oregon. I did thirty-odd states and I finished in San Francisco.

Birnbaum: One last question, how important is it for you to maintain your Irish identity?
McCann: Probably it's pretty important to me, although I pretend it's not. I'm a New Yorker because I live in New York, and that's where I will be now for quite a while, but I'm definitely, definitely Irish. And I'll always be an Irish writer. No matter what. No matter what happens. Nobody can

take that away. If I never set a book that touches the notion of Ireland or Irishness again, it still won't matter to the claim; in fact, that I'm an Irish writer. Irish identity is important to me. But I wouldn't go back there to live. But I love the stories, I love the songs, I love the sound, and I love the feel of it. I like being Irish. I don't want to become one of these "Oirish" people, if you will. Over the top, wearing my flat hat backwards and swigging pints of Guinness and singing Molly Malone. Although I do that too, every now and then. Because, why not? I couldn't become an American, if you will. I definitely could become a New Yorker. It's important to me and the sound of the language and the feel of the stories and everything like that. Although it must be said that American writing is much more interesting than Irish writing right now. There's a couple of great Irish writers who are doing really interesting things. But in general it's not the heyday of Joyce and Beckett and those sorts of days. I wonder if those days can ever come back. Is it possible to write a novel like *Ulysses* anymore?

Birnbaum: Should I quote back John Berger to you?

McCann: Berger knows that freedom begins between the ears. He's so smart. There are some great ones over here. DeLillo writes great novels. Jim Harrison. I love Jim Harrison. He's so ballsy. Yes. He pulls no punches. There's no bullshit about him. He's truly one of the greats. He's mostly recognized abroad, unfortunately.

Birnbaum: He has a great humor and humanity about him. Well, I expect we will talk again. Thank you.

McCann: I enjoyed it very much.

Zoli Interview: Q&A with Michael Hayes

Michael Hayes / 2007

From colummccann.com. A widely-published poet and expert on Romani culture, Hayes is
the author of *Irish Travellers: Representations and Realities*. Reprinted with the permission.

Michael Hayes: What did you know about the Roma before you started
writing the book?

Colum McCann: Nothing. I came to the Romani culture empty-handed.
That's interesting, now that I finally understand it. The gadjo (non-Gypsy)
comes in, swaggering, but is immediately apparent as empty-handed. What
an idiot he is. He thinks he can watch. Even worse, he thinks he can understand. He has no background to trade on.

But then again there's a freedom in that, an open doorway, if you're open
to possibility. You walk into it cold. Then you pass through a warm house.
And you realize you've been somewhere special. And then you understand
that in a certain way, you, the changed one, have turned your own clichés
upside-down. I was the one who went in with nothing. This could be called
begging, but it's not. It's searching. And then I was the one who came out—
after four years of writing and researching—if not more knowledgeable,
then at least changed.

I equate my initial ignorance with the general level of ignorance in the
wider world. I'm no different to anybody else. I knew nothing about Gypsies.
I didn't even know the word Roma or Romani. But my interest was piqued
by the Isabel Fonseca book [*Bury Me Standing*], and I just wanted to know.
I wanted to delve. I wanted to see if it was possible to tell this story that was
largely untold. It was then I found my heroes . . . the Papuszas of the world,
the Hancocks, the people in the Milan Simecka Foundation, the community
workers, the ones that effect a difference in the larger communities.

In relation to the novel, I know that I didn't get it all right. I know that. Who can? Who might want to? *Zoli* is a failure. All books are. But I tried to tell it in the most honest way possible. I tried to make a little footprint.

The thing I'd love is that a young Romani writer might look at *Zoli* and say—hey, that's okay, but it's not good enough, I need to write my own story. That would be a curious form of success for me. If it became the yeast for the bread that finally comes from the oven.

Hayes: . . . and what was the catalyst for this book?

McCann: I was literally looking for a book that would form a peak to my ideas about exile. I have written about exile since my earliest collection, *Fishing the Sloe-Black River,* when I was in my twenties. It has—though I wasn't always entirely aware of it—been my obsession for two decades. And once I realized that it was my obsession, it was time to get rid of it. One last excursion into that particular darkness. And then my wife, Allison, told me about Papusza, whom she'd read about in Isabel Fonseca's book. I couldn't get rid of her. This poet. This exile. This Gypsy. In order to lose her, I had to write her.

It was, I hope, my most complicated statement about exile. But there's no point in me sitting down to try and make intellectual sense of it. That's for others. It should be emotional. It should be felt. By way of analogy, consider the writer as being disguised as a creek. Eventually he or she meets other waters. That is the reader, or even the critic. Hopefully it hits a wider world.

Hayes: Have you had much feedback from women about the book? How did they "respond" to this story of an "unusual" woman whose life experience and minority culture background would have been quite different to the average woman's life (in either Western or Eastern Europe back then?)

McCann: For whatever reason, it seems that women have latched on to this book—and especially women who know what it is like to be marginalized. Perhaps they recognize her in a way. Some are frustrated by Zoli and her seeming lack of action in her middle age—and yet that's part of her attraction too. I can see that Zoli is frustrating as a fictional character . . . in a way she's meant to be . . . if you take it from a white European or American perspective, she never seems to fight back. She takes what comes to her. She walks away. She never entirely embraces where she has come from. And yet from a Romani point of view, what she does is extraordinary, and, I hope, true. She forges her own identity. She fights through, not back. And in the end it becomes a personal song of triumph. So much of the Romani experience seems to be captured there, or at least I hope it is.

She becomes someone else, something else, someplace else. She sees the value in the elsewhere, but this time the elsewhere is an imaginative place, a written place—and finally it becomes a poem. I tried so hard to code all this in the book. It's strange, now, to confront it as an idea. I wanted Zoli to have an emotional life. I wanted people to believe that—perhaps—one might be able to go down to Northern Italy, today, of all days, and meet her. There she is, walking outside the coffee shop! There she is in that mountainside hut. I wanted that for the reader. To see Zoli as entirely real. And that's been the response. Readers seem to somehow know Zoli.

It's a book about gender, voice, distance, media. A friend of mine said that it wasn't hip, but it was hip-high. It struck him. And I meant for it to deal a blow to the solar plexus.

And yet many other readers thought that Zoli should have a triumphant halo around her at the end. Certainly I didn't want her to become a spectacle of disintegration. There's been enough of that. But I didn't want to turn her into cliché. I didn't want for her to stand up at the conference in Paris and deliver a blow for Romani rights. No. Her victory was smaller—but no less significant—than that.

Hayes: It has been noted by some people that you are fascinated by the idea of the "Other," or Otherness? Was this always the case—i.e. from your earliest writing—or is the exploration of Otherness something which has become more important to you and your work in recent times?

McCann: I'm a middle-class Dubliner now living in New York. I sound halfway between suburbia and silence. But I've tried all my life to value the story of the anonymous other. In this case—for Zoli—I didn't think that enough had been said. Is that arrogant? Maybe it is. Probably it is. But I'd rather die with my heart on my sleeve than end up someone who patrols quietly around the perimeters. Watch those waters. They're tepid. I'm so sick of divorce stories and suburban trysts. And so I thought, Slovakia, Roma, socialism, okay, I'll try that story. I'm not trying to excuse myself. I hear writers, when they're talking about minorities, giving the excuse that they're half this, or an eighth that, or that their best friend is this shade of skin color . . . as if that allows them the right to own the story.

I don't own any story. It's my job to intrude.

And, always, in the back of my mind—whether I'm writing about homeless people in New York subway tunnels, or the gay underworld in the 1970s, or the teenagers caught in the Northern Ireland conflict—I'm aware of what I'm saying, or thinking, that I'm not that, what should I write about it, what right do I have? It's economically arrogant, culturally arrogant, sexually arrogant, socially arrogant. That's not me! That's not my life! But what am I going to do? Write about the pleasant Friday afternoon in 173 Clonkeen Road, Blackrock, Co. Dublin? Or the very nice chess game I just had with my kids on 86th Street in Manhattan? That's my immediate life, yes, but I'll leave that to a writer more talented than me.

So . . . to be the voice of "the other"? Fuck, yeah. Absolutely. No better compliment. Or to be a small catalyst of that voice? Wonderful! That's where I'm comfortable. That's where I'm best. Do I claim to *be* that voice? No. Of course not.

I write stories. That's another one of my jobs. I try for them to be good. I want them to be engaging. And on a certain level I want them to be social.

Hayes: Some might argue that Irish fiction until recent decades was somewhat insular and fixated on themes relating to a rural Ireland that has virtually disappeared—and issues as relating to sex, religion, authority, poverty, and the conflicts between different generations, etc. It appears that Irish fiction and other media, music/film, have become more "international" now—dealing with more "universal" themes. How do you feel about this?

McCann: Fair enough—but then at some stage you go back to your own. *Zoli* is an Irish novel. How can it be anything else? I'm an Irish writer. And yet it must be everything else. I realize that I'm answering by evading, but that's the job of the poet. Then again, I'm not a poet. I'm a contrarian.

People have asked why I didn't write about the Irish Travelers. Well, because I think that story is in the process of being told by others who are more inside than me, more at the center, with more access. They will tell it, and some already have told it, better than I could.

Hayes: Did you feel a burden of "responsibility" in bringing the story/voice of somebody who is now dead but who was also a woman from a "reviled" group who've been subjected to centuries of stereotype and many of whom have had no literary or public voice to date?

McCann: Yes, it was a massive responsibility. I didn't want it to be—or didn't even expect it to be a responsibility. But then I began researching and I was astounded. There were so few stories, so few novels. And they all came out the same. I wanted Zoli to fit in a certain box and yet for her to change that cardboard box utterly.

Early on in the novel I knew that it was the greatest social responsibility that I have had—as a writer—to-date. I found that a lot of the scholarship was shoddy, particularly from people on the outside who wanted to impose their ideas on the Roma.

Hayes: Is this the first book where you have written in the "persona/voice" of a woman? Was it more difficult than writing in the voice of a male narrator or the same?

McCann: I've written in a woman's voice before. My first published short story was "Sisters," in a woman's voice. But this is the first woman I truly know as a character. I am quite convinced that Zoli is alive today and living in Northern Italy, although of course she is not. In this sense, I find her to be my truest character.

Hayes: The Roma would be one of the largest minorities who have come to settle in Ireland in recent times—many with a view to making a life for themselves in Ireland settling here permanently. Was this in the back of your mind when you wrote the book?

McCann: It's a good question, but it had nothing to do with the writing of the novel.

Again . . . maybe someday I'll write the story of the Roma who have come to Ireland. I'm amazed that other Irish writers (apart from yourself) haven't had the gumption to do it . . . Why? I did at one stage flirt with the notion of bringing Zoli to Dublin, but she refused this option. She just wouldn't get on that ferry! I spent about a month writing that section and then, in the end, she tore up her first-class ticket!

Hayes: Did you find it difficult to balance writing somebody's story (albeit fictionalized to a great extent) and the duty of "informing" people about some of the realities of Roma history and their development as an outsider group?

McCann: A great question. I never felt it before. I never felt myself to be "the uncreated conscience of my race" in any manner or means. I never felt a duty to "represent" Ireland. But I felt it necessary—and maybe even imperative—to get the story of the Roma at least partway right. I mean, the thing is that I wanted to communicate that the Roma are as internally diverse as any other people. Fiction-writing is about being able to hold the essence of contradiction in the palm of your hand. I wanted the story to have wide ripples. The thing is the troughs of silence run very deep. But once you penetrate them, many other voices will emerge.

Hayes: You lived in a Roma settlement in Slovakia for a number of months?
McCann: I stayed in a few settlements, but I didn't live there. I was in Slovakia for two months altogether.

Hayes: What did you find difficult about this experience, and what was the most rewarding aspect of it?
McCann: The poverty in certain areas was brutal. Amongst the worst I've ever seen. And the racism was astounding.

Then, to have such generosity around that amazed me. I mean, these people invited me into their homes. They should have been berating me for my silence and ignorance. They should have been taking up arms against the policemen who spat on them every day. That astounded me. And we would sit in at night and sing songs. I sang Irish ballads. And the kids would lean against me and sometimes go to sleep. Possibly because I sang so badly.

Hayes: You must have heard some amazing stories while you were living there? Were there any that left a lasting impression on you?
McCann: All the stories left an impression on me. I can't remember and separate them now from the stories I created about Zoli. Hopefully her story contains their stories.

I do remember that one day I was in Svinia, in what they call "the dog eater's camp." I saw a young boy sitting near a bridge, rolling a cigarette. The bridge was a mess, put together with planks, aluminum siding, rope, tree trunks, sodden cardboard, tires, that sort of stuff. The boy himself looked part of the bridge. He was sprinkling tobacco onto the paper. Then I noticed that he had torn a page from a book in order to roll the cigarette. When he lit the smoke, the paper flared a moment, and he smoked in quick sharp bursts. When he was finished, he tore the remaining pages from the book and stuffed them in the pocket of his jeans. He threw down the cover and it landed at the foot of the bridge.

When he walked off towards a ramshackle shed, I strolled across to see what he had just smoked—it was a Slovak translation of the Romanian writer, Emil Cioran. And I thought, "Well, that says it all, doesn't it?" He had smoked the page.

Zoli Interview: Q&A with Laura McCaffrey

Laura McCaffrey / 2007

From colummccann.com. Reprinted with permission.

Laura McCaffrey: What inspired you to write this novel?

Colum McCann: Well, I'd just written *Dancer*, a fictionalization of the life of Rudolf Nureyev, a story that ranged time periods and continents and territories. So I wanted to take it easy for a while. I wanted a smaller story. But that's exactly what I didn't get. My wife, Allison, was reading the Isabel Fonseca book *Bury Me Standing* and she pointed out the story about Papusza, the Polish-born Gypsy poet who became a poster girl for the Socialists back in the fifties. Papusza ended up exiled from her people, living in a small cottage in Silesia. She died in '86. It was a classic story of the twentieth century. I couldn't get her face out of my mind. She was constantly there, along with the extraordinary plight of the Roma people she represented. I tried starting other novels, even short stories, but I kept returning to her. Eventually I had to write about her in order to find her and, I suppose, to lose her.

McCaffrey: So why Zoli? Why didn't you call her Papusza? You didn't shy away from that with Rudolf Nureyev. Why now?

McCann: I always felt that Rudi was more than able to look after himself. There have been, and will be, plenty more books about Rudi. His reputation wasn't going to stand or fall on my interpretation alone. And I didn't really care about him, *per se*. I know that sounds harsh, but I cared about the smaller people around him, those who lead more anonymous lives—the nurses, the rent boys, the soldiers, the shoemakers, the ones I made up, the fictional characters.

Zoli was always going to be a different cultural proposition. I didn't know enough about Papusza and I certainly didn't want any of the strait-jackets of traditional non-fiction. So I wanted to take just the templates of Papusza's life and turn them around, set them free. I certainly didn't want Zoli to die alone and forgotten. I didn't want her to become a spectacle of disintegration.

I wanted the story to be true and honest and accurate, but I also wanted to say that there is a future, there is a civil rights movement at the core here, there is a light at the end of the tunnel, and it's not just a train bearing down awful fast.

McCaffrey: So this is a social novel then?

McCann: Maybe. I don't know. It is rather alarming that for a culture of ten to twelve million people—who are as internally diverse as any other people—that we often have, in our imaginations, one single "Gypsy" story. Coming from a country of five million myself, I'm well-aware of the impos-sibility of one single Irish story to represent all stories. So it is astounding to me that we seem to weave one narrative thread around the Romani people: they lie, they steal, they sing, they dance. In a sense the Romani experience is one of Europe's last properly told stories, or certainly one of its most ignored stories.

We have to take into account that there are ten to twelve million Roma in the world. That's as many as there are Jewish people. Yet the public nar-ratives are so different. The memory is constructed in a different manner. Often, for example, they are just a footnote in the history of the Holocaust. And there is no real public perception of their enslavement in eighteenth- and nineteenth-century Europe.

When I was writing *Zoli*, I didn't want to brutalize or sentimentalize, but to answer your question, yes, on second thoughts, I think it's a social novel. I wanted to shine a light on a story that has not necessarily been told enough. Some great books have been written about the Roma, but not enough, never enough. Stories have to be told over and over again. And again after that. Stories are the human democracy. I have had a great time with Steinbeck, for instance; he was both a story-teller and a social novelist.

McCaffrey: The novel isn't very flattering of the Gypsies, or the Socialists, or of any one culture really. But the Gypsies really suffer here. There's death, drownings, destruction—and then they exile their great poet. Surely lots of people say that's their own fault? That the Roma brought this down on their own heads? They don't really write. They don't want to assimilate. Some people might say they've made their own bed and now they're lying in it. **McCann**: You might say that. Others might too. I might have said that at one stage. But we wouldn't if we were Roma. We wouldn't if we were being burned out. We wouldn't if our kids were being shipped off to schools for the handicapped simply because they're brown-skinned. We wouldn't if our sisters are being sterilized by the local doctor.

And that's happening in twenty-first-century Europe. Today.

Sartre said of the Jewish people, something like: "They have allowed themselves to become poisoned by the stereotype that others have of them and they live in fear that their acts will relate to this stereotype. . . . We may say that their conduct is always overdetermined from the inside."

I imagine a lot of Jewish people would feel that the inside has been significantly determined from the outside. I imagine that the Jewish people—of all people in the world—can examine and understand the Roma story. That suffering. That longing. I think Irish people can relate too.

McCaffrey: The Gypsies have a bad rap—
McCann: No kidding! This whole thing about Roma stealing? I'll be honest. When I was going to the settlements I even bought myself a new pair of trousers with hidden pockets just because I was afraid that I was going to get robbed. In the end I didn't get robbed. I robbed myself, I suppose. I robbed myself with such negative emotions. But I learned something too. I remember—I'd be in the settlements—and the children would come awful close to me, right up beside me, and I would think: They're robbing me! But I had my hand in their pockets. You know, metaphorically.

Some clichés occupy disproportionate amounts of space. That's a lot of what's happened with the Roma. And then there has been silence. Silence leads to confusion and misplaced emphasis. The media is as guilty as anyone. We love the Gypsy exotic, especially if it involves a curly-haired woman and a knife and maybe a horse with teeth filed down. We have to take individual and collective responsibility for our clichés.

McCaffrey: But we seem to know so little about the Roma. I'd no idea there are ten million or more. Is that what you said?
McCann: Ten to twelve million. That's twice the population of Ireland. I'd say there are numerous problems that emerge when talking about the Roma experience. It has traditionally been an oral culture and so the process of "remembering" is different. There was a distrust of book learning. The poets

and scholars have largely been ignored until recent years. You hear sniggers when someone says the words "Gypsy intellectual." As if it's some sort of aberration.

Maybe the story of the Gypsies is too painful to be encountered. We can't deal with it. Instead we idealize a misty, ruined past or we brutalize a terrible present. Maybe I did that. I hope not. I hope that *Zoli* goes beyond that.

Often there is a deep ambivalence about the Roma identity—they are both proud and ashamed at the same time. They are sometimes even scared to call themselves Roma. It might bring a house of clichés down on their heads. There are Romani bankers, computer technicians, philanthropists, actors, all sorts of people. You don't see the newspapers writing about them. That's what drew me to the idea of a Roma poet. I liked Zoli. I like what she became. I liked her force and her intellect and her link with her people. She became more real to me than anyone else. I even miss her now.

McCaffrey: People talk of the "Gypsy problem"? What does that mean?

McCann: What we have to recognize, eventually, is not really the "Gypsy problem," but our problem with the Roma.

McCaffrey: Can you clarify the difference between Roma and Gypsy? I'm confused.

McCann: You and me both. Even people in that community haven't pegged the language down. Roma, Romani, Romanistan. The people are the Roma. The adjective, and the language, is Romani. Romanistan is that place, if you will, where Roma feel they could come together. But "Gypsy" is a pejorative term. For some people, it's analogous to "nigger." But it is the most often used word. Things are changing. People are changing this. Ian Hancock at the Romani Archives and Documentation Center at the University of Texas is in the process of leveling out the lexicon and putting pay to some of the incredibly stupid assertions, like there are no words for "beauty" or "truth" or "duty" or "possession" in the Romani language. These are oft-repeated notions.

McCaffrey: Are the Roma still nomadic?

McCann: Depends what you mean. They don't travel around so much anymore. In fact many of them have been settled for centuries. In their intellect, or their heart songs, are they nomadic? That's a different question, I suppose. But you won't find Romani families traveling around in horse-drawn carts. Many of them still group together in settlements and areas of towns.

But others are fully assimilated. They are Roma and proud of it and indistinguishable from you and me, really.

McCaffrey: How do these ones deal with the notion that the Roma are shiftless, lazy, thieving and so on . . .?
McCann: Well, the first thing I'm going to say is that there are plenty of shiftless, lazy, thieving Roma. There are also plenty of shiftless, lazy, thieving Micks living on the south side of Dublin. And more of the same sort residing right now in the White House—far too many, in fact.

But the Roma are always tarred with the same brush. That's the problem. One person steals, and ergo, everyone steals.

Our inability to recognize the extent to which racism exists is truly amazing. Only thirty years ago I could flick through a *Punch* magazine and see the British cartoonists representing Ireland as a drunken pig in the kitchen. Forty years ago Martin Luther King's marches were only just beginning in the southern US. Why is it impossible for us to believe that there is racism in modern-day Europe against the Roma? Why is that such a stretch? Why do people want to deny that? Why do they want to just call them thieves and liars?

When I was researching, I often sat with European intellectuals and they could talk to me of Irish civil rights and American civil rights, Miriam Makeba and Stokely Carmichael and all that, and then I would say to them: "But what about the Roma in your country—aren't they discriminated against?" And they would reply, without any irony whatsoever: "Ah, yeah, but they're just Gypsies." Jesus, that could be the title of a poem. "Just Gypsies."

By the way, I'm astounded by how national newspapers all over the world still refer to them as lower-case. The gypsies. I think they're the only people in the world who don't get a capital letter. What's that about, if it's not about dehumanization? The *Irish Times* does it. I was shocked. It's in their style book.

McCaffrey: Do you see yourself as a radical writer?
McCann: Not really. I want to create texts that break through the policing of our borders, but I'm not a radical, no. I'd be in prison if I was a radical. My favorite radical is someone like Daniel Berrigan, who really put himself on the line. He's that American priest, a Jesuit, who was particularly active in the peace movement for the past forty years. He went to jail for his thoughts. I'm not that brave to put it all on the line.

McCaffrey: Tell me about your research. Is the journalist who goes to the camps a sort of Slovak version of you?

McCann: The guy who's "comfortably fat"? Yeah, I suppose! That's me. I mean, something similar happened to me, though not quite as jarring. I was there in Slovakia over the course of two summer months. I met all sorts of people. I had these guides from the Milan Simecka Foundation, Martin and Laco. They were amazing. I met writers like Michal Hvoercky, musicians, ethnographers, sociologists, and, of course, many Roma activists. I also went to the most notorious Slovakian settlements to see the conditions of life there. It shocked me—the mud and wattle huts, the poverty, the desolation. No electricity. No running water. I just wanted to hang around and get a flavor of the place.

McCaffrey: How did the Roma people treat you?

McCann: I had a lot of fascinating experiences. They liked when I sang old Irish songs. And we ate together, drank together. But most of the time I just hung out and watched. I was an outsider. I was dependent on others to show me around. I didn't have a secret key to their hearts or anything. But that's what I do best—I hang around, people invite me in, I try not to intrude on them, and I also try to understand them. It's about empathy.

But one day I was in Svinia, the notorious "dog-eater's camp," which is just another journalist's fancy name for a way to brand them, or a way to spice up things. People there have eaten dogs, yes, but—believe you me—they resist the temptation to call it a delicacy.

Anyway, a big group of kids and I went down to the local soccer pitch to play football together. We were playing away happily, quietly. But then these "white" women started shouting at us from a distance. Before we knew it we were hounded out by the mayor and the local policemen who called us "fucking Gypsies." Except they were a bit puzzled by me. They kept staring at me. As if to say, "Who's the white boy?" Anyway, we got kicked out. They locked the gates behind us. I tried to protest in English and apparently they were calling me another bleeding-heart, another European sentimentalist. We walked away, back to the settlement. A half-mile along this country road. Quietly. No fuss. No fights. There was lots of broken glass at the field near the settlement. That's why we couldn't play there and had to go to town.

But therein lies the dilemma. I could make this a story about being treated terribly by the local authorities. That's true, but it's also true that nobody smashed glass on that field other than the Roma themselves. The kids had ruined their own field. That's the heartbreak. That's the contradiction that fiction, too, has to find.

McCaffrey: Zoli at one point says: "I cannot explain why so many of them have hated us so much over so many years, and even if I could, it would make it too easy for them. . . ." Is this the point of the novel?

McCann: Well, I think a reader should become a writer at the end of the novel. The novel should be left open for interpretation. I'm mouthing off now, but in my novels I don't believe in mouthing off. I want the reader to have the dignity of his or her own interpretation of the text. I don't want to tell people how to think. I'll leave that up to others. There's nothing better than being a reader and being allowed to let your imagination go wherever it wants to go. That's freedom. It begins between the ears.

McCaffrey: Is it a novel about memory?

McCann: Well, the thing is, Zoli sings at the end. She sings something that has been forgotten. I didn't struggle with the ending. I wanted her to have dignity.

McCaffrey: Does it matter to you how a book goes down with the public? I believe I read somewhere that a million copies have been sold of *Dancer*, in something like twenty different languages. Is that true?

McCann: Yes, but quite honestly the best moment for me so far in this whole process with *Zoli* was Ian Hancock, the scholar I was telling you about, lending his signature to the book. I was on cloud nine that day. I danced around. I thought: "Well, I broke my back with this, and some parts of it still don't work, but I'm happy. I did my best. And Hancock liked it. Which means I got at least a part of it right. . . ." But, you know, it's terrifying, this whole thing. I still don't know if my brother Ronan likes the book or not. I sent him an early draft. I don't know. We'll see.

McCaffrey: Where next?

McCann: Ah Jesus, I don't know. Maybe Ireland. Maybe New York. I really want to do something where I don't have a lot of research to do. I don't want to become pigeon-holed. I spent all my writing life fighting against being pigeon-holed. I always wanted to be different. I wanted to come out with a book and shock people. Now people expect that from me—something "exotic." I'm going to have to do something low-key. Two chances, I suppose. None . . . and sweet F.A!

   I remember once I told an interviewer that writing about real-life people represented a "failure of the imagination." Well, a couple of years later I was writing about Rudolf Nureyev. That says it all. I never know where I'm going to end up.

McCaffrey: You're friends with Frank McCourt—

McCann: Who wouldn't be? He's the most generous man I know.

McCaffrey: Are you part of the New York literary scene?

McCann: You know, I can give you a list of people whom I consider, now, to be friends, but I hate doing this, and it would sound ridiculous, and I always leave someone out. My friends know who they are. I mean, I travel around, I have a beautiful family, I have a charmed life. Charmed. But it's never going to distract me from the stories I want to do. So, well, I don't know if I'm part of the New York literary scene or not. People talk about New York being the center of literary ambition as if that's a curse. Me, I think it's just a great place to live and raise a family. And I couldn't give a shit one way or the other, to be honest, about literary scenes. I just need to keep on writing. . . .

McCaffrey: Good luck—and many thanks.

McCann: Thank you.

Colum McCann

Robert Birnbaum / 2007

From The Morning News, May 3, 2007. www.themorningnews.org. Reprinted with the
permission of Robert Birnbaum.

Colum McCann: I've never done an interview in a car before.
Robert Birnbaum: OK, let's talk. We're sitting in my ragtop with the top
down, on a side street near Boston University, facing the Charles River, and
"Tow Zone" is painted in big yellow letters on the wall.
CM: [laughs]

RB: I read this book [Zoli] and it has the feel of a very large story, a big story.
Was it a much larger manuscript?
CM: It was, but not significantly larger. I thought it was going to be five
hundred to six hundred pages, but these stories find their own length, eventually. And I thought it was going to go to different places and go much
further. I cut about one hundred-fifty pages. As I say, you hope that it finds
its own length and place.

RB: What is that process of winnowing, whittling it down? Feeling some
passages weren't necessary? Or that concision is the better part of valor?
CM: You never know what's going to happen. I mean, I originally was going
to structure it much like *Dancer*, which was told from a lot of different viewpoints. Lots of different techniques, different ways of telling stories. People
approaching it from hundreds of different angles. There is a story right at
the end of the book—actually the last page, where Zoli talks about making a
makeshift chladni map using a violin bow and seeds to create patterns on a
sheet of metal. That originally was the first page of the novel. At that stage
I had a whole biography—she was born this year and in 1956 she did this
and in 1957 she did that and there were big gaps—but that was at a time she
wasn't really speaking to me. She was elusive. And actually, I was talking

65

to [Jim] Harrison about this and he was saying that same happened to him with Dalva. Early on he just couldn't locate [the character Dalva] at all, he couldn't find her voice, and then she would visit him at the most unusual times. Sometimes it got frustrating, because she would go away from his/her voice. The voice of Zoli came along and blindsided me and she sort of worked outward, and so it became a different novel from the one I had conceived. I mean, every move is a failure, I suppose.

RB: [laughs]
CM: On account, it has to be.

RB: Why is that?
CM: Well, it does. First, you can't think you have done your best work. Then there would be no real point in going on.

RB: Why even frame it in terms of best or worst work? Where does that enter the creation process?
CM: You're always scared that you are not able to do it again. And the older you get and the more you get into writing, it's really interesting how terrifying each new novel becomes.

RB: Even after you have exhibited skill and been well received? Even after that?
CM: Absolutely, absolutely. Each time you finish you think, "I'm a charlatan. What am I doing in this world?"

RB: Do you think that about other things that you do? Do you think you are a failed parent?
CM: No, never.

RB: I don't know what else you do—
CM: I play football. And things like that. But writing is my life. You realize— [John] Berger says, "If I'd known as a child what the life of an adult would have been, I would never have believed it. I never could have believed it would be so unfinished." And you think when you are twenty that if you manage and are still lucky enough to be writing novels in your forties, that you just will be able to turn around and blast them out. But it just doesn't happen that way. You sort of use up everything that's inside you. At the end of it all, you are exhausted and then you have to get ready again and stretch.

RB: That's the writing and creative part of it. But you have to fit that in a real life. Responsibilities legal and familial. What do you allow yourself in that period after you have exhausted yourself? What kind of recuperation?
CM: Then you've got to start reading and looking around and figuring out where it is you want to go. You start filling up the well again. I do other things. I teach at Hunter College in New York City.

RB: Peter Carey is there.
CM: Myself and Peter and Jenny [Jenefer] Shute—she's a South African novelist—together we do the MFA program there.

RB: Pretty un-American.
CM: An Australian, an Irishman, and a South African, yeah. But that doesn't matter—what's New York? We're all New Yorkers at that stage. Also, I write screenplays and I do journalism and so on. But the one thing I focus toward—it's got to be terrifying, in order to write something that you hope will make an impression in the world or make an impression on the reader. It can't come too easy.

RB: You don't feel that fear with the other forms of writing you do? The stakes aren't the same?
CM: Oh, no, I can turn around and write—I do a piece for *Village* magazine in Ireland every week (it's actually going monthly soon). I can do that in an hour. Write a thousand words in an hour.

RB: So part of this is your own sense of your talents and concern about what?
CM: In the sense that it lasts, and that it matters. In a sense that the book will always be there.

RB: How much do your concerns have to do with pleasing the reader, delivering for the audience? When I pick up your book, do you owe me anything?
CM: Absolutely, yeah. There is as much in creative reading as in creative writing. So my responsibility to the reader is to give her or him enough so that they go away and finish the story. I don't believe in telling people how to feel about Zoli or the Romany community. Or about Rudolf Nureyev [*Dancer*] or homeless people living underground [*This Side of Brightness*]. They make up their own minds. I paint the photograph or create the picture.

And then hopefully they walk into the picture. And they're the ones who actually complete the novel, in a way. So that the best books, to me, are the ones that leave it open to me to become the writer of it, at the end. And that's what I love. So that's where it's so very different from journalism, where you are saying exactly what you feel and putting it out there. That's more along the line of being a politician. And screenplays are a craft thing.

RB: You are not solely responsible, with a screenplay.
CM: If you write a bad screenplay, you can always blame the director.

RB: Not that they are so closely adhered to—
CM: Or get made. [Jim] Harrison wrote twenty-four screenplays, and how many of them were made?

RB: *Off to the Side*, his memoir, is one of his most amusing books. Lots of scorn for Hollywood, described in his inimitable style.
CM: The best book of poetry that came out last year was *Saving Daylight*. It's fantastic.

RB: I have that volume. I loved the essay he recently wrote for the *New York Times* called "Don't Feed the Poets," on Karl Shapiro. He was a big deal in poetry in the fifties. And Harrison takes the opportunity to talk about artists making a living . . .
CM: You know what he says about that in one of his poems? He says, "Children pry up our rotting bodies, with cries of 'earn, earn, earn.'" [both laugh] But if you read "Letters to Yesenin," that big poem, that thirty-page suicide note that is sort of addressed to Sergei Yesenin, you realize that Harrison was in his early thirties when he was writing this stuff and it's just phenomenal.

RB: He holds an odd position in the American literary world.
CM: He does, yeah. But you know he's a big hero in France. He walks down the street in Paris and people recognize him.

RB: That cuts two ways. The French like Jerry Lewis and Mickey Rourke.
CM: That's the thing. It could be like a bad Jerry Lewis joke. But it's not. They really appreciate him. They appreciate what he is trying to say about America. Sometimes you get the feeling that some of the important stuff

that is being said is only being heard outside. Although there's books now—I love the fact that Dave Eggers has come out with this book—

RB: *What Is the What.*
CM: About the Sudanese. That's fantastic. What a leap of the imagination. Also it shows, because people are buying it and reading it, that we are beginning to look outside again.

RB: I wonder if it's come at a time when there is something of a boomlet in African fiction—a number of wonderful books by young African novelists. Chimamanda Ngozi Adichie, Chris Abani, Uzodinma Iweala, Ishmael Beah—Nigerians writing about the Biafran War, child soldiers, immigrant and assimilation issues.
CM: These stories are getting told, that's the important thing. It makes me optimistic for the first time in about five or six years about what is going on over here and for my kids: that people are reading outside of their own small niches.

RB: One takes their optimistic signs where one can get them, but I am happy to inhabit this small sliver of the world that is the world of books and literature—which is marginal to most people and I try not to think about the fact that even a well-recognized, well-received book doesn't come close to even an unpopular TV show's audience.
CM: It's the quality of the experience rather than the—

RB: No question—but if you start to look at things quantitatively, which is always tempting, you can become scared. I am tempted to look at you as a hybrid Irishman. You seem so affected and buoyed by the American experience to be pure Irish. You tell me?
CM: I'm Irish. Absolutely Irish. But I am an Irish New Yorker. What I like is the notion of the international bastards of the world, the international mongrels. I look at someone like [Michael] Ondaatje, whom I love. Don't know him and haven't really met him—I met him glancingly but I would love to spend some time with him. There he is, born in Sri Lanka, educated in England, the boarding schools, goes to Canada, becomes a Canadian citizen, and writes his first book about Buddy Bolden, a New Orleans jazz musician—*Coming Through Slaughter.* I love that there are no boundaries and no borders there. Part of what being an Irish writer who writes about

other places, maybe part of what I am trying to say, although I am not fully conscious of it, is that our story is everywhere. And that's important to me.

RB: As a practical matter: Where would you live in Ireland?
CM: Good question. I was actually thinking that about it—I wouldn't live in Dublin, no. I have friends who live in Dublin, writers, but I might live in the west of Ireland or the north. My family is here now and—last year I went back six or seven times. So it's almost like a commute. This is what's interesting to me now. I first started writing in the eighties, when Ireland was completely wracked by emigration. My first collection of stories, *Fishing the Sloe-Black River*, was all about going and loss and everything like that. The most difficult thing for people to do now—people don't leave now, people return, and it's harder to return. It used to be hard to leave. Fifty years ago, it's almost a cliché now, but they used to have those Irish wakes.

RB: In *Zoli*, you keep saying, "Memory has no backspin." You can't return to where you started from.
CM: You can't go back to the place where you were before. I can't do that perfect backspin to that place. Nobody lives where they grew up anymore. It's this condition of trying to find a home—not necessarily the home where you grew up, but some other deep home where you can feel, "I belong here."

RB: Clearly that's a state of mind. It's not about geography.
CM: Absolutely, it's not a geographical place.

RB: But it does have to smell right and does have certain colors and light.
CM: Yeah, you have to be comfortable there.

RB: Directionally, you seem to be writing more from some real historical foundation—why?
CM: I don't really know. I gave an interview to *Atlantic Unbound*, about seven years ago, saying writing about real people and absolute historical situations was a failure of the imagination. [both laugh] And exactly two years later I am picking up on Rudolf Nureyev and creating a novel.

RB: And the sandhog—
CM: In certain areas you get people thinking, "Oh, well, your imagination is not big enough to create its own story, you're relying on history." But I think that is horseshit—it's just that little launching pad. I don't write about

myself as such, though ultimately all we do is write about ourselves. But I write toward what I want to know. That's what interests me. And then you get sideswiped by these notions, by stories. With *Dancer*, I think I told you before, it was like I literally heard a story about a young guy living in the housing projects of Dublin and the very first image that came on the television set as he tried to get reception in the flats was Rudolf Nureyev dancing. And I thought, what a fuckin' amazing story that is. I wasn't interested in Rudolf Nureyev, wasn't interested in dance. I wasn't interested in the history of the Soviet Union or anything like that. I just got completely swiped by this notion of this boy carrying this TV set and carrying Rudolf Nureyev in his arms. I never got that into the book, never got there. And same with this book. I didn't set out to write a social history of the Gypsies because I felt that they had been persecuted and kicked around for hundreds of years, which they have been. I simply found this photograph of this woman. And she haunted me. They are simple beginnings that turn toward complicated endings.

RB: Talk about failure of imagination—unfortunately that's usually in the readers and reviewers. There is a tendency to look at novels that have some historical reference point and the writer's intention to create a work of fiction is immediately forgotten. Usually it will say, "Blank-blank, a novel."
CM: I hate the term "historical novel." That drives me nuts. The term "fictionalized biography," I don't know what any of that means. In fact what does "fiction" mean? The characters we create in these books around us are as real, if not more real, than the six and a half billion people we haven't yet met. I know, in this respect, that my great-grandfather walked through Dublin on June 16, 1904, but I never knew him and I don't really know anything about him. But I know Leopold Bloom. Leopold Bloom is more real to me than my great-grandfather. And that's the power of fiction, and in a curious way you hope that you create characters in these books that live with people, months and months and months afterwards. Like the one nice thing that I would hope with Zoli is that people would feel that she is entirely real. And that they can carry her with them for a long, long time. And that is a powerful thing. I don't shrink from the notion that writing can change things or have an effect.

RB: Is the failure of the imagination bad training or huge distractions from our elemental interest in stories and storytelling? That we can't form or don't have a naturally intuitive grasp of someone willing a story and easing into it via some historical touchstone? People may be thinking, where are the special effects, or where's the trick? I like the way you have Zoli shying away from writing things down because the words are fixed—that's a peculiar way of looking at language.

CM: Stories have beginnings and endings but certainly the things that I happen to use have no beginnings and no ends. You have to choose where they go in. But then you come upon a book like Eggers's *What Is the What* and you just think, "Fuck me, that's great." That's the story we're looking for. That's the edge.

RB: I've had trouble reading Eggers in the past—a little too much irony and coyness is slathered into his stories.

CM: Not this time. No, no, no, no, no. It's lean and it's all moving in the right direction and full of empathy, and I really like that. These books come along and you are shifted. It's nice.

RB: You talked about not pushing the reader to conclude something at the end of a story. I frequently read a story and I will go, "Yeah, I think I want to know more now." And then wonder if the writer is finished with the story.

CM: I'm not interested in taking the characters up again. I spent my three, four years with them and it's time—but this could be one of those *Atlantic Unbound* moments where suddenly five years from now I take one of the characters I would like to take out of the cupboard. I have a character in *Dancer* called Victor Pareci.

RB: Didn't he die?

CM: He dies of AIDS, yeah, yeah. But we can exhume him.

RB: You could do Victor, the Middle Years or The Wild Years.

CM: [laughs] Yeah, yeah, I am actually looking at New York in the seventies right now and the story sort of centers around there. And I keep coming back, I keep turning the corner and Victor is there. But I'd prefer to stay away. For me, writing a book, you go out into unknown territory and you have to consent to the fact that you are not going to see land for quite a long time.

RB: And your family?

CM: I have to do research generally—with this book I had to go away for two months, to Europe, and that was tough. And of course I went to the camps in Slovakia—see these horrible trousers with these zips and all these pockets?

I bought these because I knew I was going to get robbed, so I could hide my passport in here and money down here. But of course I didn't get robbed at all. I was treated really well in the settlements. They took me in. They guided me around. But being away from home for a while and having to travel through Europe, to me that's part of the joy of it. I see myself sitting down writing a story about being a fat, middle-class writer living in New York—

RB: Where nothing happens.
CM: Or a campus novel or divorce novel, it just doesn't interest me. I want to be—as a reader I want to be thrilled and excited, but also as a writer, if I'm going to spend four years on something, it better be something I have a real interest in discovering. Quite honestly, I feel like I go back to university each time. For example, I knew nothing whatsoever about the whole Gypsy culture before I started this.

RB: Apropos of nothing, Isabel Fonseca [whose book, *Bury Me Standing*, McCann used as research—ed.] has just written a novel.
CM: Has she really? I'd love to see her, I'd love to meet her. I believe she is in New York right now. [Fonseca's husband] Martin Amis was there. I bet it's a great novel. She is a nice writer.

RB: So says Amis—who's going to argue?
CM: I could argue with Amis, but I don't know if I'd argue with her. You know, the whole book tour thing seems to be dying out.

RB: You think so?
CM: Well, in England it's completely dead. Why do you hope so?

RB: It's an adjunct to the celebrity thing about writers, and the readings themselves are usually boring. Most of the time the audience has not caught up with the book, so they have no readily available questions. So there has to be a better way of letting them get to know the writer—
CM: How do they get to know the writer then unless—?

RB: More Q&A, or conversation? More talk, less reading.
CM: That's great. In England now, the only literary venues are festivals and there are moderators and so on. Edinburgh and Hay and all that sort of thing. But I have to say that I like getting out and about. Spend a couple of years in a room sitting—

RB: There are also many writers who seem not to like it. But maybe less so as the job description has changed, including the tour as part of the gig. Greater responsibilities to the publishers, the competition is greater, and so writers want to make everybody happy. This is your first book for Random House. You probably want to match their efforts and do whatever you can to help the book—

CM: That's exactly how I feel. I also feel if someone is going to buy a book I'd like to get out and have a chance to talk to them for five minutes. When I sign a book, I actually always put bits and pieces of poetry or quotes. If they are going to put out twenty-five dollars, I appreciate it. There's two ways to do it. Fuck all and hide away, right. Which works. [both laugh]

RB: It only works for a few people. If everybody did it, I don't know.

CM: Or do everything. And you can't be choosy. You can't say, "I don't want to go on Oprah or don't want to do this"—that's just stupid. And this whole—I hate this position, you probably see it sometime, "How difficult it is to be a writer? I have to live in my garret. I have to wear my blindfold." Give me a fucking break. It's difficult being a plumber living in the Bronx or a turf cutter in Donegal and this stress about writing—

RB: I don't see that much anymore. No more suffering artists posing . . .

CM: Really?

RB: Maybe it's self-selective—the writers I meet are out there and happy to be talking about their work. Maybe the ones I don't meet are the ones who are suffering?

CM: What about the position of having a family? Like, writers actually having a life and not destroying their lives with drink and drugs?

RB: Writers have become much more middle-class—paying rent, trying to make a living.

CM: I love the fact that I can have a life, have three kids. I can have a mortgage and live this semi-normal life. But then when I get into the fiction, that's when the madness emerges. And you're living with it a long time. Sometimes four hours a day. Sometimes eight hours a day, sometimes twenty hours a day, toward the end. And to me that's the sort of travel—I don't have to go out and do Dylan Thomas and eighteen whiskeys, although every now and then eighteen or nineteen whiskeys goes down very well.

[laughs] But no, in general you can balance these things out and you don't have all these grand narratives about writers destroying themselves as much as you had thirty or forty years ago. Is the work worse?

RB: I think not. But who is to say? The unanswerable question is what work is going to last.
CM: Right.

RB: There seems to be the same claims about depression and creativity. The assumption that Dostoyevsky or Van Gogh wouldn't have produced without some pathology—that you need to be afflicted to be creative. Peter Kramer in *Against Depression* argues that that is false and it contributes to a very misinformed and unproductive response to depression. It's seen as an existential choice or attitude—
CM: Something really interesting I found out recently: In the west of Ireland, they had the highest concentration of schizophrenia in the world. It's called a "black triangle" of schizophrenia—

RB: Was it the water?
CM: You're absolutely right.

RB: Or some environmental thing.
CM: They just recently also found out that is the highest percentage of celiacs in the world, these are people with wheat intolerance, right. So people are eating bread, potatoes, drinking Guinness, things like this. And what happens is that it brings about or plays with the body in certain ways. And so they used to think it was the farmers coming down from the hills who had been sleeping with their sisters and things like that, [both laugh] but now they can map it with the diet and what we are drinking.

RB: Geez. Martin Amis told me that statistically Europeans are getting taller with no causal link, no scientific explanation as to what causes it.
CM: Somebody is stretching them out in bed. [laughs]
[RB and CM pause to pick up RB's son Cuba from school.]

RB: The poem attributed to Zoli in the book, is it yours? You wrote it.
CM: Yes.

RB: What's it based on? Loosely based on the poetry of—
CM: No, not even loosely based on—the story is based on Papusza, who was, in the fifties, a Gypsy poet who became quite famous under the socialist government. [Her given name was Bronislawa Wajs—eds.] She was fostered by Jerzy Ficowski, who later trumpeted Bruno Schulz. [Ficowski was] a serious figure who only died last year in Poland. I really wanted to meet him and interview him and see how he felt about what happened to Papusza but I wasn't able to. I went to Poland to interview him and couldn't get to him. He was too sick. I really wanted to know what sort of guilt lay behind all this, because here was this beautiful woman who wrote simple, elegant, gorgeous lyrics. But the problem was when I was looking at her poetry, it is so simple that if I tried to replicate that simplicity it would have become an absolute parody. Because stuff like moonlight and Gypsy superstitions, that wouldn't have worked if I had tried to replicate it unless I used, exactly, one of Papusza's poems. It would have been against the whole push of the novel. I was trying to fictionalize, break the story out from Papusza. So I waited two and a half years to find that poem. And I didn't know if I was ever going to get it. I don't write poetry. But it sort of came very quickly then. Once it began to work on the page for me, I wrote it inside of about two weeks. It was really interesting; at the launch in New York, the Gipsy Kings—the band—came along and played. And they wanted to put that poem to music. So I went up on stage and we set it to music and it was really great.

RB: Cool.
CM: And then all this Romany stuff—the interesting thing about my readings over here in particular is that Romany people are coming along and they are actually standing up and saying, in Romany, "Thank you for writing this book," because these stories, in general, have not been told. One guy in New York told me he said it was the first time he had ever stood up in front of an audience and admitted—he used the word "admitted"—to the fact that he was a Rom. It's a really hard thing to do for him. Because you say it, it means (to other people) that you are a liar and a cheat, you steal—all that baggage.

RB: "Gypsy" is not the word they use?
CM: They will use it amongst themselves. But it's like the N-word in many ways. We (the Roma) can use it but you don't use it because if you call me a Gypsy we know what you mean. Even the phrase "to gyp" comes from "Gypsy." All these things—it's really, really, really extraordinary—if you go to

Europe and see some of the prejudices going on, you'd be amazed—I went into these small little towns where women had been burnt out with their families by, they said, the local town mayor. I met women who had been sterilized. They hadn't been told. They had babies and then had their tubes tied in hospitals in Slovakia in the 1990s. Skinheads writing "Burn, Gypsy, Burn" all over these settlements. There are towns in the Czech Republic, where they are building walls, even today, to keep Gypsies in or out. And the story I am very fond of, in a terrible way, is that Miss Czechoslovakia got up on national television in the early nineties and she was asked her ambitions in life, and she said, "I want to become a public prosecutor so I can clear my town of all its brown-skinned inhabitants." The further I got into this, the more I realized there is an extraordinary story there, and *Zoli* is just is a tiny part of it. The only thing I hope for the novel is that it opens the door. You know, something really strange has been happening. I have never had this happen to me before. People are sending me paintings; three different people have sent me paintings of what they think Zoli is, looked like. And they just arrive in the post—I don't know, that's a very heartening thing to happen.

RB: It's the case that there are Romany people in every country in the world?
CM: Yeah.

RB: Is the bias against them universal?
CM: More or less. The estimate is that there are about a million Romany people living in the United States but nobody draws attention to it because they don't draw attention to it themselves. They live at the edge of Indian and Pakistani communities. Even in Canada where there is a significant population but they fit in with the Indian communities there. Often, I have been hearing, there are Gypsies living on Native American reservations. When I was growing up in Ireland, it was, "Be careful, the Gypsies will come and take you away." And when I was in Slovakia—I was in this little place, Hermanovce, I heard this woman say to her little boy, [chuckles] "Be careful, or the white man will take you away."

RB: Yeah, everyone has a boogeyman. Isn't there a Charles Simic poem about having two fathers and being raised by the Gypsies—
CM: We all need somebody to hate. It really seems extraordinary to me that in this day and age and contemporary Europe that kids are living on toxic dumps and it's okay to say, "The Gypsies do this and that." I don't know

of another culture that has a lowercase letter attached to it. If you go to the *Irish Times,* for instance, they still refer to Gypsies with a lowercase g. And it just annoys—

RB: They never use "Romany"?

CM: Now they are starting to. But that's a minefield. Roma, Romany, Rom, Romanistan, it's a linguistic thing. There are scholars like Ian Hancock at the University of Texas, who started up the Romani Archives and Documentation Center, who are changing all that. He's extraordinary. And really in Budapest and Bratislava and Dublin and London, there are these young poets who are getting up and saying, "I'm Romany and this is my story." But for a long time it wasn't written down.

RB: What language do the Romany/Gypsies speak?

CM: It's their own language. Romany. It comes originally from an Indian language because they all came originally from Northern India—it's the Gypsy language and there are so many dialects because it uses up the host country's language, also. It was interesting for me when I went over to the camps—I don't have any Romany or Slovak, and when I went to the Czech Republic I didn't have any Czech.

RB: Doesn't Ireland have Romany?

CM: Sorry, I meant I didn't. I had two guides who could speak Slovak but sometimes I was left on my own and the places I went were fairly rough. Like, Hermanovce is on the edge of a town—

RB: As described in *Zoli*?

CM: Yeah and I sit in there and sort of—but they really looked after me. And I tend to sing—Harrison says I do sing but I can't sing [both laugh], but I'll tell you those old Irish songs were part of my passport to get people around and talking to me. Or just singing, and I used a tape recorder, a small one, and I have a lot of their songs on tape. It was a fascinating thing—we tend to forget the Romany population is as internally diverse as any other population. So there are scholars, there are doctors, psychologists, but—

RB: It seems to be normal to look at minorities as monoliths.

CM: Exactly, and I think it's a big story right now. Maybe because I am right in the heart of it right now, but we'll see some significant changes in the next ten years.

RB: What happened after Isabel Fonseca's book?

CM: There was a lot more public awareness. An awful lot more public awareness. And there was a lot of infighting amongst the Romany people. Certain scholars said it just reinforces certain prejudices. I didn't think it did that in any way. But there are certain things that happen. If you look at the history of the scholarship, there was a nineteenth-century ethnographer who went in the camps and settlements in Bulgaria. He decided even though he didn't speak Romany that were no words in the Romany language for "truth" or "duty."

RB: Didn't somebody, Ronald Reagan, claim that about Russian—there was no word for "freedom" or "democracy" in Russian? [In 1985, Reagan said he had been told there was no Russian word that translated to "freedom." There is such a word: svoboda.—eds.]

CM: It allows the stereotypes to exist. Of course, [they used to say that among] the Gypsies, "there is no such thing as truth." "There's no word for duty." "They don't have possessions because they don't have a word for possessions." It's extraordinary! And Ian Hancock comes along and plows that argument under. It's just a matter of more stories being told, the more developed our relationship to the whole culture will be—

RB: Is this experience of writing this story and being in touch with a very different world, is this haunting you?

CM: I think it will be with me forever. It changes how I look at the world. There is no way I can forget it. It just deepens my experience of life. And I don't think it will be terrible baggage—I am happy that I got a chance to do it. How much fun is that, to be able to make a living at what you really, really want to do, at your most honest core, and get to meet people, do exciting stuff, see places, see the darkness, and then try to create—

RB: Don't be so happy about it. You can't be that happy.

CM: I know. I am not that happy; I'm in therapy.

RB: If, in this day and age you try to quantify that—how many people get to do that, what they want and care about? How many people, really? Not many.

CM: Very few.

RB: Looking out at the world, can we wonder why there is a long list of societal ills? And why is it not the goal of social organizations to enable people to do that?

CM: It would be wonderful, wouldn't it?

RB: So why don't we have such goals and or organizations? When I am in a grocery store or department store, I look at people and they look grim—and this is big recreation in this country.

CM: Wouldn't you say it's our duty to find a moment of hope? And say that there is something there beyond all that everyday torments, that there is something more behind that?

RB: Duty? Looking for meaning and importance and relevance sounds worthwhile.

CM: I was with the homeless people in the subway tunnels, I got to talk to them in various different situations, they were out of hospitals, mad, mentally ill. Others were refugees from the Vietnam War, hiding away, wounded. Others were temporarily there—they had lost a job or had a divorce or whatever. Something big had happened in their lives and they were trying to get things back together again. No matter who they were, across all spectrums—race, gender, economics—every single one of them said, "When I get out of here." Not "If I get out of here." "When I get out of here." There is that deep place—no matter how dark the darkness, there is a part of us as humans that says, "We will eventually get to some sort of light." That's what keeps you going.

RB: The hope chromosome. There is also supposed to be a resiliency gene.

CM: Why do you think we need shrinks?

RB: Uh, we don't know anyone. Our communities are devoid of natural, meaningful conversations.

CM: We shouldn't have a need for shrinks. We are storytellers and listeners—

RB: How many significant, enjoyable, pleasant conversations I would have in a year if I wasn't talking to people who are writers and storytellers—which makes me want to talk to many more people in all sorts of situations.

CM: Yeah, it's just a matter of opening up—

RB: Right, but I don't recall doing that for large parts of my life. Nor are we trained to do that. By the way, try having those offhanded, off-the-cuff conversations on the streets of New York.

CM: Ah, I think you can do it in New York. I actually find New York to be a strangely friendly place. Because people are coming from all over, there is a sense of the everywhere there. It doesn't even feel to me like it is part of America at all. It's its own place. All these refugees are coming from different places. All these stories that are there. I love that energy.

RB: When we were talking about the village aspect of NYC, I was thinking that is true of most large metropolises, they are subdivided into neighborhoods. Growing up in Chicago, it was the same sort of thing, very distinct neighborhoods, which are enclaves unto themselves. It seems to be the natural order of things, that people break them down. On the other hand, there are huge tracts of high rises, skyscrapers, gated communities where people are isolated from their city, their environment—

CM: The thing is, we all have a deep need to tell a story—that's the thing. Everybody needs to tell a story, whether it be to your shrink, whether it be to your publisher, whether it be to whomever, that's the vast democracy— the only democracy, in fact, that we have that goes across every geography, every age group. We tell stories in different ways, obviously, with the clothes we wear, with the car we drive, and things like that. But at heart, everybody wants somebody to talk to and to be listened to. That's the function of literature. This is why we do get charged up about talking about books, because it's somehow how we have our finger on a pulse that's alive.

RB: It is a sign of life.

CM: It's not like working in the bank. It's not working in the insurance company and going home and sticking in the DVD and not talking to anyone. So it seems to me the writer and the good reader, they are almost the same thing. [Each] gets out and does look for those stories. And then they find them sometimes in books, too. That's why you like Harrison. Why do you enjoy reading Harrison or Peter Carey? Or John Berger or Ondaatje or Toni Morrison, it doesn't matter who. Louise Erdrich. Because you feel like you are being talked to, you are listening, and it's dignified.

RB: Did you ever see the story that Jim Harrison wrote for *Men's Journal* about the Mexican Border, "Life on the Border," prompted by the

death of a nineteen-year-old woman, the discovery of her body—he might have written a poem about it—
CM: Yeah, yeah, yeah. He did write a poem about it.

RB: It was an incredibly compassionate and powerful take on immigration, a wonderfully formed political broadside, humane, and you see how moved he was by the woman's death and his rage at the hypocrites and bloated pols. It was as if he was talking to you, telling the story of this land theft that has been legitimized, and now the bizarre criminalization of the victims.
CM: There is an Irish writer, Ben Kiely, who was one of my big heroes when I was young—*The Collected Stories of Benedict Kiely*. He is sort of ignored, as he is of an older Irish generation—criminally ignored. You meet him in his house in Donnybrook in Dublin, and God, could he spin a story! He was at the heart of the matter. He told wild, discursive stories. He would bring you places. He would put you in to the pub and then out of the pub and up the hill and around the back and then down to the poteen still, where it would be poured into the river.

RB: The what would be poured into the river?
CM: Poteen, Irish moonshine. It's a scene from one of his stories. And then say things like, "All the fish were swimming along the banks of the River Strule [in Northern Ireland]." He would tell stories and they would go on forever. And just full of music and the same sort of thing in his fiction, too. You just wanted to be around him. He was also a deeply political writer. [Kiely passed away in February 2007.—eds.]

RB: As an undergraduate in philosophy, I would come upon the issue of what was essentially human and concluded there wasn't such a thing. But if there is something that comes close, it is the storytelling imperative. Socialists could argue that man has become so alienated from his best interest—
CM: I don't see what's socialist about that.

RB: It's an anti-capitalist line that I am happy to toe.
CM: I'm happy to toe that line, also.

RB: There's something wrong out here, right? Marx got communism wrong but he didn't get capitalism wrong.

CM: There you go. One of the things about his character Swan in the book is that he comes from the left, he's a naïve Socialist whose beliefs become more important than the truth and you look around what we have today: We have all sorts of people who embrace things so tightly that they become a terrible lie. It was Fitzgerald who said something about the essence of intelligence being the ability to hold two conflicting ideas at the same time and not fall over and collapse. [both laugh] That's the job of the writer. And that's where you go in and don't tell people how to believe but you paint the landscape enough that people go in and understand it. Isabel Fonseca and her book—fiction operates on another level. Her book was really fantastic and gives people a wonderful introduction into the world of the Romany people and culture. And *Zoli* will hopefully work on a completely different level. And also [Fonseca's book] is not very complimentary, and doesn't sentimentalize the whole idea of the Gypsy culture. Zoli gets booted out—

RB: You say that at your readings people have come and said they are happy you have written this book. But they come from a non-reading culture.
CM: That's the thing. We have created this whole background that they don't read, they don't write, and it's so fabulous and exotic that it's become part of the myth—

RB: Zoli is an example of that.
CM: She is, but what's happening now is that there are real issues of memory here. And people are recognizing that, and at the beginning of this century and end of the last, people really started to see—it's time for us to tell our story, if we don't tell out story, the others will tell it, and they'll tell it wrong, and we will be even more brutalized by these mistruths. So people are recognizing that it's time to tell the stories. A half-million Romany people died in the Holocaust.

RB: It appears nobody cares.
CM: Right. It's our job to start telling the stories so people will care.

2009 National Book Award Winner Fiction: Interview with Colum McCann

Bret Anthony Johnston / 2009

From www.nationalbook.org. Reprinted by permission.

Bret Anthony Johnston: First, congratulations on *Let the Great World Spin* being named a finalist for the National Book Award in fiction! Do you recall the inception of the book? Was there any image or incident or memory that triggered the writing process?

Colum McCann: Thanks so much. One only has to look down the roll-call of nominees through the years to realize what an incredible honor it is. It's humbling and thrilling.

As for the writing process, it's hard to say where anything really begins or ends, isn't it? I suppose the novel itself is a contemplation of what it means for life to be unfinished. Things spin. We are made by what we have been, and at the same time we become what we desire. This past and present is braided together with a beauty and an uncertainty.

But to answer on a practical level—even though the book takes place primarily in 1974—so much of it began for me very shortly after 9/11. I had read Paul Auster's collection of essays *The Red Notebook*, where he wrote about Philippe Petit scribbling his name across the sky between the World Trade Center towers. Then—when the towers came down in 2001—the tightrope walk popped out of my memory, one of those Eureka moments, and I thought, "What a spectacular act of creation, to have a man walking in the sky, as opposed to the act of evil and destruction of the towers disintegrating." I certainly wasn't alone in this. It was almost part of a collective historical memory. The same image ran true for a number of people, not least, of course, Philippe Petit himself. And I wanted to write a song of my adopted city as well, and maybe to confront some things that were on my mind about issues of faith and recovery and belonging.

Johnston: When you wrote *Let the Great World Spin*, did you have an audience or reader in mind?

McCann: I always have a few different audiences in mind. Most of all, it's an older creaky-boned version of myself. I want to be able to turn around in twenty or thirty years and not be embarrassed by what I've written. The test of time. So I don't want to have to hide my own books away from myself! Then on a practical level, there's my wife, Allison, who's always my first reader, and my father, and my children, and my friends: I write for all of them. And there's also my heroes, people like Michael Ondaatje and John Berger and Jim Harrison and Peter Carey, a part of me always wonders what they might feel if they got a chance to read it. I don't assume that they will read it, but I dream that they will read it.

Johnston: Did writing *Let the Great World Spin* feel any different from what you've written before?

McCann: Yes and no. Yes, because on one level every book has to be new, and you encounter new voices and new territories every time. No, because . . . well . . . I'm not sure . . . but essentially it was the same old process of sitting down in the chair and trying to work towards some modicum of beauty. That's what it always is. You sit, you work, you imagine, you hope to achieve something you are proud of.

Johnston: Did you encounter any blocks or unexpected difficulties in the process? How did you push beyond them?

McCann: *Let the Great World Spin* wasn't a particularly difficult book for me to write. I suppose I had to juggle a number of different voices, but that's just part of the job. And I had to do a good deal of editing, but again that's par for the course. Losing sections is always difficult—I had, for example, written stories about a hot-dog vendor, a Muslim shopkeeper, and an elevator man, and I had even invented a chess game that I was going to notate and put in there. I had worked with a chess grandmaster to figure out a game where black and white come to a mutual stalemate, but in the end it didn't fit in the novel, and I didn't want to shoehorn it in there either. I wanted the book to be organic and for it to flow.

I had some difficulties finding the title, but then I came across the Tennyson quote: "*Let the Great World Spin* forever down the ringing grooves of change . . ." And, as luck would have it, Tennyson had been influenced by a series of sixth century pre-Islamic poems, the Mu'allaqat, which asks the question: "Is there any hope that this desolation can bring me solace?" And when I found that line, my heart skipped a beat or three, because it was exactly what I wanted. But I can't claim any intelligence on any of this. It arrived for me. I feel like so much of the novel just fell in place, that all I was doing was opening up the windows and letting it come in. I don't mean this in any sort of false modesty, or to be disingenuous—of course, I had to work to get the book where I wanted it to be—but like a lot of work, it really begins to make sense in retrospect. We open up our windows for emotional reasons and then the intelligence of it, the fresh air, comes later.

Years ago, I wasn't able to admit that I never really knew what I was doing, but now I'm able to say that, most of the time, I'm flying on a wing and a prayer. One only hopes the wing holds out and that the prayer has music.

Johnston: In the novel, you negotiate a number of characters' consciousnesses in an elegant, commanding way. How did you manage this with such grace? Were any of the characters more difficult or more rewarding to inhabit than others?

McCann: Grace? Me? You should see me dance! Or the way I write. Push together, pull apart, tape together, pull apart, break, reconnect. And, honestly, I'm not sure how these voices come about. I teach writing at Hunter College in New York, and my first lesson to my students is that I can't teach them anything at all. They look a little stunned at first, but then I tell them that it's all about desire, stamina, and perseverance, and if they have that, it will feed their innate talent. And I also tell them to try to write outside of themselves. It is my philosophy that we shouldn't write what we know. That's boring and ordinary. Rather, we should write towards what we want to know.

As for the characters in the book I like Tillie, the thirty-eight-year-old hooker. And I like Claire, the Park Avenue mother. And I'm fond of Corrigan, the Irish monk. I suppose in the end I like all the characters, flaws and all. In a funny way I still think they're all alive, that I could turn the corner any day and say, "Oh, there you are." There's that great line from Anna Akhmatova, who says in a poem: You're late. Too many years have passed, how glad I am to see you. I'm paraphrasing, but the essence is there. It is in fiction and poetry that we extend our lifetimes. What a great privilege that is for a writer, to be at the heart of that process. There we go, inhabiting another body. In fact, there we go, creating another body. There is no end to the possibilities we have with language.

Johnston: The image of the tightrope walker crossing the space between the Twin Towers becomes the touchstone for most of the characters in the novel. What was it about that iconic event that you found so inspiring, especially in light of the Towers falling?

McCann: Yes, it was the catalyst for everything. A man a quarter of a mile in the sky. But the further the novel goes along, the less important the tightrope walk becomes, until it disappears from sight altogether, and the thing that holds the novel together is the very low tightrope of human intention that we all negotiate. Some of us walk very close to the ground, but we can hit it awful hard. We are all, in the end, funambulists.

I live in New York. I was there on 9/11. And there was so much happening—it was a deluge of images. It's probably the most documented couple of days in all of media history. Not just the big picture, but the small intimate moments too. The car outside my window that got a parking ticket on September 10, and another early on the 11th, but then one day it got a flower instead of a ticket, and then you knew, you just knew, until eventually it was just covered in flowers and the parking tickets were obscured. Or the supermarket shelves that were cleared of eyewash. Or the little film of dust that sat on your windowsill and you wondered what it might contain. Or the bagpipe players who were exhausted from playing at funerals. Or my own father-in-law escaping from the World Trade Center towers and coming home, his clothes covered in ash from the cloud of dust he had to run through, and my four-year-old daughter hiding because she thought he was burning. It was a whole collision of the personal and the public. I wrote plenty of journalism about 9/11, and it was all right, but what I felt down deep was that I would have to try to write a novel. But what was difficult for me as a writer was that everything was so very full of meaning that it seemed so difficult to write a sentence, or take a photo, or draw a picture without it having some heft or meaning. And it just kept gaining momentum, with Iraq and Afghanistan and Madrid and London, and all that justice turning into revenge. My question was, "How can I write about this? How can I discover how I, on a personal level, feel?" I really wasn't interested in trying to draw out a moral landscape, or to make some big comment on 9/11. I leave that to others. But I wanted to discover what all this meant, to me, and what it might mean for my family.

Then came the moment when I thought that I could go backwards in time to talk about the present: that's when the tightrope walk came in. And the deeper I got into the novel the more I began to see that it was, hopefully, about an act of recovery. Because the book comes down to a very anonymous moment in the Bronx when two little kids are coming out of a very rough housing project, about to be taken away by the state, and they get rescued by an act of grace. That's it, not much maybe, but everything to me. And there's hardly a line in the novel about 9/11, but it's everywhere if the reader wants it to be. I trust my readers. They will get from a book what they want. It can be read in many different ways. In this sense I hope it works on an open poetic level: Make of this child what you will.

Johnston: Did you set out to write such an allegorical narrative or was the doubling of the narrative and its mythic or symbolic implications something you saw emerging as you wrote?

McCann: It was both. I knew it was allegorical from the beginning, but then the allegory deepened for me the further I went along, and even became more complicated, layered. I hope it doesn't give too much away that two of the major characters die in the first section. I was very annoyed when I was writing it, but I couldn't stop it from happening. I wanted to shout, "No!" Every time I tried to resurrect these characters, they just refused to roll back the stone. I tried and tried to rescue Corrigan in particular, but he wouldn't put on his shoes. And then—about two years later, when I was coming to the end of the novel—it suddenly struck me that two human towers had fallen early on in the novel, and we spend the rest of the time trying to build them back up again. To me it was all about healing. We learn and then we move on.

And then, of course—from the get-go—I was well aware of what the words "World" "Trade" "Center" would do on the page. They are sponsored less by sentiment than they are by history. They have a specific weight for everyone, not just in New York. And I was interested in the mythic proportions of the story—especially if I could tell the stories of the forgotten corners, the Tillies, the Jazzlyns, the Glorias. I wanted to say that what happened on the streets of the Bronx that morning was just as important as any fancy tightrope walker, which is kind of saying that what happened in Basra is just as important as what happened in downtown Manhattan. World. Trade. Center. A complicated trinity. But what began to overwhelm me was the fact that life goes on, that even grief finds its own level.

I recently heard a story of a man in Ireland cutting his grass on 9/11 when the phone rang and he went inside to answer, and he just crumpled to his knees, because his daughter was gone, and he left the grass uncut, one-half of it long, one-half of it short. But the fact of the matter is that the grass will find its own level. It will grow back, it will level out. And eventually I'm sure that the man went back out to cut the grass, maybe wept for his daughter but also got that new-mown smell.

Johnston: One of the elements that all of this year's fiction finalists share is a deep sense of place, a narrative focus on how time and setting both form and inform the characters' lives. Did you always know that place would play such a large role in *Let the Great World Spin*? How did you go about evoking a landscape that would imbue the book with such power and resonance?
McCann: The place was made for me already. New York is such a vibrant place to write about. Eight million stories colliding all at once. And what a landscape to operate in. The eye never gets tired. Even the garbage can be acrobatic. So I just look for the language that will reflect that. Our language is so deeply influenced by landscape, and vice versa. But mostly for me it has to do with rhythm and sound. As a writer you have to try to find the music of that place. If it's the west of Ireland it's a different music to what it is in New York. So I went out and listened to the different instruments that the city plays . . .

Johnston: Along those lines, what kind of research did you do for *Let the Great World Spin*?
McCann: Well, I love libraries, so I did a lot of work in the New York Public Library. I read about tightrope walking and computers and Vietnam and theology and all these things that the book tries to look at. Then I went out to the Bronx with cops, to see if I could soak up a language that would relate to the streets. I even spent time with homicide detectives, though there are no murders as such in the book. I just wanted the language. And I looked at boxes and boxes of rap sheets. And I read novels, looked at films, searched through photo archives. After all, I was in Ireland in 1974, I was a nine-year-old kid, I certainly had no idea about the Bronx at that stage. But I love research. I feel that I go to university each time I write a new book. I revel in getting away from myself.

Johnston: What writers do you enjoy reading? Are there other artists or art forms that influence or inspire your fiction?
McCann: If I gave a list of writers I admire we would be here for a decade of Sundays. My bookshelves at home are stacked three deep. I can't get rid of a book. And I love flicking through them. The art form that most inspires my fiction is photography. I love looking at photographs. I feel that in some ways my job is to become a photographer with words, or to paint with words.

Johnston: As a professor in the Hunter College MFA program and as a writer of such distinction yourself, you have a unique perspective on the state and future of contemporary literature. What advice do you give your students?

McCann: I teach alongside Nathan Englander, Peter Carey, and Claire Messud. That's just the fiction program. We have had Don DeLillo come visit class, Ian McEwan, and younger writers like Jeff Talarigo, Nat Rich, Rivka Galchen, Nicole Krauss, and Darin Strauss. Seamus Heaney is coming in a few months. As a result of such a strong faculty, we're lucky to have some of the best students in America. And I love seeing them succeed. Their success is so much less complicated than my own. My advice is for them to develop stamina, to look outside their own lives, and write, write, write. Develop empathy but have some anger too. Have an adventure in the skin trade. Read your contemporaries. Knock that older writer out of the sky.

Johnston: This year is the sixtieth anniversary of the National Book Awards. How do you feel having your book celebrated among the luminaries that have preceded you? Are there previous NBA winners or finalists that you've found especially powerful over the years?

McCann: This is the most significant honor I have had in my writing life. As writers we get our voice from the voices of others. There is a domino effect. I feel like having a handshake with the past. I hope to continue to acknowledge that debt.

Colum McCann in Conversation with John Kelly

John Kelly / 2010
South Dublin Libraries READISCOVER Podcast, County Library, Tallacht. Printed by permission of South Dublin Libraries.

In his first interview in Ireland after winning the National Book Award for *Let the Great World Spin*, Colum McCann spoke on April 20, 2010, as the guest of the South Dublin Libraries, Tallacht. His appearance was nothing short of a miracle due to disruptions in air service caused by volcanic eruptions in Iceland.

John Kelly: What was it in your background or your family that led to you becoming a writer?
Colum McCann: I grew up in Deansgrange. My father worked for the Irish Press. We lived in a suburban, semi-detached house on Clonkeen Road. I was thinking about this recently, and first of all, it was my father, who worked as a features editor and brought home books. There was no wallpaper in the house, it was books everywhere.

But then there were my teachers. I think it's important to remember the teachers in my schools, both at St. Brigid's in Fox Rock and Clonkeen College. I even remember a teacher called Mr. Hill, when I was in first class. What was I, six years old or something? And he had to retire. I remember him coming into the school grounds every day and wanting to get back into the classrooms. Maybe he just wanted to teach. Then one day I noticed they actually had to lock the gate on him. And I was looking out the window—I did a lot of that in those days [Laughter]—and I saw Mr. Hill, who must've been seventy, trying to climb over the school gate at St. Brigid's with tears in his eyes, trying to get back in and do what he wanted to do.

So I got it from my father, from my parents, from my teachers, and then from all the writers like Ben [Benedict] Kiely, who was one of the writers when I was growing up. He took me under his wing. He used to take me down to his house in Logansport, Donnybrook, where we would sit and talk, and I could see the writer's life close up. And there was nobody like Ben to tell a story, as you know. He was so discursive, bringing out all these songs and tales, and eventually it would all come around to an absolute focal point.

And it was nice watching in the late seventies and the eighties to see people like Roddy Doyle come along, and Neil Jordan doing the Irish Writers' Cooperative, and I would think, oh, it was possible to do that.

I remember being in a pub—too many of my stories come from being in a pub, I suppose that's not very proper—and sitting there one day was Sebastian Barry, after he'd published a very small novel called *The Engine of Owl-Light*. I read it and thought it just amazing. And I wanted to go over and talk to him. I sat at the counter for about two and a half hours, trying to figure out what I could go up and say to him. I wanted to say something smart and clever, but I had nothing smart and clever to say to him, except "I liked your book." And he left. I never got a chance to say something to him until ten years later. I met him in Toronto at a book fair, and he said, "Why didn't you tell me? Nobody had read that book at that time."

Everybody has a story. This is the democracy of our times. This is the absolute most democratic thing we have, because everybody has the ability to tell one, and wants to tell one and to hear one but doesn't have the actual ways and means to get it down. It takes a lot of desire, a lot of stamina, a lot of perseverance, a lot of failure as well. I have books in the drawer from the early years. But every time I start a new book, I honestly feel I'm not going to be able to do it again, that something's been lost. And then you sort of build up again. You know, you have to get your body and your mind back in motion again.

Kelly: Do you recall, Colum, the first time you wrote something and you thought, I've got some kind of a purchase here, something's happening? I can do this. You'd got a sense of confidence that you'd achieved something. You know, maybe it'd been a school composition.

McCann: My father took me to see my grandfather, who was living in London at the time. He was in a nursing home, and he was dying. It was a spectacular moment, for it was the first and only time I met my grandfather. I went back to St. Brigid's school the next Monday, and my teacher asked me to write an essay about the person I most admired. So I went home to my dad and said, "Would you mind if I wrote an essay about my granddad?" And he said, "No. Fire away." At the end of the week my teacher actually read that essay out to the rest of the class. But now, thirty or forty years later, I realize I wasn't really writing about my grandfather as the person I most admired. I was writing about my father, who allowed me to meet my grandfather. I remember thinking at that stage this writing stuff is a way to get at the pulse.

Kelly: I see you turning to journalism. Did you see that as part of the same procedure, or as something separate, as a way of earning a living?

McCann: I saw it as absolutely part of the same procedure, and I still argue that there is no difference between poetry and prose and play-writing and good journalism. When you get the really good journalists, and they're working well and putting words together on the page in a perfect sort of order, like Ben Kiely, Flann O'Brien, and Con Houlihan would be doing, like so many writers still do, I have a value for journalism, and for me it's just another way to tell a story. I started working in the papers when I was seventeen and got out when I was twenty-one, and went to the United States, just out of curiosity, and took a bicycle across the United States for about two years, and that's when everything sort of opened for me. I began to meet all these people, and think, maybe I should put these stories down in another sort of way.

The very first thing I did was an article called "The Back Street Kids," where I went into the flats. This was completely different for me going from suburban Dublin into the flats in Finglas and Ballymun, and talking to community groups, mothers who had been abused by their partners, and for me to walk in there was a whole new landscape. The very first article I got published was an investigation into the battery of women and kids. I don't know what led me to do that. I mean, maybe it was some kind of empathy my teachers allowed me.

Kelly: Do you think if you hadn't gone to America that any of this would've happened?

McCann: It's a great question. I don't think things would've happened for me in the same way if I'd stayed. There's a certain part of a writer that needs to wound herself or himself. Things would have been distinctly much easier for me here than they ended up being over there.

The whole process of being an emigrant is a process of wounding yourself, and forcing yourself to another place, not necessarily that you have nostalgia for what's gone, but you remember sometimes more acutely what it is that's gone. So even though I went at a time when lots of people were being forced to leave, I went out of curiosity. It was being over there that allowed me to do what I couldn't have done here.

But a lot of writers stay here now. Look at the great work coming out from, say, Sebastian Barry, Joe [Joseph] O'Connor, Roddy Doyle, Anne Enright, all these people who made their choice to stay here so they're doing spectacular things. But for me personally, I have to get away.

Kelly: Does it help being away so you can be taken seriously at home?
McCann: No, the funny thing is I never felt that, even in the early eighties, when I was writing short stories and won the Hennessy Award, and I came back. It was almost as though mine was the first generation that could go away, and come back and be accepted at home at the same time.

One of the great things about being an American, especially as a novel-ist, is that they will accept you and still allow you to be Irish. And they do have numerous people like Alexander Hemon, who's from Sarajevo, who is an American and from Sarajevo at the same time. And there are writers like Chimamanda Ngozi Adichie, who is Nigerian and American at the same time, all sorts of younger writers who are getting "incorporated" into the system of literature but are allowed to be where they came from. If I weren't allowed to be where I came from, I couldn't handle it, and I'd have to come home. Part of me feels, I'm always and can only ever be an Irish writer.

Kelly: From your position of success now, can you say you ever felt utter despair?
McCann: I think I did at one stage wallpaper a bathroom with rejection slips, and it's the only thing you should wallpaper with rejection slips, because when you go in to sit on the throne you can look at the rejection slips and think about all those people who said no. [Laughter] I think if you're a writer, you will write no matter what.

And I said to my wife, this was after I'd done my cycling journey and we'd lived in Japan for a time, and I looked at her and said, "We're going to get married, and you have to let me write no matter what," and she said, "Well, of course. After keeping close to our family." That was one of the decisions we made together. I wonder if I'd still be writing books if all the others had gone to the slush pile. I think I would. And I think I would be angry and go to all the bookshops, and say, "Why the hell haven't you . . .?" And I'd be checking the ages of people: "Twenty-five, and you've got a book published?" [Laughter]

When I teach now in New York, I say, "You have to be able to take people on and go to the extremity of your desire and your experience, and I always quote Beckett: 'Ever tried. Ever failed. No matter. Try again. Fail again. Fail better.'" And that's the thing. Every book's a failure, and then when you turn around, you want to fail better the next time. Even though it never may approach perfection, you have to at least have the idea that someday it'll approach perfection.

Kelly: But if a book fails, there's been a hell of a lot of effort in something that results in nothing.

McCann: All things that are difficult are rare and necessary at the same time, and I think it's good that it's so hard. I like the idea of forcing myself toward excellence, and having those three or four years, when it might not work. I'm entirely honest when I say every time I finish a book, a month or two afterwards, I wake up in terror, thinking I'm never going to be able to do it again. And that terror is part of the thing that fires you up, like being an athlete, in certain ways: You want to beat your previous record.

Kelly: Did reality ever interfere with this desire you have?

McCann: I've waited tables, I've bartended, I've dug ditches, I've taught, done all these things. My first book, *Fishing the Sloe-Black River*, had a print run, I think, of 1,500 in England. And I remember I'd been in Japan and I went to England, and it's publication day, and I walked into the offices of Orion Publishing, and I thought I was going to be cool and trendy and wear my long, black coat, like [Sebastian] Barry, and people would say, "O, hail The Author," and nobody gave a flying fig.[Laughter] I wandered around, and I was virtually in tears, and then get this: This spectacular woman, whose books I had read, was in the office having a tête-a-tête with her editor. Edna O'Brien walked through the corridor, she was introduced to me, she had read one of my short stories, and she put her arm around me, and said, "Why don't you come with me tonight? I've got a reading in London, and you can introduce me."

She gave me my first taste ever of literary life, and I think I read for twenty minutes, which is way too long, and Edna was probably [he makes a gesture of impatience]. But that's the generosity that's interesting to me now.

And I think of the generosity of the Irish literary community. I heard Roddy [Doyle] and Anne [Enright] went down to Cuirt when people had to cancel [because of the volcano's disruption of air traffic], and Jennifer Johnston too, they just picked up a lot of the slack for people. I think we're in a good space, as long as we don't start patting ourselves on the back—"Oh, aren't we wonderful"—because that's no good either.

There's that quote from [Kurt] Vonnegut I really like: "We should be continually jumping off of cliffs and then developing our wings on the way down." And that's what it feels like to me. I've got to go to the hardest point and then fly up. It seems to me a lot of Irish authors are doing that. I don't know if it will continue.

Kelly: I think there was a moment when younger writers felt there was nothing happening for them.

McCann: And exactly what will happen is what we did in the 1970s when [Neil] Jordan got together with [Ronan] Sheehan and those others and formed an Irish Writers' Cooperative, and said, "Okay, they're not going to publish us in Britain. We'll publish ourselves. They'll find new ways on the Internet to get their stories out." I firmly believe that when good literature gets done it has an impact, and it will get written, and it eventually somehow gets read.

It helps if it gets read by one hundred thousand people, sure, but even if it's read by one thousand people it makes a difference. It has a knock-on effect. We read one story, and it shifts people's lives, or maybe just their relationship to how they live in the world. Maybe it makes them happy or sad. We can't despair that the publishing industry is not serving us in the way we want it to serve us. We've got to get out there and find new ways—stick it on iPods and cell phones and things like that.

Kelly: How important is an editor? A lot of the young writers are saying there seems to be no editors around like there used to be, nurturing writers.

McCann: Every writer has to find a very good friend, be that your wife, your father, somebody in a book group, who's entirely honest with you, who can say to you, "This is a pile of shite," or "This is fantastic, this is working." You've got to have one reader who looks at you and says, "Right. I understand what it is you're doing." Sometimes it's an editor. More of the time it happens to be a friend. Editors pass through these houses very quickly, but that's a shifting shape.

I remember being terrified in the mid-eighties: Oh, I wouldn't get published, I wish I was like the guys in the sixties and seventies when they were so much luckier than I was. So I think this is a cyclical thing. We will find ways to get over and around it, and then before you know it this'll be the golden age of literature.

Kelly: When I look at your website, Colum, I can see you have a whole system, an organization around you of agents for screen writing, agents for novels, etc. Is it hard for you to keep your business, as such, on the road, while spending presumably a lot of time writing novels?

McCann: Yes, it is because the further you go along, the more you have to do. I like to go to high schools, especially poorer high schools, say, in New York, and spend a day talking with kids there, and then I'm writing a screenplay for *Let the Great World Spin*, and I'm actually writing a ballet right now with a guy called Alonzo King, who's an African American . . .

Kelly: Got a role for me?

McCann: You'd look perfect in tights. [Laughter]

Kelly: Listen, I'm not just being smart. Now what in hell do you know about ballet?

McCann: Well, nothing. I wrote a book called *Dancer*, but even then I didn't know a thing about ballet. But once you write a story that inspires a choreographer . . . it's all about language, putting all this language down on the page, and it inspires a choreographer who's taking it and abstracting the thing. We're doing it with the Monte Carlo Ballet, of all places. Maybe it will come to Dublin, there's good potential it'll actually come to Dublin. But this is a really cutting-edge, African American choreographer who uses dancers in all sorts of weird ways, and he asked me, "Will you write me a story?" So I say, "Okay, yeah, I'd love to."

That to me is part of the excitement, the journey of getting out and doing new things. Sometimes you can get overloaded, and you have to hide away and get back to the real work—the novels. I have a new novel I'm researching right now, and then I have another novel I'm also researching that will actually take place in Ireland, and I'll do that over the next couple of years too. Sometimes it just gets very, very noisy, but there's beautiful moments in writing too, where you're into a voice, and it's just going, it's fantastic. I've told this story before, but I really like it.

I was working on a chapter in this book *Let the Great World Spin*, about this prostitute in the Bronx, a thirty-eight-year-old grandmother, and she had this voice, and the voice suddenly came to me, and the sounds were sort of in a frenzy, and I was sort of channeling this voice, if you will. I was typing away, and a note slips in under the door, from my then-twelve-year-old girl, who is a big soccer player. It was like whooosh under the door, and it said, "Daddy, let's go play," and I'm thinking, I can't play soccer in Central Park . . .

I'm a thirty-eight-year-old hooker in the Bronx. How can I have that life and this life? Which you can have, that life and this life. [Laughter]

In *The Poppies* [Chapter 13, pp, 109–10], Cyril Connolly says, "There is no more somber enemy of good art than the pram in the hall," but I don't agree with that. I look at writers like Michael Ondaatje, who says, "You can have a life, and you can live outside your book, and you can have a beautiful life." And it's not all about drinking and drugs, and the "literary life goes to literary parties," because at a certain time you just have to go into a room, close the door, and work. And sometimes that means, as you know, working twelve, fifteen hours a day and maybe only getting one sentence. I mean, I've done that! But when the one sentence comes, and it's the right sentence, then you're off and moving.

Kelly: Where do you work?

McCann: Well, I have a little office in my home. I also work in the New York Public Library 42nd Street. I should say I work on 42nd Street, and then people can work that out.

Kelly: Is the room in your house a small, cluttered, messy room, is it a clean room, is it a white box, is the music on?

McCann: Funny thing is everybody's going to get a chance to see it on May the 4th because RTE is putting on a documentary. They came into my disaster of an office. It's like completely messy, with photos all over the place, books three deep on the shelves, and papers on the floor. As small as the room is, I change it around for each novel; you know, take down various photos, try to create a new space each time. Yeah, so Charlie McCarthy, who's with the film, and Seamus Heaney came over, and we spent ten days together in New York.

Kelly: Now, when you go to the office, Colum, do you say to your kids, "Daddy is going to leave you now, and I'm going to be here for, what, an hour, three days, six months." How does that work? Do you say, "Leave my meals at the door?"

McCann: I'd say I have a fairly normal life outside the writing life. I think when I write, I journey, so I can close the door for eight hours, be in an absolutely alternate universe, but when I go out the door, then I have to be an ordinary dad, pay the bills, get the notes from teachers saying my son's been messing up the school. Can I tell you the story about Johnny Michael?

Johnny Michael is eleven years old. I went to his school bag a few months ago, and it felt pretty heavy. What in the world's in here? I found a few copies of *Let the Great World Spin*. One of them, in particular, was very thumbed through, and particular pages were turned down, so I said, "John Michael, what's the story?" He said, "Sorry, Dad." "Sorry about what?" "Can I tell the truth?" "Yeah, of course, you can tell me the truth." "Well, Dad, I was showing all my friends the f-u-k parts." He's going to have to learn to spell. [Laughter]

Kelly: Do you get in the eight hours?

McCann: I would push to get the eight hours. They know not to open the door. Often in summer time, they will go away for a couple of weeks, and I will just come home, especially at the end of a novel, and I literally will put in eighteen hours. That's when the office becomes a spectacular mess, pizza boxes, whiskey bottles, and all sort of things. And that's really concentrated time. But at the start of a novel I'm sort of fidgety, two hours here, three hours there, researching, but at the end of a book, that's when I really need the space and time.

Kelly: Do you have a pot of coffee, do you go jogging in Central Park before you start?

McCann: Yes, I do. My dream day would be to wake up at five o'clock, six o'clock in the morning, get two hours in before having coffee, before checking internet, before reading the newspaper.

Kelly: Is that what you actually do?

McCann: Sometimes I do, but it would be a dream day. Then I would have coffee, breakfast, get kids off to school. I'd work for another three hours, check messages, go for a run in Central Park. I try to run every day and get the toxins out, and then I'd work up to late at night, have a whiskey late, then go downstairs and check out . . .

Kelly: Can you sleep at night? When you go to bed, do you still have this stuff going around in your head?

McCann: No, no, no, after that, I go to bed and go to sleep.

Kelly: How important then is it that you're in New York? If I lived in New York, I'd enjoy jogging in Central Park every morning. I'm just wondering if you'd be as mentally sharp, as focused, if you were living somewhere else. Like Mayo.

McCann: I'm not sure. It would be a different sort of focus because language is influenced by the landscape in so many ways. But part of living in New York is really expensive. Jim Harrison has this line in his poetry: "Children prop up our rotting bodies with cries of 'Earn, earn, earn.'" So I do have to earn a living, you know, and part of that is like being in New York. I could leave New York, and take it easier and be more comfortable by going to Mayo. I used to live in Castlebar, in fact. But I love the energy of New York, to walk out onto the street, and everybody's colliding and . . .

You know, New York feels like a sort of elsewhere to me, all these people coming from all these different countries. On my floor, there's a Russian woman across the way, there's an Armenian couple next door, there is Greek couple across the way from us, an Israeli woman downstairs—it feels like the United Nations, you know, but I love that clash and energy so you're almost away at the same time you're at home.

That the world is that big and that small is one of the things that really interests me as an Irish writer. I can be writing an Irish novel, but none of it takes place in Ireland whatsoever. So it could be about a Slovakian Gypsy woman, who wanders around Europe, and there's no mention of Ireland in it whatsoever. But it's still an Irish novel because the borders of our imagination are so much bigger in particular because we have people coming here now, and I think the novelists of the past twenty-five years have gone outward, as people have come inwards, and we have wanted to tell our own story by accepting or not accepting the stories of others as they've come into us.

I love the fact that now I'm a member of Aosdána. I shouldn't have become a member of Aosdána because I'm living abroad, but they voted me in. Aosdána can operate in New York, you know, so I can hold onto what I was given here and at the same time try to expand it outwards. That would be my function.

Kelly: Is there any downside to where you are now? I don't know what your relationship with your agent is, but suppose you said your next book is this [*Let the Great World Spin*], and they say, "No way, Colum. Don't write about that stuff anymore, write about this, or write another *Let the Great World Spin*, or whatever." They must be pressures that come. What are they?

McCann: It frightens the daylights out of me. First of all, because you feel like you don't deserve it; second, because you're in the middle of it, and you're thinking, This is everything I wanted, but now I have seven hundred emails I have to respond to. And all those people that wanted me to read their books and blurb their books now they're mad at me because now I don't have the time. But that's part of the joy of it as well. I think I'm damned lucky, and say, I'm glad to have all of this happening to me. When I get down and out, as I have done, my wife Allison—she's very good about it—she says, "Will you ever stop worrying for crying out loud? All this good stuff is happening." And it'll calm down. I have to find, somewhere in myself, the way to write the best book that comes along next time.

But it is great to be able to be in New York and end up going on a committee for the Irish arts community over there. It gets me to meet someone like Gabriel Byrne. Gabriel Byrne is fantastic. Generally when you say "Gabriel Byrne," you hear a lot of ooooo's in the room. Is he a big ooooooo in Ireland as well? [Laughter] He's also cultural ambassador for Ireland, and he's doing some incredible stuff. So I get out and get to meet people like that.

Kelly: Is there some big guy with a cigar in your life that says you're not common, you're big, and this what you've got to do?
McCann: There's none of that. I just signed a two-book deal with Random House, but it was the two books I wanted to do, and in the end what're they going to do? They can't fire me. It's a fact of life. Nobody can take my job.

Kelly: When you sign this two-book gig with Random House, is it a foregone conclusion that they're going to take the two books?
McCann: More or less . . .

Kelly: So it's not the case that they're going to say, "Let's check this book out first and see what it's like at the end." They will take you on because . . .
McCann: Yes, they will take me on, and hopefully things will go on down the road. But I've always felt that even if I'd sold two thousand copies of this [*Let the Great World Spin*], it's always going to come back.

One of the ways I sprung into this book was that my previous book *Zoli* didn't do very well, especially in the States—people weren't interested in Gypsies—and I was sort of angry because I didn't think people were embracing the story of the other. So I said, "I'm going to go in there and tell a story that goes right to the heart of, say, 9/11 and see how people respond to that, and so part of this was fueled by anger—and desire."

But that's the thing I don't want to lose—the desire to write a good book. People I admire who are in for the long term, like Roddy [Doyle], who started outside the SFX [City Theater] Center, hawking *The Commitments* (1987), self-published. He knew what he wanted to do—bravest writer in Ireland—took on topics normally people wouldn't engage in, like *The Woman Who Walked into Doors* [domestic violence], and stayed true to himself.

The absolute necessity for arrogance, which all writers have, and the huge necessity for balance with as much humility as you can possibly get—so you have those two things. If you let the arrogance overpower the humility, then you're in real trouble. I've seen writers who expect things to happen to them.

You know, sometimes I don't think it's even me who's written these books, and I've got an obligation to my readers. My readers finish the books. That's not playing to the audience. I really truly believe a book should be good enough that it doesn't know its own intelligence. It's only when the reader comes to it, and she or he expands it with their own intelligence that the book actually becomes good. So in a way the writer is the facilitator.

Kelly: Just before we get some questions from the audience, one of the things you say, particularly about this book [*Let the Great World Spin*], you're an Irish writer in America, and a lot of the great American writers were all given a hard time for not writing the great 9/11 novel. They all got into the act, but nobody seemed to be able to do it. Does this draw attention to this book?

McCann: Joe [Joseph] O'Neill wrote a great book [*Netherland*]. Claire Messud [*The Emperor's Children*], sure. I think [Don] DeLillo's book *Falling Man* is a fantastic book. I don't think the great 9/11 novel's been written yet.

Kelly: It's been said that this one [*Let the Great World Spin*] is.

McCann: It's been said, but I paid a lot of money for people to say that. [Laughter]

I knew I wanted to write a 9/11 novel, and whether it's the best or not is not up for me to say. But if other people say it, I'm completely flattered by it, but it doesn't mean that it is, or will be. Or perhaps it is. But it means nothing in large scale that I could sit back, and say, "Oh, isn't that great?" And I don't like that sort of attitude.

And this book [*Let the Great World Spin*] was about trying to find grace, a moment of beauty, trying to find a moment of healing, a moment of redemption. Amongst all the shit and the grime and the everyday torments of trying to live in a city and just try to find a little chink of light on the outside. That could be criticized as being sentimental, but I really find it anti-sentimental because to be truly optimistic you have to go through the really,

really, really thick darkness and come out the other side—changed. But you have to go through the thick darkness in order to come out and find some sort of filagree of light.

Kelly: We're about out of time, but we do have time for some questions.
Questioner: I developed this habit when I was fifteen: every time I'd read a book I really enjoyed, I would underline specific lines so I could take the book off the shelf later and find the lines. I totally defaced your book. [Laughter] I'm just wondering about why people write and how much easier it might be if you're successful. I write, and I've worked it out for myself. It's getting that one line, the elation of getting from nothing to something you're happy with. But I wonder how you've worked it out.
McCann: That's the crucial moment. The writing doctor says writing is like driving at night in the fog with your headlights on: You don't absolutely know where you're going, and you can see only just so far ahead, but you're going to get somewhere anyway. Then comes that moment. It hits you! A line, just like, "That's it." Of everything I've worked for, this feeling is as good as anything. There are very few human moments, it seems to me, as powerful as the feeling when you hear a voice. It's not yours, but that voice seems entirely true, about to tell a story, and I love that!

Don DeLillo actually came to a class of mine at Hunter College to talk about process and how to write and all that stuff. He was answering questions, talking actually about mystery—I love this mystery—but then he tilted back his baseball cap at one stage and said, "Well, I seem to be the beneficiary of another revelation."

And sometimes it's just like that. You're sitting there, and you work hard enough and you become the beneficiary of a revelation, and you didn't know it was inside you. I think we're all bigger than what we actually know, and we've more expansive hearts, and actually we do understand other people more than we know. Books enable that. I love stepping into books and having bigger lungs at the end of it all. Basically, that's how it feels.

Questioner: My first encounter with your writing was *Fishing the Sloe-Black River*, and I've never forgotten those characters. Those characters are so strong, even now as I'm talking I'm thinking I'm thinking about them. [*McCann:* Wow!] How do you excise those characters from your past when you finish the book?
McCann: Wow, that's a great question. I wrote a character called Zoli, and I think I could still go to the mountains in Italy and knock on this door, and

she would be there somehow. I suppose I could say the same about other characters. I could go down through the tunnels of New York and meet Treefrog. Sometimes you think that they're still alive.

I think the way you excise them is that you give them to other people, and the other people take on the responsibility for them. [Questioner: Lovely answer.] By publishing them, for example, and you reading them, then you take on the weight, the responsibility, and take some of it off my shoulders, and that's what reading is all about. Thank you.

Questioner: I loved the book [*Let the Great World Spin*], really enjoyed it, but I was confused about the man with the camera. I love the rest. What was he doing in the book?

McCann: Okay, we're talking about the chapter about the man who has a camera, and he goes around underground and takes photographs of graffiti. His name is Fernando Yunqué Marcano, who's only mentioned once, and it seems to be he never comes up in the book again.

Now turn to page 237. At the bottom of the photograph, there is the character Fernando Yunqué Marcano, who has stepped out of Wall Street. He has a camera with him, and he has taken a photograph, which is the man on the wire, and the two towers on the other side so he's halfway between them. [Colum reads from the chapter "Roarin' Seaward, and I Go."] So he's there in that chapter, he takes the photograph, and she [Jaslyn] later owns the photograph. There are lots of little threads in the book that come together. Some of them I don't tell people about.

Questioner: I loved the book but I didn't get that.

McCann: My editor didn't get it either, and she read it twice. She said, "What is this tag thing?" So I have to decide: should I take it out or leave it in? Should I make it more obvious?

The photograph was taken by Vic DeLuca. I phoned him up and said I'd bought the rights to the photograph, and I said, "I'm not going to put your name on it but the character's name, do you mind?" He said, "No, fire away." That was the crux of the novel for me. You have this tightrope walker and this plane in the background that could smash into the towers, but, of course, it doesn't. Thank you.

Questioner: You talk about not wanting to write about yourself. Does this have anything to do with the "channeling" you mentioned? Is "channeling" something that comes off you?

McCann: I think it's the desire to be someone else. All of us want to be someone else at a certain stage of our lives. Actors do that most supremely. The best actors can become someone else. Sometimes you have to work at it.

There are different forms or different ways for getting into a character. For me, it's about, yes, divesting myself from the story, and yet you're obviously there in all sorts of ways because you're the one who's choosing the way the words go on the page. So you're both that person and another person, but it's the ability to be Other.

I think the most significant political thing we can have, the most significant social thing we can do, is to understand the Other, whether that be the single mother down the road who is not putting the proper clothes on her child or allowing the child to go wild, whether it be the idiot businessman who just ruined our economy or whatever it happened to be. If we can have some degree of empathy to try to understand, then I think we can deal with our own faults at the same time. If we just look at other people and judge them, then we have to be perfect ourselves—somehow? But we're not.

I think to channel others is to acknowledge that you yourself are flawed, and deal with some of the guilt.

Questioner: When you get to the end of a book, do you ever go back to the beginning and change things?

McCann: The book is always in flux, and the last sentence will sometimes change the first sentence. And I will read it over, and over, and over, and over obsessively, and wander around my house, reading it aloud, but it's never such that you have a first chapter in place and it never changes. Everything that comes along afterwards will change what went before as well.

In a certain way, it's like a piece of music, like the violins come in here, the drum's in there, the guitar's in there. Ooh, does that mean I should put a little bit of violin at the beginning to get the violins ready at the end? It's in a constant flux.

Question: I'm reading your book [*Let the Great World Spin*]—themes of obsession in it, Corrigan and Petit, the tightrope walker, and maybe you want to look at the documentary *Man on Wire*, which raises its own questions. Did you ever meet him?

McCann: I have a message on my answering machine. "Allo, thees ees Philippe Petit." I talked to him on the telephone and told him what I was doing. I sent him the book, I said if he had any changes I'd be very willing to entertain any changes he wanted. He's not mentioned in the novel as such, but it's obviously about his walk and the character of the tightrope walker is different to Petit. When he jumps off into the snow, for instance, I'm sure Petit never did that. But I never heard from him. I hope someday to meet him, but I might stand a few paces back 'til I know exactly how he feels. But he comes out really well in the book. He didn't like the documentary.

Questioner: Well, it did portray him as an awfully obsessed character.
McCann: And narcissistic. The beautiful thing about what Petit did was—of course, it was beautiful in itself; it was a crazy thing to do, to walk across a tightrope a quarter of a mile in the air, eight times back and forth. But it's become even more beautiful because now that the towers are down it's absolutely unrepeatable. That's what's so really gorgeous about it.

Kelly: There's two questions emailed in. How did you find the voice of Tillie?
McCann: Six months of work, lots of rap sheets, lots of hanging out with cops, went to the Bronx, talking to women who'd been around in the seventies and were willing to admit they'd been a hooker, working, working, looking at films, looking at photographs, and then trying to get it working, and it wouldn't. Then one night she said—talk about "channeling"—she's talking about traveling to New York: "The skinniest dog I ever seen is on the side of a Grey Hound bus," and once she gave me the line I knew her voice. That was it! Out of that came everything.

Kelly: The character of Corrigan is roughly the same age as you, Colum. Does he reflect you in any way?
McCann: No, he's way too good. Now [Ciaran] the brother's more like me. [Laughter]

Questioner: What has the response been to *TransAtlantic* here in Ireland?
McCann: I have to say that *TransAtlantic* did better here than anywhere. Actually I'm so proud of that! I hit the *New York Times* best-seller list, but being on the list here, that's a kicker. The essence of what I'm saying is that it's nice to come home and be recognized by your own.

"A Country of the Elsewheres": An Interview with Colum McCann

Joseph Lennon / 2012

From New Hibernia Review 16.2 (Summer 2012), 98–111. Reprinted by permission of Joseph Lennon.

Joseph Lennon's conversation with Colum McCann developed over several years through face-to-face contact and e-mail correspondence.

Everything in This Country Must

Joseph Lennon: I'd like to begin with a few questions that Eóin Flannery has passed along about your short story collection, *Everything in This Country Must*, which seems to have been overlooked in scholarship. What do you make of its critical and scholarly reception?

Colum McCann: A lot of people have been telling me that *Everything in This Country Must* becomes a better story the older it gets. Well, certainly it seems to get more attention. Part of this is because we made a short film that got nominated for the Oscars, but another part is that there is the beginnings of a new study of stories that relate to the North. And when I wrote the story there was still that embarrassment in Irish literary circles that someone had written a "Northern Irish story." Imagine that, and he's from the South! How dare he! As if it's five million miles away. As if I was writing about Mars. I could take on the gay underground in New York, or the killing fields of Russia, or the Mexican landscape, but God forbid I try to go to Derry, one hundred miles from where I was born. This embarrassment with Irish history and the Troubles will soon be a thing of the past.

The collection is about the accidental blows that children get from politics, but it's also about the development of political consciousness, how we get to the stage where we have to start answering the questions.

I have heard that the story is now being studied in universities in Beirut, in South Carolina, in Sydney, in Tel Aviv, in Dublin, and in New York. There's a universal aspect to it. Carver says that short stories should tell us what nobody knows, but everybody is talking about. I like to think that stories can get to the pulse of the wound. I suppose I was trying to explain the situation in Northern Ireland to myself, but in a certain way I was also trying to explain it to my children, so that years from now when they ask me why that happened (as I asked my father after the Miami Showband murders) I will sit them down with the story and hopefully it will capture some ongoing essence.

I'm always flattered that anyone would study my stories, sometimes just flat-out amazed. I don't discount it at all. I learn from scholars. Mine is a text (or at least should be a text) that opens up other texts. This is the function of good criticism, to spin outward from the story. This is not the exclusive territory of poetry. And the story must be left open enough to allow a creative reading. I don't want to be told what to think. The world is full of that already. I'd rather be allowed to feel and then make my mind up from within my own experience. Didactic writing is automatically diseased.

I have to say this, though. The story was better received in the North than it was in the South. And the film too. It got a huge round of applause in the North, in Belfast, where they thought it was "true," that was the word they used, but in the South a large number of people just slinked away from it. Maybe it was just the weather. I doubt it, though. There was a real sense of, oh Jesus, Northern Ireland, how Neanderthal is that? We're turning the corner now. The silence won't be accepted.

Lennon: Also, short stories (as well as poetry) frequently represent the Troubles, as with Eugene McCabe's "Christ in the Fields." Why did you choose to represent the Troubles in short form?
McCann: The North has always held a fascination for me. I remember going up north from Dublin with my mother, to her family home, and experiencing the simple amazement that a post box was red. A red postbox. Years later I wanted to write a derivative poem that began: "So much depends on a red postbox . . ."

And so much of my youthful questioning revolved around the North—I just wanted to know why it was happening, why were people being kneecapped, why were girls being tarred and feathered, what happened to the Miami Showband, where was Doctor Herrema? Why did I have to disguise my Dublin accent when I was on the streets of Garvagh town? To answer these questions, the short form has worked for me so far, both in "Cathal's Lake" and "Everything in This Country Must." But I would like to write a novel about the North. That's a three-or four-year commitment, but one I'm getting very close to doing. I feel like I've been preparing all these years to go home, or should I say "come home"?

There's plenty of good short fiction about the North, and, yes, Eugene McCabe is one of the very best. But more, please, more. I remember the review in the *New York Times* of "Everything . . ." and some moron said that I was just taking the route of every other Irish writer, that we seemed morally compelled to write about the North. I wish it were true. I only wish we could have taken it on in better and deeper ways, maybe we would have been more aware, as a nation, of the horrors we were doing to one another. Does fiction have the ability to heal things? I doubt it. But it might show us where some of the bandages are hidden.

Lennon: Lastly, in *Everything in This Country Must* did you intentionally build parallels to *Dubliners* (using adolescent protagonists; weaving in themes of paralysis; representing fractured families; creating alienated characters)?
McCann: No, there's no intentional parallels. I think the prose would creak if I intentionally set out to mirror such an important book.

Zoli

Lennon: *Zoli*, your 2006 novel based on the life of the Romani poet, Papusza, has received wonderful reviews around the world. How has it been received by Romani?
McCann: Well, the best thing about *Zoli*—which is probably as a work of art, my biggest failure—is that it helped change more things than any other book of mine. The novel was brought up in discussions in the European parliament and some politicians/lawmakers have told me that it helped change their perceptions of the Roma. And the Roma themselves—those who read the book—have been incredibly kind to me. I stepped into their territory, stole from them, tried to create a story or a myth, and they allowed me to into their homes, their lives. I am humbled and blessed by the reaction to that book from the Romani people in particular.

Lennon: So why was it a "failure"?

McCann: In many ways I feel that I was too responsible to how I felt the culture would receive it. The anxiety of influence, but in a cultural context. When I wrote about Nureyev I didn't give a damn about him, he could look after himself, but when I wrote about Papusza (through the character of Zoli) I felt an enormous responsibility to get it right. And I think it put certain gates and walls around my imagination. If there's any novel that I could get back, to rewrite, it's *Zoli*. And yet I don't want to step backwards. It's the old Beckett thing: No matter, try again, fail again, fail better.

Besides, every work of art is a failure. When you sit down to write it, it always falls short of what you want it to be. This is good news, though. The failure, as Beckett again would say, has a vivifying air to it. There's a great charge in promising yourself that next time you'll get better.

Lennon: You have just finished a novel, which we will get to in a moment, but first a question on work that may be gestating. You've been a commentator for the *Village* in Ireland. Will your next novel deal with issues of immigration and the "new" Irish in Ireland? If not, what are you working on at present?

McCann: After finishing a novel, I'm generally exhausted and need a few months to recover, read, discover again. And then I get terrified that I have nothing to write about. And then I place my feet down into that painstaking tar, and start to create. But I really think it will be back to Ireland in some form or other, preferably something that ties in Northern Ireland and the new immigration as well. But who knows? It's dangerous to talk my way into it right now, even more dangerous to talk my way out of it. Think of it like I've just finished a long marathon. I'm at the end of the track and I'm still panting, but I'm beginning to think about next time around.

Let the Great World Spin

Lennon: Your last three novels have had characters at their centers based on actual people: Rudolf Nureyev, Papusza, and now Philippe Petit. Why do you choose this route of fiction, one that skirts biography?

McCann: A good few years ago I gave an interview to *Atlantic Monthly* and in it I explicitly stated that writing about "real" people somehow showed a failure of the imagination. A year or so later I was trying to step into Rudolf Nureyev's shoes. Go figure. What does it mean? Nothing except that you cannot really trust anything that I, or any other writer says, especially when it's an absolute. We move on, we grow up, we make mistakes, we enter new territory, we embrace flux.

I do think there was an unconscious political intent here, however. I went through *Dancer*, then *Zoli* and now I've taken the events of Petit's walk, and shaped them. I was in a way questioning the notion of fact. I have always said that facts are mercenary things. They are at the core of manipulation. This is the era of "The Fact." Colin Powell stands up on TV and shows the world a photograph, and says it's a photograph of a chemical tanker and therefore it must contain agents of warfare and therefore we must send our children to war to protect us from the evil within the "fact" that he holds in his hands. The only fact is that he holds a photograph. But out of that photograph we extrapolated a whole legacy of death. That was his fact. Death. And George Bush's facts.

So the fiction is saying: Question the facts. Question who owns the facts. Question who puts a logic on them. Be angry at his facts. The job of fiction is to get at the texture and the truth and the deep honesty of what it's like to live inside your own—and other people's—skin. The job is to hold up a photograph to ourselves, and to walk around it, through it, and question it, and if possible find beauty there.

Some people seem to think it's cheating. That it would be better somehow to ignore the real world and just create from scratch. But I do create from scratch. I try to create from a scratch that has become a deep wound.

Also, this look at "biography" questions the technology of remembering. And so it's an examination of storytelling too, and notions of memory. *Dancer* is a very obvious example of this—who owns Nureyev's life? Well, in most history books it's the elite. In the novel it's the ordinary people, the nurses and rent boys and gravediggers.

And with *Let the Great World Spin*, of course, just mentioning the WTC has a whole baggage to it.

Lennon: *Let the Great World Spin* brings us into the lives of twelve different characters (plus one) from many walks of life, from judges in mahogany-paneled chambers to street-walking prostitutes. It is a fine paean to the creative urge of life embraced by the diverse mass that is New York City. It is a lyrical tapestry of experience.

McCann: It's a city in many ways. Not a whole Whitman city, as I would like some day to do, but there's the spirit of a city there, I hope. And the intimate connections. For every atom belonging to me as good as belongs to you.

Lennon: All of the narrators seem to be gifted wordsmiths, each after their own fashion. Why did you organize the novel in this fashion?
McCann: Well, there's the kaleidoscopic influence of the city for one. Hence the desire to be in a lot of different heads. And the desire to find their voices, so that they whisper in the reader's ear. If we hear a fabulous voice, we are more or less prepared to go anywhere with it. The different narrators are gifted on different levels. Tillie, the prostitute in the Bronx, speaks a lot differently than Claire, the mother on Park Avenue, but hopefully they both surprise us, like life surprises us. The stories don't end. And the angles from which they can be seen are infinite, but the most important angle is that of the human heart.

On a more practical level, this is the way I like to write—to change the tempo, sometimes sound out the contrabass, sometimes bring in the creaky old cello, every now and then have the violin become an upstart.

Lennon: Much of the novel takes place when the World Trade Center Towers were just being completed in 1974, not when they were destroyed. This novel seems to be less about grieving and more about creation—you have characters at their most daring, at the moments when things are beginning or about to begin—artists pushing frontiers, technicians developing the ARPNET (the internet's precursor), and characters such as Philippe Petit (the man who walked between the Twin Towers on a tightrope in 1974) doing original, daring, and innovative acts. Discovery is a kind of genius to the young photographer character—who later photographs Petit's walk as a plane passes overhead, its nose seemingly about to hit one of the Towers, which eerily echoes for us today, even though it was taken in 1974. When this young photographer sees the new style of graffiti, "wild-writing," in the early 1970s, it seems to him like finding "a new frontier" and "like discovering ice." Why did you make artistic discovery a main theme of this novel? Is this a tribute to things that have been accomplished, not to things destroyed?
McCann: This is the question I fear and dread, partly because I think I've answered it in the novel and I'm fearful of making pedestrian sense of it, and partly because I'm still not entirely sure what I've done here, so close to having just finished the novel (just a few weeks ago). Yet in some ways it's the only question and it's dogged my mind for the past few years, all throughout the writing process. It's dangerous to be too aware of what you're trying to do.

But to begin in the beginning. My father-in-law, Roger Hawke, was in the WTC on September 11th, on the 59th floor. He was one of the lucky ones, he got out. And he came to the apartment where my wife and I were living, uptown, and he was covered in dust, and I remember my daughter Isabella smelling the smoke off his clothes and she said: "Poppy's burning," and I said, "No, no, love, it's just the smoke on his clothes from the buildings," and she said—out of the mouths of babes—"No, no, he's burning from the inside out." And it struck me immediately that she was talking about a nation. Or that's what I thought at first anyway. She's right, we're burning from the inside out.

And I began to wonder, Who's going to write about this? I did some essays for newspapers and so on, but everybody did. Susan Sontag was the bravest of all. But every piece was poignant: every journalist, every poet, every gossip. And everything had meaning: it was like the whole city was infused with meaning. The lone fire hydrant. The flowers on the window of a car. A bit of ash that tickled the back of your throat. You couldn't help thinking that everything held importance. Even the child's painting of the two buildings holding hands was a powerful image. In fact, it was a level ground of meaning. Meaning came down, it was leveled into dust. The over-world, the underworld. I felt it was quite impossible to write something that would break your heart, because anyone with any sort of heart had it broken that morning. And I'm not just talking about the hands-on grief, that horrible look-at-me-I'm-burning sort of grief, I'm talking about what it meant for the world, the horrors that the Bush administration would unfold in its name, the terrible way they turned justice into revenge, the dark mark of hatred that reared itself both in the Islamic world and in Britain and here in the States. I mean, I just recall being so very hopeful for the first few days, thinking that maybe now we would understand grief, maybe we could be empathetic, maybe we could turn some good out of this. But then the months went on and it kept getting worse, until of course they unfolded the map of Iraq to level it, and it turned into a tragedy of Shakespearian proportions. And still the question was: how do I write about this?

I remembered the Petit walk pretty early on, and I knew that was my novel—that had to be it. Originally I was just going to write the novel and have him fall, mess with history, the facts, the textures. I was raring to go. But I had already embarked on *Zoli* and I wasn't willing to throw all that work away, so I tucked the Petit thing in the idea drawer. Not that it's a tremendously original idea anyway. First of all, he did the walk. He himself wrote a book about it after the Towers came down. Then came a children's book. Then a play. Then a documentary. I mean, it's the obvious image.

Lennon: It was even on the cover of the September 11th *New Yorker* two years ago on the fifth anniversary.

McCann: Yes, that great drawing where the city becomes a ghost at his feet. The walk across the World Trade works on so many levels, it even has that Nietzschean ring to it, the over-man stuff. But I always thought that at the heart of my novel it wouldn't be "about" Petit's walk. I knew I was writing a 9/11 novel, one written in advance. But it was an emotional response, rather than a measured intellectual one. And the fact that all this stuff took place thirty years ago was perfect, because I could lay it over the present, like tracing paper. And let the reader decide. And my benchmark was my father-in-law. He couldn't stomach anything about 9/11. He hated the books and the screenplays and the rah-rah-rah industry that grew up around it, the missiles slammed into Baghdad in defense of the dead, he was, like a lot of Americans, disgusted by it all. He woke at night dreaming of those young firemen running up the stairs past him while he escaped. He said he'd never read a 9/11 novel. But he eventually read mine and he knew what was going on with it, he felt it, he felt all that grief, and yet it's exactly as you say, Joe, he recognized immediately that it was a novel about creation, maybe even a novel about healing in the face of all the evidence. He liked it. In many ways, it's his book. It's my response to him. Look at that, you're alive, your grandkids are jumping in your lap. This is powerful stuff to me. This is the glue. This is what we were meant for. And we fight off the evil with whatever small good we can do.

I'm not willing to say that this is an accidental 9/11 novel. No way. From the get-go that's what it was about. You caught me at a raw time. I haven't yet talked about this. I haven't formulated a defense. I haven't learned to talk around it. I hate hearing about "accidental" 9/11 novels. You know, DeLillo, one of my great heroes, went right to the heart of it with *Falling Man*. The first sentence of my novel, long before I read DeLillo's book was: "The prospect of a falling man." I had to put a red line through it when I read his novel.   On another level, I'm not interested in the triumph of destruction. There's enough of that. The White House is filled with that. I'm interested in how we move on. I grew up in Ireland. I saw what the bombings could do. And I lived long enough to know that peace could come out of it. And I know enough to say that peace is complicated and tough and proper. None of it's easy. I'm proud of this novel. I might hate it next year when the critics get at me, but for now I have said all that I want to say. Sometimes I want to run away and just spend an afternoon in the pub with my characters, or walk through the Bronx with them. I suppose that means that they're alive. I can only imagine Tillie hoisting one with Corrigan, or Ciaran having a laugh in the background, and Claire picking up the bill, and Jaslyn over in the corner watching Barack Obama on the TV.

Lennon: You seem to quietly allude to a story of Salman Rushdie's "The Courter" in *Let the Great World Spin* when you mention that Albee was a grandmaster of chess from Hungary. Is this a case of intentional intertextuality, or am I just making it so? If so, are you a fan of Rushdie's and of "postcolonial" fiction? In any case, why does chess figure so prominently in your fiction? I know you and your children are accomplished chess players, but is it also as a metaphor for cultural politics?

McCann: I don't know Rushdie's story. I should, because I'm fond of Rushdie and what he has done, his political intent, his work against the colonial grain. It's quite simple, really, chess is a great metaphor. In fact, I was going to include a whole game in this novel, a whole notation, a mutual stalemate that Albee was going to create, and it was going to come towards the end of the novel. But it never fit in. There's no point in shoe-horning it.

I use chess in my novella "Hunger Strike," where the boy eats the queen with a sort of savagery. What is it a metaphor for? I don't really know, but here's a clue. While writing this novel, I also wrote a short story that was never published. It's the account of a game between Hillary and Barack, where Hillary plays black and Barack plays white. I loved that story, but I never got the correct narrative frame for it, and so never published it. So, yes, cultural politics, indeed. But I'm loath to talk about metaphor. In the end it all can be metaphor. Sometimes a kick in the chest is just a kick in the chest.

Lennon: In a 2007 interview in the *Montreal Gazette*, you said that the key flaw in American foreign policy has been "a failure of empathy." This seems to be a key to much of your work, treating fiction as a tool for developing empathy.

McCann: The greatest thing about fiction is that we become alive in bodies not our own. If it isn't about empathy, then I don't know what it's about. The courage to read nowadays is not such a frequent thing. Let me say it again. The courage to read.

As I tried to explain a moment ago—on my soapbox, God, I hate my soapbox, but I can't get away from it sometimes—I feel we must fight against the absolute of despair. Of course, all of this leads us into the sketchy area of situation ethics and morals, spiritual entropy and lack of meaning. But fighting it off has meaning. Isn't this what all the great fiction has been about? When it comes down to it, that's where Joyce is, and Dostoyevsky, and Steinbeck. It becomes a stay against meaninglessness and despair.

Lennon: So how does this novel attempt to do this?

McCann: What this novel is trying to talk about, I suppose, is the courage to look at the horror, recognize it, and the equivalent courage that it takes to move on. But we only move on if we have understood, and if we have cared enough to change things. The whole time I was writing this novel, there was only one other novel I wanted to write, and that was about a woman in a market in Baghdad, that would be the only novel that could have twisted my heart backwards in the same way.

I'd love to have Dick Cheney in a room and read to him from a novel about an Iraqi woman in a fruit market, with a missile approaching and left in mid-air. That would torture him. For him to know what it's like . . . Cheney, that bastard . . . that would be his torture. Is it naïve to think that a book could change his heart, or Bush's heart? Probably. First of all, you'd have to locate their hearts, I suppose.

Lennon: I want to briefly reference two other works: In 1913, a Sophia Bryant wrote that the Irish were "other-conscious as a matter of course" in her book, *The Genius of the Gael*. This is a stereotype—that for the Irish "the other man's hurt hurts him"—but it seems to have some resonance in your fiction, especially your latest novel. And the second reference: in *Phenomenology of the Spirit*, Hegel wrote that intersubjectivity occurred when one recognized the self-consciousness of another. Your characters in this novel display both great self-awareness and haunting self-consciousness. Is it a goal for this novel, to plunge the reader into the consciousness of others, those with different identities? Is it to help your readers recognize a sense of sameness in the other? Does Irish literature do this particularly well?

McCann: It is a goal for the novel, yes, to plunge the reader into the consciousness of others, but I suppose all novels are. I think, then, through our sameness we can recognize our difference too. Good novels briefly whisk you from the world and make you glad to be alive, no matter how difficult the territory they plow. It comes down to recognizing the hurt, sometimes even closing a book and checking your skin for the fresh wound. There's a peculiar joy in recognizing that you don't have it quite so bad. Oh, look at that, I haven't been hacked, but I know what it feels like to be hacked.

In relation to Irish novels, who sings "I've been down so goddamn long that it looks like up to me"? I'm honestly not one to harp on about the Irish, and our understanding of suffering, but the fact of the matter is that we did get kicked around, there was genocide during the Famine, there were horrible years of colonial oppression. I recall on a personal level going up to

Northern Ireland and having British soldiers spit at my cousin's feet. I used to go to England with my father to watch football matches and he would tell me to be quiet. And there was something in the Irish spirit that wanted to be elsewhere. We are, or at least we were, a country of the elsewheres. But we have long wars and short memories, don't we? Ireland now—the Ireland of the 21st century—is one of the most prosperous and arrogant countries around. Do we still feel the "hurt" that Bryant talks about? I don't know. Do you need to be hurt in order to understand hurt? I hope not.

And I think when it comes to Hegel, he's talking about a heightened sense of empathy, which is almost saintly in a way, and very rare.

Lennon: You have been lightly criticized for writing aphorisms into your fiction. From your new novel, you have a character, Ciaran Corrigan, state tersely—"If you think you know all the secrets, you think you know all the cures"—when he mistakenly thinks he's understood his brother. Do you see yourself writing aphorisms—morals for your readers to take away from the fiction? Or, more broadly, do you see art and fiction as inherently political, Brechtian in a way (perhaps without the class-consciousness program)?

McCann: What is it Brecht says? That art is not a mirror to reflect reality, but a hammer with which to shape it? I wish I could be as deeply and overtly political as, say, Steinbeck. I don't shape things. I react. In my reaction I hope that others might shape things, or be moved to shape things.

Writing novels is a form of entertainment, but it can't just be entertainment. I'm fond of quoting DeLillo when it comes to this. He talks about the danger of writers becoming just one beat away from elevator music. The writer must work in opposition, he says. It's the dying section, dear Reader, not the living section. He isn't interested in being facile. If this means having an opinion, then I'm all for it. I don't like the idea that it would be aphoristic. It makes me want to dive back into my novel and get at it with a scalpel! But the fact of the matter is that people have opinions, be they right or wrong. People judge. People say things like, "That's the pot calling the kettle black."

I don't see myself as a moralist. I do, however, see the reader as a moralist. I want to write something that he or she can interpret and walk away with. It's the act of creative reading. I provide the text, you take from it what you want. I have to trust my readers to do this. Of course I also want them to be entertained. But the idea of being preachy goes against the grain for me. I'm not that clever. Most of my readers are cleverer than I am. So take from the novel what you will. I mean, the fact that you immediately saw that it was a novel of creation was a huge shot in the arm for me. The fact of the matter is that in the very first chapter, the two subsequent pillars of the novel—Corrigan and Jazzlyn—come tumbling down. The whole novel is then spent building them back up. I wanted to find the moment of joy. To twist Whitman a little: Do I sound sentimental? Very well, then, I sound sentimental. Because deep in there is a contradiction also.

Lennon: In your new novel, you have a character, Corrigan, who sets much of the tone. He seems to shadow many characters in Irish literature—religious (yet not as expected), alcoholic (and eventually abstemious), sacrificial and other-conscious (perhaps to a fault). Also in this and other works, names often have real significance. I have some thoughts and questions about this particular character and his name. First, is he a character you admire? One whom you want your readers to admire?
McCann: I loved Corrigan all along. At one stage it was going to be a novel only about him. But he would have hated that. All along, he was whispering to me, "Don't just write about me, what about all the others, they're far more interesting." And yes, he's other-conscious to a fault. But what I enjoyed about the book, and what surprised me, is how Jazzlyn and Gloria and Claire began to take it over. I think Corrigan would have understood this. When I got Tillie's voice—I mean, when I heard her and she started telling her story—I could feel Corrigan in the background saying, "On you go, sister."

Lennon: We often see others—his mother, brother, father, friends—literally calling his name in search of Corrigan, sometimes even beseeching him. This name, however, is not his first name, John, but his family name, Corrigan, the name of his estranged father who lives in England. His called name, therefore, seems particularly significant. John suggests an evangelical dimension, although one that is hidden (like his name) or at least dressed unfamiliarly (as his monkish character is). His brother calls him "the origin of things" and "a lost saint," even as Corrigan wrestles with leaving his order. He is also a sacrificial figure and therefore Christ-like. So a pointed Dedalusean question: why bring religion into this? Have we not had enough of Christ in Irish literature?
McCann: I'm no holy roller, that's for sure. At the best of times I'd call myself a col-lapsed Catholic. I suppose I have a Christ obsession, but that's me and three billion others. I've used these references (which I suppose come naturally from my youth) in a lot of my work. I'm thinking here of *This Side of Brightness*, for example, where we spend forty days and forty nights

with Treefrog, a brown man who lives underground, a man who scars his hands, a man who finds out that "our resurrections aren't what they used to be." And Corrigan is like an above-ground version of Treefrog. His struggle with Christ is a mammoth one. Christ, the communist. Christ, the lover of Magdalene. Christ, the man who knows his flaws. If there's any person to be, then be Christ. Be poor, be decent, be haunted, be angry, be understanding. Of course we all fail at even the most simple of these things. But it's an eternal theme in literature. I don't think we'll ever get too much of it. Hear me tout it one more time, the great John Berger: "Never again will a single story be told as if it were the only one."

As for Irish literature, I think we could do with a dose of Christ now. He is, in the end, far more interesting than our navels.

Lennon: Corrigan, his more Irish name, seems, however, to actually be a reference to the famous "Wrong-Way Corrigan" who flew an unauthorized flight from New York City to Ireland back in 1938. If so, what can this character tell us about contemporary Ireland and the emigrant experience?

McCann: I never thought of it that way. Of course I know Wrong-Way Corrigan. And here's the rub. While I never once let him cross my mind, maybe it's there. The beauty of criticism is what it finds, not necessarily what was intended. So I don't know if Corrigan's story is "about" the emigrant experience, but if a reader finds it there, I say hallelujah.

The truth of the matter is that I got a letter many years ago from the Jesuit priest Daniel Berrigan. It was about *This Side of Brightness*. The most extraordinary and generous letter. And I got to know him, and read his poems, and I fell in love with the ideas of Berrigan, his ideas on liberation theology, his activism, his radical Christ. I find him extraordinary. And when I first started writing this novel, I called my character Berrigan. Of course, it's not him. So I had to change the name. Corrigan came close. And after a while he just couldn't be called anything else. And of course his first name gets swamped. The John in him gets lost.

Lennon: Corrigan's brother, Ciaran, (with Lara, his American wife) eventually returns to Dublin for the boom times, and tries to get Corrigan to return, but Corrigan never expresses a desire to return. He does not display what Shiela, a minor character, does: "that emigrant's sadness—she would never go back to her old country, it was gone in more senses than one, but she was forever gazing homewards anyway." Toward what is Corrigan metaphorically gazing in the development project in the Bronx where he lives?

McCann: And now your preceding question makes absolute sense. Corrigan is the original "international bastard." He is comfortable everywhere. He doesn't gaze home. His home is in others. He can return there any time he wants. Corrigan is the man of elsewhere.

If he had lived, I imagine that he would have gone to Guatemala with Adelita. And if he were alive today and was given the opportunity to go one more place, I think he'd return to the Bronx. But he'd never lose the Irish in him. If anybody asked him where he was from, he'd simply say: Dublin.

Lennon: Is Corrigan also a way for you to explore otherness? Corr in Irish means odd, queer, peculiar, random, weird—as he is generally perceived both by the middle-class world in his association with prostitutes, drunks, and junkies—who, in turn, also perceive him as corr. Is he odd and other, or someone representing the unknowable (perhaps spiritual) core of us all?
McCann: I forgot that about "corr." And then the word "currach" comes from "corr," as well. Unsteady, out of balance. The Brendan character coming across the ocean. It all becomes so laden with meaning. I wish I could say I intended it. Corrigan wouldn't find himself to be "other" at all. He would see himself as deeply flawed. His goal is to fit in and be ordinary. He says: "One day the meek might actually want it."

Lennon: Tragedy bookends (literally and figuratively) this novel—the tragedies of lives lost, unlived, or unfulfilled. In some ways this seems an advance 9/11 novel—you have suggested that Corrigan's death evokes the fall of the first tower. Why did you choose this character for that fall?
McCann: I was never conscious until I'd finished the novel that I had Corrigan and Jazzlyn becoming two towers. Small and ordinary towers, I suppose, those lives that fall. And they are the only ones who never get to tell their stories. Everyone else tells the story for them. But they go on living. This, I suppose, is the art of how we come to survive.

Lennon: Corrigan is often referenced and described by other characters, yet we never hear him in the first person (except in reported speech) as we do with so many of the other characters. We don't learn what makes him tick to the same extent as other characters—we never hear his voice inside his head—his own self-consciousness. His mind and voice, in short, creates a kind of absence in the novel. Why did you depict him solely in the third person?

McCann: On a practical level, he dies. But in a way he inhabits all the voices. He's the force around which the voices spin. For me he was one of the main reason to write the novel: I wanted a story about a spiritually engaged character going through a crisis, and not another pedophile priest story either, enough of that. I wanted to feel the pain of being lost of God. I think that when I got Corrigan right he led me to Tillie, the hooker, who's my absolute favorite character in the book, but then again I'm just finished so the dust hasn't fully settled.

Lennon: We have discussed how the title of the *Let the Great World Spin* alludes to a line from Tennyson's "Locksley Hall," a text inspired by translations of a set of pre-Islamic Arabic poems, the Mu'allaqat. The main character in Tennyson, a soldier, longing for youth and his lost childhood home, hankers after a new world order and unified world government and idealizes the European sense of progress ("Better fifty years of Europe than a cycle of Cathay"). How does this resonate in a post-9/11 world?

McCann: The title *Let the Great World Spin* was an accident. I can't even remember how I found it—I had fooled around with a lot of names and somehow stumbled upon it, somewhere on the Internet. So I read the poem and I thought that the idea of a young man returning home from war, pondering the nature of the world, might fit. And I was stunned by the aerial imagery. To be honest, I was a bit uncomfortable with the fact that it was Tennyson, and there was this implicit talk of a new world order and an idealization of Britain and Europe.

I would have rather used a title with less colonial/territorial implications, but then the poem had been inspired by the Mu'allaqat, or the "Suspended Poems," those seven long pre-Islamic poems. And the texts seemed to dovetail into each other, as if they were in a strange historical gyre. And the Mu'allaqat asks "Is there any hope that this desolation can bring me solace?" So it fit. It was an accident, but I suppose some of these accidents happen for good reason. Still, I want to leave the 9/11 aspect up to the minds of readers: they can get from it what they want. It doesn't have to be a 9/11 novel—it can just be a look at New York, primarily in 1974, all the different people who collide with each other, a novel of grace in the face of reality, and the capability of reconstituting new myths.

Lennon: Perhaps the links between the two poems points to interconnections between our cultures—ones that are not immediately visible to us? In this sense, there is a certain revolution or "spin" of meaning (but not in the sense the media uses it) that occurs with your "suspended" title. One last post-script question, if I may impose—and great thanks for taking the time with all these questions.

I am struck now, in going back over the book and our above interview, how the life of every character somehow dovetails with other characters, and in particular, radiating from a single moment of tragedy and trauma. Perhaps my earlier question on intersubjectivity was wrong-headed, and I should have been asking about interconnections. In life we rarely see how we connect with strangers, just as none of the characters see all the connections that link their lives with one another. In fiction such connections can be observed, however.

Could you say more on why you made this plot with such connections between all of the characters, both known and unknown, both witnessed and unnoticed? Is this a novel of unseen dovetails, where the characters—the mortises and tenons, if you will—cannot themselves see how they beautifully they join?

McCann: The older I get, the closer I get to myself. I don't want this to sound like any mystical wisdom. It's very simple. I've been around longer. I understand more things, and hopefully I understand them better. One of those things is the realization of how "unfinished" life is. Another of those things is the capability of beauty surviving even against the darkest elements. This does not deny the darkness, but it says that we can survive it. Another of these things is the realization of how many people I happen to be—father, son, brother, writer, friend, enemy, teacher, the list is endless. That these things can resolve themselves in one life is extraordinary to me. And I'm interested in finding out these connections that we have with others, and how these connections can rescue the beauty in our lives. Known and unknown, as you say. Witnessed and unwitnessed. Bidden and unbidden.

The characters in this novel do not know how latticed they are in the world. But they fight on because they feel some ancient music there. There is a sort of memory in connectivity. There is also a memory in survival. A grand, ancient, human memory. Again, against the dark. That's where we are.

"Embracing the World by Inventing the World": The Literary Journey of Colum McCann

John Cusatis / 2012

Ernest F. Hollings Special Collections Library at the University of South Carolina. March 14, 2012. Reprinted by permission of John Cusatis.

The following interview between Colum McCann and John Cusatis, author of *Understanding Colum McCann*, was conducted in front of a live audience. McCann was invited to USC to participate in the first annual "Open Book" series, sponsored by the College of Arts and Sciences and hosted by novelist Elise Blackwell.

John Cusatis: I first met Colum in Ben Greer's novel writing class in the fall of 1997, while I was a Ph.D. student here. Colum was on campus to give a reading from his first novel, *Songdogs*. He spoke to our class and answered our questions. Afterwards, a small group of us took him to Hannah Jane's on Five Points for lunch, and he and I stayed in touch over the years. So I'm going to start, Colum, with the question I asked you during that class nearly fifteen years ago. At that time you had published two books—a novel and a short story collection. I'm interested to see how you would answer the same question five books later. I asked, "When you start a novel, to what extent do you lay down the scaffolding beforehand: map out the plot, determine the symbols, plan for character development?" Do you want to know what you said?

Colum McCann: I hope that I said the exact same thing I'd say today . . . that I have no clue.

Cusatis: That's correct. [Laughter]

McCann: I suppose it's like being on a journey. When you start the journey, you sort of cast out to sea, and you don't really know what land you're going to hit or going to find. But you know that eventually, if you go long enough and hard enough, you'll hit land. Or you'll run aground. You can use any number of metaphors. But I like the idea of not really knowing where it is that I'm going. With *Let the Great World Spin*, I thought that I was going to finish with another tightrope walk by Philippe Petit. I believed the novel might need a certain circularity. In the end, it didn't work that way at all, but it gave me an idea that I wanted to get somewhere. I knew I wanted to write about grace and recovery. So it was in the process of moving towards a false end that I found the various voices. To me it's like playing a piece of music. You play it over and over again. You try to get that chord right: "Ah, that sounds right. Let's go there." And then it takes on a rhythm. Especially a novel, I think, takes on a symphonic intent. You discover as you go along. Then these things sort of meet each other. They collide and affect one another.

Cusatis: In your comments to the MFA students this morning, you talked about your unconventional approach to writing fiction: not writing about what you know, but, as you just mentioned, taking this journey. What have you learned along the way, writing a book like *Let the Great World Spin*? You say you may discover things that you knew but didn't know you knew. Can you talk about that discovery process?

McCann: I think I've found that you don't know what the hell it is that you've learned. [Laughs] It never gets any easier. One would think that you accumulate this experience, and that suddenly you know, then, how to write a novel. But in the end you find out that you're starting from scratch again. You're carrying around the bricks and you're looking for a place to build a home. Then you have to teach yourself again, because each book should be a contained home, unto itself. It should have its own rules and regulations and landscape. I always think, "Okay, the next one is going to be easy." Because, you know, you have that dream vision. If you're writing something, you think, "Ah, Eureka! This is what I'm going to do." And you can see it very clearly. You can feel it in your soul. You can feel the texture of the thing. And you think, "Nobody's ever done this before! This is magnificent! I can't wait to get at it. I know exactly what it is that I want to do." And then you get home, and the thing just won't come through your fingers. [Laughter] You know you have it inside you. It's like: "Come out!" It doesn't happen that way. You keep carrying the bricks.

And that's part of the joy and the terror. I agree with Yeats's idea of "the fascination of what's difficult": putting yourself in a position to do something that is almost impossible. Nathan Englander talks about the impossible being the only thing that he's truly interested in. The fascination of the inexecutable. I like that notion because you push yourself into new space, and you learn things that you knew but you weren't entirely aware of. So there are degrees of consciousness here. Access to the mystery, if you will. Very few writers talk about this, but there is a joy in the exploration as well. Even the dead ends can be vivifying. Sometimes I get so serious: "Oh, it's about degrees of consciousness; it's about mystery; it's this or that." But the truth is that sometimes you just want to write these stories because you can engage in the world in a new way. It's about turning up the temperature on what fascinates you. For example, I used to travel a lot. I actually traveled through this area, twenty . . . six years ago—Oh, my God, yes, twenty-six years ago—on a bicycle. I went right across the United States. And now I can't travel quite as much. I live in New York. I've got three kids. It's harder to do those sorts of trips. So in some ways you learn to go on adventures in the heads of your characters. You're actually embracing the world by inventing the world. You fill your lungs with imagination. You create what wasn't once there. In my twenties I took a lot of risks. But now, I suppose, I go to dangerous places, but they happen to be more in the imaginative sphere. Writing about Rudolf Nureyev, for instance, was an incredible journey for me. I adventured my way into that world.

Cusatis: The poet Dana Gioia has written that during the mid-twentieth century "an academic bureaucracy" replaced "literary bohemia." You experienced many bohemian adventures, and now you teach in Hunter College's top-ranked MFA program. How do you think the prospects differ for a writer who gets started in an academic rather than a more bohemian environment, in other words, for one who may not get the chance to get out "on the road," in the way you or many of the Beat writers did, before he begins his serious work?

McCann: It's a question on the mind of virtually every MFA student that you meet: "Should I be here? Should I be doing this?" I didn't really go to an MFA program. I attended a few classes at the University of Texas. But I defend the MFA experience because it's a great time for people to experiment, to come into a hothouse environment and spend two years creating. They can decide whether or not they really, truly want to be a writer, if they really can be that person. And you've got a small community. They're looking after you. They will read what you've written. You don't have to work in isolation. However, there is a slight problem in this whole academic thing in the sense that you get these kids who are coming straight from undergraduate programs. So they're twenty, twenty-one, and they go immediately into an MFA program. They finish when they're twenty-three, twenty-four, and their mums and dads say, "Well, look, I paid all this money. Where's your book?" [Laughter] And then they're thinking, "Oh, Jesus, I have nothing to write about." So when we choose at Hunter College, we like to choose students who have a little bit of life experience, someone who has seen the raw and rougher edges. In the end, though, there are no rules for becoming a writer. None. You make your own path. You don't have to have lived a bohemian lifestyle. You don't have to have gone to all these different places around the world, but I think it helps a bit. I would like to have a nice meld of the bohemian and the academic. But I have to tell you, I have three kids, as you know, and I'm terrified that they're going to do what I did when I was younger. [Laughter]

Cusatis: I remember you telling me, when we were having lunch at Five Points fifteen years ago, how you had recently ventured down into the New York City subway tunnels and spent time among the homeless in preparation for the novel you had just completed, which, of course, was *This Side of Brightness* [1998]. The spirit of daring that made that novel possible must have been rooted in these early reckless days you are referring to.

McCann: Yes, well, I think the bicycle journey helped me enormously in that I could meet and talk to anybody. But really, ultimately, what those people wanted to do was to talk about themselves. They wanted to tell me a story because, in a weird way, vicariously, they were becoming novelists. They saw that I was moving through their town, and sometimes they would tell me the most intimate things about themselves. Or they would tell me the most harrowing things because they knew that I was taking it down into my belly and literally moving it down the road. It wouldn't necessarily have repercussions for them in their hometown. I was like a vagabond psychologist, meeting these people and learning how to talk to them. And also, quite frankly, being Irish helped an enormous amount. I was never as cool in Ireland. When I was walking across Ireland, people would say. "What are you walkin' across the country for? There's a bus, for cryin' out loud!" [Laughter] "You're three sandwiches short of a picnic!" But over here, it's like, "Ohhhhhh! You're from Ireland! Sing me a song!" [Laughter] Of course, I like talking to people. But one of the things that disturbs me is that, increasingly, I talk about myself. I'm so sick of myself. Up here, on stage, yapping on. I like the moments when I get to hide away, and I don't have to deal with myself anymore. That's where fiction comes in. I get to be someone else. I'm more honest that way. When I'm "other," I feel like I'm telling the truth.

But in regard to the tunnels, I would go down to the tunnels, and, yes, it was dangerous. But because I was Irish, I wasn't part of the system that had "oppressed," quote unquote, these homeless people. And I could stay, hang around. The longest I stayed down there was a few days at a time, but over the course of a year and a half, I got to know the homeless people living in various parts of the tunnels, like Broadway and Lafayette, where there was a crack tunnel. I was in a tent one time, and this guy wanted me to smoke crack with him. Misery loves company, and he wasn't going to let me out of there. Big, tall University of Alabama football player. [Laughter] I'm thinking, "I am in trouble here." I got out eventually, but I had to talk my way out. There were lots of adventures underground. I'd meet all sorts of people—hookers, Vietnam vets, runaways. They fascinated me, one and all.

I'll never forget this story. This woman loved getting those little packets you see on an airplane, what do you call them? Hand serviettes, hand towels? I'd go down the tunnels, and it was filthy. So I'd have these little towels, and I'd clean my hands sometimes, and this woman noticed. Denise was her name, I think. Anyway, one day she said, "Can I have one of those?" So the next day I brought her one of these airplane sachets. She was so happy, she kissed me on the forehead. "Thank you, Irish, thank you." Then I got to know her a bit more, and I'd bring down these packets on a regular basis. "Thank you, thank you." And then one day—I thought it would be really nice—I brought down a big box of baby wipes. She started crying. It was an affront to her dignity. I hadn't thought about it at all. She wanted the little packets, which she could secret away. To bring down this big box and make a presentation of it was wrong. You have to think about those things, and all these people in these situations.

But, also, we aren't so far from it ourselves. I mean homelessness. It happens so easily. You write a check and it bounces. Suddenly the bank is after you, right? So then you write another check. And then you steal your brother's check book. And then suddenly you get kicked out of your brother's house. Then you sleep on someone's sofa for a while. And then, one night you get drunk and the door is locked, and you have nowhere to sleep. And then you find yourself sleeping on the street. And then you find yourself sleeping in the tunnels. It can happen. We aren't that far from it. And I think we have to empathize with these people. We have to look at their story and try to tell the story in order to know who we ourselves are. We get to the story of ourselves by listening to the stories of others.

Cusatis: Ian McEwan is going to be here in a few weeks, reading from his novel *Atonement*. One particular passage from that novel makes me think of your fiction and relates to what you are saying. The young girl, Briony, is trying to write a story, and she thinks, "It wasn't only wickedness and scheming that made people unhappy, it was confusion and misunderstanding; above all, it was the failure to grasp the simple truth that other people are as real as you. And only in a story could you enter these different minds and show how they had an equal value. That was the only moral that the story need have."

McCann: Yes, Briony is making a justification for telling her own story. That's a good quote. But I don't think it's only in literature that we find value in story telling or find value in others. I mean we do have a chance in books to become other. That's great. That's one of the beautiful things about re-recognizing places and looking at geography differently. I told the MFA students that as I was coming into Columbia I was reading E.L. Doctorow's *The March*, a great book, superb book. But Lord above, just as I'm flying into Columbia, Sherman comes into Columbia! [Laughter] It deepened my whole perception! Why are there no antebellum homes down here? Why does the city look the way it does? And Doctorow gave that to me. I knew about the march, of course. I studied American history in college. I knew, but I never felt it. And what stories do is put you in the body of another. We become alive in bodies not our own. Literature provides this extraordinary leap into new territory. So I think McEwan's character is correct, but I think McEwan would also argue for the value of extending the literary experience to the lived experience. We must learn how to listen as well as imagine.

Cusatis: One of the MFA students this morning asked if you felt that trying to better the world through fiction was as worthwhile an ambition as trying to do so through hands-on actions, such as working for the Red Cross. You never brought it up in your response, but along your bicycle journey you devoted a lot of time to working with juvenile delinquents in Texas.

McCann: Making them more delinquent than they already were! [Laughter]

Cusatis: Interestingly, a few years ago, I was listening to NPR, and you were being interviewed after having won the National Book Award. A young man called in and said you had mentored him in the eighties in Texas.

Apparently he had been listening to the radio, heard you being interviewed, and decided to call in to say what an impact you'd had on him twenty-five years earlier. He expressed gratitude for your having read books to him and the others. I thought that was a great testimony. He had clearly gone on to . . . well . . . he was listening to NPR. [Laughter.] I'm sure your later writing was inspired by that stay. Of course, you wrote a short story, "Through the Field," in which a teenage boy boldly commits a murder, and after hiding in the woods for a few hours, turns himself in to the authorities, ironically, because he is afraid of the dark. Can you talk about how your experience working in Texas impacted you?

McCann: Yes. It was a seminal experience. Those days still wake me up. I carry them with me. It began while I was cycling through Texas. I went through a sort of mini-crisis of faith. If you've got a lot of time on a bicycle, you tend to think about God a lot. "Good God, I only have canned ravioli for dinner tonight!" [Laughter] "Good God, where am I going to sleep tonight?" No, seriously, I did have a crisis of faith, and I stopped in a lot of churches. The Catholic Church, which I had grown up in, was too structured and formal for me at that stage. I wanted something new and expansive. So I'd stop in these little churches along the way, and I'd pull in on my bicycle. Also, it was a great way to get a good meal, especially in the South. On a Sunday?! Afterwards you'd get all that cornbread and barbecue. But I was genuinely interested in the people and the experience. I wanted to understand how they lived.

One day I pulled in to this church in Independence, Texas, outside of Brenham. There were all these rough-looking kids in the back of the church. I thought, "Wow, that's really interesting." Of course the pastor called me out and he asked, "Who's our new guest today?" I said, "I'm traveling across the country." And I saw the light in the eyes of all these kids. It turned out they were part of a juvenile detention program run by the Baptist Church. They wanted to be out on the road with me.

After the church ceremony, the director of the program approached me. Terry Cooper. A visionary. A child-care revolutionary. He said, "Listen. We're going to Big Bend today. I don't know you, but I'm trusting my gut and my instinct. Why don't you come with us? We're going to go down for two weeks and we're going to canoe the Rio Grande and go rock climbing. Just stash your bike here, hop in the van, and come with us." And I said, "Sure." And out of that came a relationship that has lasted all these years. He opened the lungs of the world for me.

I stayed about a month and a half, working with these kids. And after I finished my bicycle journey, a year or so later, I went back to Texas and ran a wilderness program. I would take six boys at a time—kids who had been in prison or juvie in San Antonio, Houston, Dallas—out to the middle of the woods, and say, "This is your new home for the next three months." And it was great. I had a Vietnam-era tent that we stayed in for the first week. I said, "Guys, this tent is coming down next week." They didn't believe me. They're all like, "I'm gonna run away. I'm gonna kill you." I said, "Don't kill me. Seriously, don't kill me until you've learned the way out of here." [Laughter] "Here's the map." And then I began showing them how to find the North Star, that sort of thing. They were hooked. They'd never seen anything like it before. They thought I was stark raving mad. Maybe I was. After all, I was only twenty-three years old, and I was dedicating my life to living out in the woods and working with a bunch of teenagers who professed to wanting to kill me.

In the first week I was building my pine-pole shelter, and I said, "Guys, I'm gonna take the tent down!" They were like "Sure! Sure." And I did. I chopped the tent down on the seventh day, making it all biblical: "On the seventh day . . ." [Laughter] And they're like, "Man, what do I do? Where do I sleep?" And they all slept in my shelter that first night. Then they started to build their own pine-pole shelters. And their shelters were so much better than mine. So much more imaginative. But I had to show them the way. And beautiful, beautiful, things happened: these kids changed. They opened up. They confronted their fears. They learned survival. I read them books at night. They taught me about their world.

I'd read *Grapes of Wrath* and *Catcher in the Rye*. I read a book called *Fup*. And these were sixteen-year-old kids! But it worked, most of the time anyway. There were nights when they'd tell me they were going to run away. Then I'd sit with them, and I'd give them stuff: "Here's twenty dollars. It's forty miles to the nearest town. You're going to need this." And then I'd point out the North Star. They didn't know how to deal with me. They'd parade off into the dark. But then they'd come back about an hour and a half later weeping because they were scared of the dark. Scared of the dark. And they were all kids who were like, "I'm gonna kill you, man! I'm gonna rip you up!" [Laughter] But I loved them. They were good kids.

There is one thing that I will never forget. I'd have a smoke at night, just to get away from them. I'd go three or four fields away. But apparently the smoke would drift across the camp. [Laughter] They all wanted to smoke, of course, and one night they stole my cigarettes. I was like, "You can't do that." Then they started smoking grapevine leaves. [Laughter] It smells like marijuana, so they got this false, vicarious high. [Laughter] I said, "Okay, guys, there's no more grapevine leaves. If I catch you with grapevine, you're not going to graduate, lads!" Then one night they came along and stole my knife, and that was a big deal. I've got to get my knife back. I said, "Lads, you're not going to graduate and your parents are coming, and I don't care! I don't care! I know you have my knife, give me my knife." And then they came to me, three or four days before they were due to graduate, real sheepish. They had fashioned me a bamboo pipe—stuffed with grapevine. [Laughter] And we smoked it together. [Laughter] It was disgusting. [Laughter] I kept this pipe for years and years and years, and then, last year, I moved. I moved just down the street, but I lost the stem of the pipe. The funny thing is that the pipe has become even more important to me because I've lost the stem. So I only have half a pipe, but I have all of the memories, which goes to the heart of storytelling. Blossom, stem, root.

And, yes, I get phone calls from those young men. Every few months someone calls me out of the blue. For a couple of years I would get calls from prison, but then those calls died off. In fact, most of them got out of the wilderness program and did very, very well. I don't think any of the kids are in prison anymore. They've all made something of their lives. They may have spent one or two months in prison and got into a bit of trouble, but in general they got out. It worked. That life, out there, under the stars, was a form of storytelling. Nowadays they call me and they are fathers themselves. They boast about their relationships with their sons.

Cusatis: This morning we were looking at a map trying to figure out what parts of South Carolina you rode through, what route you took south.
McCann: Norway, Sweden, Denmark [South Carolina], all those places. [Laughter] I went all the way down to the Okefenokee.

Cusatis: Did you think that twenty-five years later you'd return as a National Book Award winner?
McCann: No way. No way. No way. I mean, I prayed at the time that I'd be able to write a book, a single book. Nowadays, I'm constantly surprised at my life. I feel genuinely very grateful for all the stuff that's happened. But there's no way on God's green Earth that I would've thought, then, that I might be living the life I'm living now. But it becomes ordinary when you're inside it. When you're living outside of it, it seems fantastic. Now I'm in New York. I have three kids. I have these books. If I could step outside myself and be that twenty-one year-old, twenty-two year-old looking at myself now, I'd be completely flabbergasted. [Pauses, then continues quickly] I'd also say,

"What happened to your hair?" [Laughter] "I remember you used to have this big head of hair, head bands. You'd go around with a big, scruffy beard." [Laughter] I used to be really scruffy. Now look at me.

Cusatis: Although your fiction tends not to be autobiographical, I imagine you can relate to the emigrant experience of your characters. You came to America with ambitions Ireland could not fulfill, but I'm wondering if you ever feel as if your coming to this country was a mixed blessing. A few of your Irish characters realize that they need to be in New York City, but at the same time, they miss their homeland. Could you comment on how you've reconciled this ambivalence?

McCann: Yes. I think the emigrant has a secret desire to hurt himself or herself in order to know fully where he came from, or where she came from, what that place was. Emigrating is a form of memory-making. In a way, you leave home in order to remember home. Part of being an emigrant, especially twenty, thirty, especially fifty years ago, was the notion that you always hold on to what you once had by leaving it behind and becoming acutely aware of it. It's as if you cut yourself, and you have this cut that you carry on your hand all the time, and you rub it all the time to remember what home was. That is a nostalgic notion of home, I know, but it is one that I still believe in. So I'm constantly returning to Ireland. I've been spending the past twenty years getting ready to return to Ireland. Of course, I go home all the time. I go home three, four times a year. But to really return and to write a big Irish novel, that's the thing I would love to do, eventually. Maybe at that stage I'll have come to terms with having left it.

Cusatis: *The New Yorker* will publish an excerpt in April from your next book [*TransAtlantic*], which is partially based on a trip that Frederick Douglass took to Ireland in the nineteenth century. Would you tell us a little bit about how you prepared to write this novel and how it is progressing?

McCann: I'm working on it right now. Last week I was three quarters of the way through; this week I'm only halfway through. [Laughter] This novel just keeps changing on me. It involves three distinct trips. One is the incredible transatlantic journey of Alcock and Brown, who took the first flight across from Newfoundland to Ireland, the first ever transatlantic flight, eight years before Lindbergh, in fact. Lindbergh's flight was in 1927, and these guys flew in 1919. Another portion of the story involves Senator George Mitchell, from Maine, the great, incredible George Mitchell, the best politician of our time, who was Senate Majority Leader during the Clinton era. His relationship to

Ireland leads him to travel across to work out the peace process. And then the third major strain of this transatlantic trinity is the trip that Frederick Douglass made in 1845 to do an anti-slavery lecture tour. He's there for four months. I think it's an incredible story that you have this black slave who goes to Ireland, and in the time that he's there, the Irish famine starts to unfold at his feet. It's really touching. And full of incredible contradictions. So I wanted to write about all that and then try to match them all, bring them all together, tie them all together. So that's been fun. [Laughter]

Trying to write about Frederick Douglass kicked my arse for a long, long time. I think that was because his voice is so powerful anyway. It was almost like he was saying, "But wait! How dare you do this? I've already done it. I've already said what I wanted to say." But nobody had really written about his trip to Ireland. I found it difficult to penetrate the story. But I would go to it and work at it for two or three months, then leave it, and go back to something else. I'd be despairing because the only thing I really want to do is write about Frederick Douglass. He haunted me. I wanted to try to beat him by finding him, I mean finding the right voice. And it probably took me ten or twelve tries. I really beat myself up. But I tried to get it right. And it's only a short section. It's only forty or fifty pages of the book, but it's something I am enormously proud of. Of all my writing, that particular section is the thing I'm proudest of at this stage. By the way, I also like a little book called *Everything in This Country Must*, which is about Northern Ireland, because it's kind of like my little orphan child. Nobody knows about that book. Anyway, I don't suppose we should prefer any one piece of writing. The writing that we're about to do should be the one that we like the best.

Cusatis: Speaking of *Everything in This Country Must*, the title story of that collection was made into a short film, for which you wrote the screenplay, and the film was nominated for an Academy Award. You've recently written the screenplay for *Let the Great World Spin* and are working with the director J. J. Abrams. What's the status of that project?

McCann: Oh, jaysus. [Laughter] I've done many drafts but, officially, I've done two drafts. I love J. J. He's fantastic. He's beginning to make *Star Trek* right now, and he wants to make what he calls his "serious film." This serious film would be *Let the Great World Spin*. We hope that he's going to be making it in the next few years. But you never know. Don't hold your breath. Please. With films it's always dodgy. But films are interesting. You're sitting beside someone on a train or plane, and they say, "What do you do?" You say that you write books, and they say, "Oh?!" And then you say, "But I also write movies," and they say, "Ohhhhhh!" [Laughter] I suppose that goes to the heart of the fact that movies are so available to everybody. If you write a book and you sell a few thousand copies, it's a joy. But if you have a movie, and the movie comes out, it hits millions of people inside its first week. That's an extraordinary thing. But I have to adapt the book, and murder it. I have to take this book, lift it up in the air, let it drop, shatter it to pieces, and then start to recreate it again. I think part of the problem with Hollywood is that sometimes they're actually too loyal to the book. And so for me, I really have to tear the thing asunder and create something different. So I'm doing that with J. J. right now.

Cusatis: The more one reads *Let the Great World Spin*, the richer it becomes, partially due to all the intertextual connections with other great books. I want to ask you about what seems like a fundamental biblical connection. In the opening pages, you write regarding the tightrope walker, "The man above was a word they seemed to know though they had not heard it before." A little later, John Corrigan mentions to his brother that he "wants to put flesh on his words." Both lines call to mind the opening chapter of the Gospel of John: "And the word was made flesh and dwelt among us." Logos is the original Greek term for "word," and it is an epithet for Christ. Much of the imagery in the novel suggests a connection between Corrigan and the tightrope walker, both of whom act as dauntless, savior figures, directly or indirectly. Did you intend for the tightrope walker to evoke "the word" and Corrigan to represent "the word made flesh"?

McCann: That's a good question and a difficult question in the sense that I have the tightrope walker and then I have Corrigan, and I wanted his faith to be tested in the same way that the walker wants his body, his flesh, to be tested. This was a central issue for me, yes.

Cusatis: So maybe in distinct ways both characters embody the "word" that the people on the street "seemed to know" but had not really heard, and perhaps needed to see, incarnate. Did you have the Gospel in mind when creating Corrigan?

McCann: Well, I first based Corrigan on Daniel Berrigan, the great Jesuit priest from New York. Then he evolves and becomes this sort of Christ-like figure, tainted and tortured, flesh and faith. Of course, mixed into all of this is my own interpretation of the Gospel. So the Gospel is there, yes, but I think most of that is an emotional energy, an unacknowledged deeper emotional intelligence that I have from years gone by, having read this stuff while growing up Catholic. So it was not entirely conscious at the time. I was not thinking, "Ah, this is the Gospel; this is John's Gospel." But you're hoping that embedded in there are all these little shards of learning that you have. Everywhere we have been is everywhere we are now. We gather. We throw off small shards of history and meaning.

Going back to the bicycle journey, I still think the reason I haven't explicitly written about it is that I am still writing about it every day. I am still being influenced by the experience, twenty-five years later. It's entering all the characters in new ways. When I actually write about the bicycle journey—if I ever write about it—it'll be finished for me as a source of inspiration. The degrees of consciousness here are really interesting, but I don't want to be too conscious of it either because otherwise it would paralyze me. You can become paralyzed by overthinking these sorts of things. What is it? "The unexamined life is not worth living"? Right? Well, the over-examined life is not worth living either. [Laughter] It's not necessary for the writer to know what he or she means. Does that sound outrageous? Possibly. But I think so much of it is fueled by mystery. Other people, our readers, make the conscious connections in the end. The "word made flesh" for instance.

But that's the beautiful thing about art: your readers become the writers. They open up the book, and at the end, they become more intelligent, more engaged than you are. For me, I spent these four years writing this book. I'm really cleaving to every word. The rhythm, the sound, the pace. I control it all. But once it's done, once people start to read it, it's their book. It's not mine anymore. And then they recognize allusions and intricate meanings and subliminal connections. They finish the book in incredible ways. They start to think about 9/11, for instance. And this is not my doing. It's their doing, right? I present it there for them, or hopefully for them. It was a very conscious decision for it to be a 9/11 novel. I also wanted it to be about beauty, recovery, grace, decency, and optimism. But if I start telling people that's what it's about, the work becomes tired and old. It's their work. So the people who read it work at it, and they create something out of it. And that reading you have—the word, the flesh—is a proper reading, and maybe I think it's more intelligent than my own creation. [Laughter] You're writing my book, John. I like that notion.

Cusatis: I've noticed a few motifs that seem to span all of your fiction. One I'd like to ask you about goes back to Celtic mythology as well as the New Testament. Characters fish a lot in your fiction. Even in *Let the Great World*

Spin, a character with no line on his fishing rod stabs at the litter floating outside his apartment window.

McCann: I don't know how to fish. I have no clue how to fish. I did fish when I was a kid, but it was basically just throwing a line off Dun Laoghaire pier and waiting, waiting, waiting. Good times. Maybe I'm just returning to those times. I did spend a lot of time in *Songdogs* talking about fish and fishermen, and the fishing of men, and I think it does have a religious implication. I studied how to tie flies and do all that sort of thing. My son went fishing in Sun Valley, Idaho, this past summer. It was a beautiful thing to watch him fly fishing. I just think it is a gorgeous image. I'm wedded to the idea of what you could do with it with language. This rod, this twine, this hook, and you have this body that sets it all in motion. I like the idea of it. But, you know, I have to be careful. Somebody told me once "you know, you've got a lot of maps in your books," and I did. I had people creating maps of faces and all this strange stuff. I couldn't write another map after that. Next book, if I have a fishing image, I'll say, "Cusatis said that all my books have fishing images! [Laughter]. Ah, what do I do now?" [Laughter]

Cusatis: The desperate fishermen in your work seem to connect with references to T.S. Eliot in *Let the Great World Spin*. A passage from *The Waste Land* reads, "I sat upon the shore / Fishing, with the arid plain behind me / Shall I at least set my lands in order?" In addition to its biblical reference, Eliot's line calls to mind the legendary fisher king, trying to find hope and restoration, a connection with the way things once were, which seems to be a theme in a lot of your work. Tillie, in *Let the Great World Spin*, is one character, though, who says, "There ain't no such thing as getting home," whereas most of your characters seem to be confident that they will again find a sense of home.

McCann: Yes, they are trying to find home, but they're not necessarily trying to find things the way they once were. I find that to be sort of nostalgic. And while I flirt with nostalgia, I don't want to embrace it. I want to question it. "Home" is the ability to create again what was there before, but perhaps something newer, something more fortified. And I think that's a non-nostalgic notion. I don't believe that all our redemptive moments took place in the country of the past. I do still believe that they can take place in our own present and in our immediate futures. Otherwise, why have hope, why have desire? Why do all this work? And I believe that an optimist, which I am, has to be a really, really deep cynic. You have to be deeply cynical to be a really good optimist. You've got to get out from under the shoes of that cynic, stamp everything down and then rise up above it. And I think that's where really good work comes from, where really good poems come from, from being cynical and vaulting beyond your cynicism.

Cusatis: The young John Corrigan tells his brother that the drunks he hangs around with are all "looking for some type of Eden," and "when they drank, they returned to it." Maybe your characters are searching for Eden, but Eden might mean different things to different characters.

McCann: Yes. He says at one stage, "Someday the meek might actually want it," which I think is a good way to look at the world. Not only should they have it, but they might want it. We have to create the world this way, so that the meek might actually want to dwell in it.

Cusatis: You've discussed working on the movie version of *Let the Great World Spin*. But why didn't they recruit you to read the audio book, or at least Ciaran Corrigan's part?

McCann:[Laughing] I absolutely love reading. I'm a ham. [Laughter] But–in relation to the recorded version of the book—I wanted to do the chapter in Ciaran's voice. So I call up the woman from Recorded Books, and I say "Hi, this is Colum." And she says, "Oh! Is it?" And I say, "Listen, I'd love to read that first chapter." Not the whole book, because obviously I want somebody else to read the Tillie section or the Adelita section. And she says, "Oh!" And I'm like, "Oh?" And she says, "Well, then yes, ah, great. Would you like to come down for an audition?" Well, what the hell? I've got to audition for my own book! [Laughter] I say, "Okay, all right, I'll come down for an audition." I go down to the studio, and I really like her. She's very nice, and she puts me in the booth. She says, "Read this." Then she says, "Stop. Now read it again." And guess what? I didn't get the job! [Laughter] So, I've never listened to it. I've never listened to any part of it! [Laughter] I'm sure the guy who did it probably read it a hundred times better than I could ever have. But, yeah, I didn't get the job for my own book. [Laughter]

Cusatis: We've got time for a question or two from the audience.

Audience Member: When did you decide you wanted to be a writer?

McCann: Well I'd left a job in Dublin as a journalist and gone to Cape Cod, and sat down to try to write a novel. Of course, after six months, I realized I really had nothing to write about. I knew that I had to embrace some other sort of experience. I had to get out and live in the world a little bit more. That's why I went on the bicycle trip. But I also went for fun and adventure. People thought I was a little crazy, and I thought I was crazy. There were times when I would sit in the silence and just weep. I'm not ashamed to tell you that I was quite sure—at the age of twenty-one—that I was throwing my life away. I'd be in Wyoming on this long, straight road thinking, "My friends have jobs on the paper; they have medical insurance; they're making money. I'm out here being ridiculous, sleeping in a tent. What am I doing?" I often questioned myself like that. But when I finished the journey, I wrote two books. Thankfully they never got published. They were awful. But I knew, probably from a fairly young age, maybe even as young as ten or twelve-years-old, that I wanted to write. But that meant, at that stage, to be a journalist, because my dad was a journalist.

Audience Member: I've read five of your books, including *Everything in This Country Must.*

McCann: Thank you. That's punishment for you. [Laughter]

Audience Member: Thank you for writing every one of them. You do an impressive amount of research. In *This Side of Brightness*, tunneling, the homeless. *Dancer*, the ballet, both Western and the Russian tradition. *Zoli*, the Romani people during the 1930s in Eastern Europe. At what point in the journey do you begin your research? How do you entwine the writing process with the extensive depth of knowledge and detail that you convey in your writing?

McCann: That's a great question. There is a point where you can over-research these things, and it can feel too researched. You can feel the writer straining to put in details because he or she found them in some sort of weird, obscure place. They sort of go in tandem. With Zoli, for instance, I had this idea for this Gypsy poet based on her true character. So I wrote for about a year and tried to imagine what it would be. You use your imaginative gifts, whatever is available inside your DNA. You try to figure out what the story might be. Then I went over to Slovakia and stayed in the camps and used what I saw to impress a reality on what was already imagined. That's nearly always what I do. I try to imagine it first, as with the tightrope walker in *Let the Great World Spin*. I tried to imagine what that walk was like and then went in and started researching. So using language and poetry, if you will, to try to recreate the experience from something that we don't know, and then finding out, yes, absolutely, and then putting those ideas in, and melding the two together. That's what's fun, too. Welding the imagination to the reality and vice versa.

Elise Blackwell: I'd like to thank both John and Colum for doing this special session today. [Applause]

The Rumpus Interview
with Colum McCann

Alec Michod / 2013

From The Rumpus, June 4, 2013. Reprinted with the permission of Alec Michod.

Colum McCann: I prefer to be interviewing you than have you interview me.
Alec Michod: And here I thought you Irish writers all loved to talk and talk. "It is one of their beauties, the Irish, the way they crush and expand the language all at once," you write in *TransAtlantic*. I love that.
McCann: We're a bunch of loudmouths. We are good at not shutting up. We're also good at not saying that much in the end. "Whatever you say, say nothing." But during the peace process of the late 1990s, language was everything. And George Mitchell was in the heart of things. The Irish people used language and flung their stories against him. But Mitchell's great beauty was that he operated like the great carnivorous reader you're always hoping you find, if you're a writer. He allowed the text to work upon him. And when they exhausted themselves and said everything they could possibly say, he turned around and said, "Okay, you told me all your stories. Now it's time to achieve some peace." And that was great because they were mangling the language. And he knew it was time to create a whole new language, or a new allowance for language.

Michod: Whole new language—how so?
McCann: It goes to the heart of the idea of cathartic storytelling, what stories can do for us in terms of healing. Other countries had it, these Truth and Reconciliation Committees. Mitchell allowed us to tell our stories. The result is we've had fifteen years of a really strong peace.

Michod: Mitchell, being an American arriving in Ireland, is very much a stranger in a strange land, right? An outsider. One of the other narrative threads in *TransAtlantic* spins around Frederick Douglass, who's in a position of power, in a way. But he's also the ultimate other. And Alcock and Brown are the other aviators.

McCann: They're all coming from someplace else, but the thing that struck me is that you can't have somebody like George Mitchell without Frederick Douglass. Douglass is ahead of his time anyway, even the way he talked about slavery and women and human rights and certainly the way he talked about the politics of freedom and dignity. Let the human be human. He's put in a situation where he has to deal with this tremendous contradiction: he is a black slave in Ireland, but he is being hosted by the Anglo-Irish gentry. He is actually in a position of privilege for one of the first times in his life. At first I didn't like him for it. I had to get my head around these notions. Dealing with Douglass was really, really tough. It took a long, long time. It was probably the toughest thing I've ever written. When I first heard the story, I thought, Wonderful. You know, visionary black man goes to Ireland. Thousands attend his lectures. Then I started to wonder why that wasn't talked about, why the story was largely hidden in history. His big contradiction is: Do I look after my three million people who are still enslaved, or do I speak out on behalf of the poor Irish? And I think that's a rather beautiful moment. It is full of shades. When he gets caught up in that tension and has to resolve it somehow. And I think in a certain way that's where fiction can get in and negotiate the gray areas. As Joyce says, one by one we are all becoming shades.

Michod: Was writing about Douglass so difficult because he was a real character, whatever that is. A historical character? Even in DeLillo's *Underworld*, the historical characters take second stage.

McCann: You have to doubt everything you say. I used to think writing about so-called real people showed a failure of the imagination, but then I started writing about Rudolf Nureyev [in *Dancer*]. So I directly contradicted myself, and I've been doing that for ten years now. I've been writing about "real" characters and placing them in a shaped, or fictional, world. Writing *TransAtlantic*, there was never really a plan, at the early stages, to question the line between fiction and nonfiction. I just went on instinct, and then these worlds started to braid. My friend Sasha Hemon says in Bosnian, there's no words for "fiction" or "nonfiction." It's all "storytelling."

Michod: I'm really interested in the writing of history, not as a record but as narrative, as story being told.

McCann: I suppose that's where the novel comes in, because it's actually quite forensically correct in the "nonfiction" parts. Take, for example, the transatlantic journey of Alcock and Brown. On the Internet you can find many accounts that they went wing-walking and so on, which is completely untrue and impossible. But that's what happens when you take accounts from Alcock and Brown themselves, which they gave to their sons and relatives and spread like rumors. But if you talk to anyone who knows anything about aviation, you know you wouldn't be able to wing-walk at eleven thousand feet in a Vickers Vimy. So for these narratives I had to do a lot of work to get it as correct as possible.

And then in the midst of this forensic "reality," I bring in two characters—Emily and Lottie—who are completely fictional, if that's a good word. That's what I was interested in, writing this book, to achieve a sort of mirror effect. One side of the book is very male, the other very female. Nonfiction, fiction. All these things operate against one another so that if you fold them in and collapse them in on one another, it becomes a sort of middle ocean. Anyway, that's some of how I was thinking about it.

Michod: That's a pretty complicated structure. Did it just unfold organically, or did you jump around trying to keep up with it all?

McCann: I wish I could say to you that it all works out organically as planned, but they never do, these books. Writers constantly—you know this—fly by the seat of their pants, and you just go along. You're open to the mystery. You're open to the possibilities.

When I was writing *TransAtlantic*, actually I was also working on another book. A completely different novel, about high-tech surveillance in New York, so I'd go back and forth, back and forth, but ultimately I knew between the two—I was writing the other one too easily, and that's how I knew. It just felt formulaic and a little stilted. So I'd go and work on it for weeks and weeks and sometimes months on it, and then decide I really wanted to work on what I called the Douglass book. The problem with Douglass, of course—not only was he this character in history who's been written about extensively, but he also wrote about himself extensively. And beautifully. So I was searching for a way to find a language that would work, both for me and for Douglass.

It's complicated when you're talking about voices and trying to create voices, or trying to create an atmosphere around a voice. I think eventually the voice is heard deep, deep into the work. There's one line there—if you can recognize it, you can bring it back to the beginning.

It's like music, right? You find the right note, the other notes will follow. That's how the voice things work in a book. You're like a conductor who goes into the pit, and you bring all the musicians and the instruments together, and you have to strike them up. Most likely you need a few days with them to find the texture of the music you want to play, or perhaps months. Am I bullshitting here? Probably yes, I am. But essentially what interests me is the music of the voice. I have to write something that I want to listen to myself!

Michod: There's that Gaddis [William Thomas Gaddis, Jr.]quote when he was asked why his books are so difficult, and he said if they weren't, he'd fall asleep at the typewriter.
McCann: Exactly. "The inexecutable is all I am interested in." My friend Nathan Englander said that once to me. And I love that notion. It's what I plow into my students' heads over and over again until they are sick of me. "No matter. Try again. Fail again. Fail better." Beckett, right? But it's so true. It all feels like one big, long, complicated failure. Until it doesn't. It's shit until it isn't. So these virtues that you know as desire, stamina, perseverance—they are the key things to be able to sit with it until it tells you how to read it or write it.

Michod: With all the narratives colliding in the book, that must have been a monumental task, just keeping your head above water.
McCann: They're going and they're leaving, they're shifting back and forth, and yes, a lot of the time I feel like I am drowning. One step forward, two steps back, and then a sudden plunge off the cliff. But I remember when I discovered that it was Lily who was going to hold the various strands together, that was a moment when I felt conscious of the overtones the name Lily had, from James Joyce's "The Dead." I felt as if I was weaving things together. Ultimately, you have a responsibility to your characters.
The thing with nonfiction, though, is that you're dealing with people who could still be alive. George Mitchell is still alive. You can't swerve with your character if he's still alive. He's not as elastic as a made-up character. There's certain factual truth to adhere to, whereas with the made-up characters there's more of a latitude. But that's terrifying, too. In the end, though, real or fictional, you just want them to be "true." I think if we write our characters well, we will meet them some day in the most unusual place. I still think I can go back to the Bronx and meet Tillie from my novel, *Let the Great World Spin*. I still think of her as being alive. Of course, that's ridiculous, isn't it?

Michod: Isn't that part of the haunted nature of writing? Your writing is so-like *Underworld*. It's English but not English, in a way.

McCann: Ultimately, it's only ever down to the right word used in the right place, the most surprising word. Form comes out of content, I think. Language is the only thing we have. The music of the sentence. Whether it be cut down, carved away, whatever it is. I don't have a prescriptive way to talk about what I really like, except you know it when you hear it. DeLillo, for instance: "He speaks in your voice, American."

Michod: DeLillo's talked a lot about how, in this day and age, there's so much content, yet less patience for language that stands out.

McCann: Isn't that what everyone always complains about all the time? Of course, he is right. With such great capability to expand, we should be expanding constantly. But we're not. We are stepping inside and closing the curtains. Still, for me the novel is actually in fine shape, or at least the future of the novel. I just wish the publishers were more open, but with the Internet it seems to be quite thrilling what you can do. The novel can contain everything. It's always been able to contain everything. Maybe now even more so.

Michod: You go back to Laurence Sterne, and he's as postmodern—more postmodern than just about anyone writing today. It's insane.

McCann: You know . . .

[At this point in the interview, a man passed by, talking loudly into his cell phone: "Better get out here quick, man," he said, "or I'll start murdering some beers."]

McCann: Did you hear that? Just listen. That's one thing I've discovered recently. I used to keep notebooks with me at all times. I don't anymore. It's just the process of absorbing it now. That's going to come out somewhere else. You absorb it and then it gets squeezed out into your language. The question is when are you a writer? Are you a writer only when you're sitting down at the table writing, or are you a writer when you're out in the world? I kind of like the idea that there's a time when I'm not a writer. I'm just listening. Better get out of here quick, man, and start murdering some beers.

Two Interviews with Colum McCann

Cécile Maudet / 2013

Originally published in *TransAtlantica*, January 10, 2014. http://transatlantica.revues.org. Reprinted with permission.

While working on her doctoral degree at Rennes University, Cécile Maudet focused her research on Colum McCann's fiction following his fall 2008 reading at Rennes. In spring 2013, Cécile interviewed Colum at his home in New York, paving the way for extensive correspondence, leading in turn to her inviting him to Rennes the next year as guest of honor at a conference devoted to his work.

First Interview (April 22, 2013)

Cécile Maudet: You have written mostly novels, but their composition is always fragmented into different stories told by various narrators. Their structures are thus somehow reminiscent of that of collections of short stories. I would like to understand the interest you find in resorting to so many voices within the same novel. What kind of spaces would you say that these condensed stories create for you as opposed to a longer story that would be told by one narrator? And what do you find in the novels that you don't find in the short stories in terms of writing possibilities—because you've gradually left the genre of the short story aside these last few years, right?

Colum McCann: I suppose first of all you write the books that you want to read. That's the most important thing. People ask you: "Who is your reader?" Well, ultimately your reader should be yourself, twenty years from now. So you hope not to be bored by your stuff, and you hope that it still has the electricity that runs through it. And also, I'm very interested in the kaleidoscopic notion of storytelling and increasingly interested in it as a political idea, especially the notion that it can be an all-embracing sort of democracy, so that if you go to a kaleidoscopic point of view you can see

145

things from several different angles. I have quoted this many times before—I'm sure you've seen me quote it—but John Berger says: "Never again will a story be told as if it were the only one." When I came across that, it was really interesting for me because I was writing. I think the big moment for me was when I was just starting writing *Dancer*. Do you know the story about how I got to write *Dancer*?

Maudet: A friend of yours . . .

McCann: A friend of mine, he was in Dublin, his father came home drunk and he saw Rudolf Nureyev on TV and he sort of fell in love with Rudolf Nureyev. I thought that's a beautiful story, an absolutely gorgeous story, really powerful. And I started to think: that particular story would never make it as a part of the official biography, the official history of Rudolf Nureyev because it's a supposedly anonymous story. But if that story captures a life, or a part of a life, it captures not only Jimmy's life—my friend—but it also captures Rudolf Nureyev's life, right? It's also a story about fathers, about cultures, about drink, it's about Dublin, it's about Russia, it's about all these different things coming together. So each individual story has its own sort of kaleidoscopic moment, its own crystal, if you will. You look at it, you shine the light through it and you see it fractured in several different ways. But the accumulation of those things can tell a sort of biography.

I'd just written a very small book called *Everything in This Country Must*, which was tight. The geography was tight, it was gathered all about Northern Ireland, and I wanted to sort of expand my lungs, but also I wanted to write very much an international novel. And the origin is kind of stupid now when I think about it, but originally I wanted to write a novel that had every country in the world mentioned somehow. But then it became a device. I started it and then I thought: "No, this is a device, this is not good." And it wasn't true, even though Rudolf Nureyev would have been the perfect person for that because he was sort of all over the place. So the project started, I suppose, when I started *Dancer*. And then after *Dancer*, *Zoli* was a much more controlled book and much more focused book, and yet it still had different points of view.

Well, maybe it's because I'm influenced by cinema in certain ways because you have the high angle, and then you have the close up, and then you have the fish-eye lens, and then you have different lenses. If you're making a film, you never use the same lens all the way along. So there's something cinematic about it, there's something to do with politics and democracy, there's something to do with just the kaleidoscopic nature.

And quite frankly I don't want to bore myself or bore the reader, and I love shifts in pace. So that's kind of like music: things become contrapuntal, and they're moving in and moving out and then they bash up against one another. Sometimes it awakens the sleep in you in certain ways when you can't write that way. That's the sort of writing I enjoy reading. So part of it then is just logical, part of it is political, part of it is aesthetic, and part of it is just because that's the way I want to do, and maybe it's the only way I know how.

Maudet: You've just mentioned the political aspect of your writing. You once said that "[you] don't know what [the term fiction] means"[1] and that "you don't like the word [fiction] anymore"[2] because, for you, stories are windows onto history. Could you elaborate on this a little? With this assertion, would you go as far as saying that your literature is akin to a historical testimony in a way, or archive?

McCann: Well, I don't say that all fictions should be this way. One of the things that I think is really important to say is that I have my point of view and I will not impose it on anybody else. I don't want to make any grand sweeping statements about the nature of fiction or anything like that, but I do think that writers, especially when they embrace the anonymous corners, are creating a new history. They become the sort of unacknowledged historians in a certain way. I think it's really important. Their story has to be told over and over and over again; otherwise it gets distorted and forgotten. The Jewish culture is really interesting in the sense that it has always known that it must tell a story over and over and over again. Otherwise you'll have people appropriate it outside; they'll say it's untrue. Writing about the Holocaust they've done the most incredible things. They've told it from so many different angles that you can't really deny its truth. Anybody who tries to deny its truth seems ridiculous. If they hadn't told their story, like, say, the Romani culture didn't really tell their story, the truth would have been created for them from the outside. It's like that Sartrian notion of the stereotypes,[3] you know, that society conforms to its own stereotypes. If the truth is formed from the outside, that's a real problem. The Irish culture forms its own truth much like the Jewish culture because we are storytellers. But there are certain things that we have avoided too like the famine. The Irish famine has been sort of avoided. So, in a certain way, I do find that there's perhaps even a truer history involved in all this. I wrote an essay about *Ulysses*. I don't know if you have had a chance to read it?

Maudet: Yes, I've read it. You're alluding to "But Always Meeting Ourselves,"⁴ right?

McCann: Right. And in that, I sort of assert that this fiction *Ulysses* is a more important history to me personally than that of my actual ancestors themselves. So that Leopold Bloom—the fictional character—legislates my Dublin for me, because he's there on June 16, 1904. My great-grandfather, who I never met—but it pumps through my blood, right?—walked the same streets on June 16, 1904. Why do I know my great-grandfather? I really know him because I know Leopold Bloom. That's very interesting to me. The imagined is real, if not even more real than reality itself. I think that's been my project for the past I don't know how many books since *Dancer*. This new book, *TransAtlantic*, is very much like that project too. I think I've finished. I'm at the end of that. I've pushed it as far as it can go. I don't know where I want to go next. Maybe off the cliff or out the window or something, I don't know! But yes, I think we have a responsibility to history, and we also have a responsibility to our characters. Much of the history, I get it right, as for example in *TransAtlantic*. I get it minutely right and then I insert fictional characters.

Maudet: It's how you do, isn't it?

McCann: So I talked with Sasha Hemon—Aleksandar Hemon—about this and he says that in Bosnia, there's no word for fiction. I think that's really cool. He says it's all called storytelling. So there's no word for fiction or non-fiction; it's just storytelling. And I think essentially that's what we are engaged in.

Maudet: Talking about engagement, your political stances are not dissimulated in your press articles, especially concerning the Bush administration and the socio-economic changes that Ireland has gone through during the last decades. You said you wished the voice of today's writers was more influential, and you deplore the "acute crisis of disengagement"⁵ from both readers and writers. You've also insisted on wanting to give a voice to "the anonymous corners of the world."⁶ Such a recurring treatment of balkanized countries, the margins and migration leads me to ask you this: in what way would you say that your literary production is also politically engaged?

McCann: I will have to say that it's politically engaged right down to its very core. But I'm not interested in telling anybody what sort of politics they should live, nor am I necessarily interested in anybody knowing what my politics happen to be after they finish the book. I think they have a fair idea. But what's more interesting to me is that you allow a human experience through the function of writing. So tomorrow, for instance, I have possibly the best day of my literary life, the biggest thing that ever happened to me, because I'm going to Newtown, Connecticut, where those twenty-six kids were killed in the shooting last year.[7] The high school there used *Let the Great World Spin* as the text to navigate the grief for the high school children, for the seventeen-and eighteen-year-olds. They've been studying *Let the Great World Spin* for the past two months. They are talking with counselors, they're talking with themselves, amongst themselves, with their teachers about *Let the Great World Spin*, but they're also using it to navigate this horrible thing with their brothers, their sisters, the kids that they babysat for, who were killed. And to me that's where literature comes in and has this moment of healing. This is where it becomes political because I'm sure that healing is political and engagement is political. And I don't want to become a politician obviously—it's so boring to be a politician, right?—but to be somebody who just talks about these human things that [William] Faulkner talks about: the human heart at conflict with itself; love, pride, pity, compassion; these things that he quotes in his 1950 Nobel address.[8] In fact, I always think it's very interesting to look at the writers. When they receive their award, that's when they become the most optimistic. They can be quite dark in their own work but virtually every writer worth his or her salt believes in the power of literature. And that's fascinating to me. I mean, there's no point to do it otherwise. We'd just be solipsistic or sort of onanistic. So, I would say that I would like to think that it is politically engaged but it's not—hopefully—it's not didactic.

Maudet: Sure, you don't want to be didactic. Yet, literature is or has to be for some writers. Frank Norris said that the novel "may be a great force that works together with the pulpit and the universities for the good of the people."[9] Conversely, Richard Ford wrote that short "story writers—more so than novelists—are moralists at heart. The short story enables to kind of show the reader some path to follow."[10] According to these two writers then, it seems that literature—whatever form it takes—has an educative role to play. As it is concise and generally very efficient, I would personally agree with R. Ford to say that the short story could indeed be envisaged as an adequate way to convey a moral message. Would you acknowledge this congruence between literature and morality? And would you agree that literary texts are forms to, if not convey a moral message, at least trigger in the reader a situation of moral questioning?

McCann: For sure, yeah, yeah, yeah. Well, first of all, I don't see a massive difference between the literary forms, between short stories and novels. I also don't even see a huge difference between novels and journalism, nor poems and playwriting. I believe that the well-chosen word properly put down upon the page can be as influential in no matter what form it happens to be. I can do short stories and I can do novels. I've tried plays and they're terrible, I've tried poems they're really terrible, they're unbelievably bad. I don't want to show them to anybody! It doesn't really bother me what form it happens to take in all the forms that I love the most, but I think the most expansive form, the biggest form of all, is the novel, because it can contain everything. But in relation to its moral purpose and its moral parameters, I think it's dangerous to say that the novel must be moral, but I will say the novel must be moral!

Maudet: I am currently working on the concept of rupture in your work. I think it applies thematically first of all. You always envisage historical events from a distance, so rupture is temporal. Would you say that, like historians who think they cannot legitimately investigate the history of the present time—as they think they need hindsight to deal with historical events, you want to wait for objectivity to operate—an objectivity that is only made possible with time? In *Let the Great World Spin* you don't deal with 9/11. I mean, you deal with it, yet only very obliquely. So, do you think that writers, or at least you, need a distance to write about historical events?

McCann: Yes, I think that this is where the difference comes in between, say, journalism and prose which I was just talking about. I think that one needs about twenty, twenty-five years before writing about events. That's why with *Let the Great World Spin* it's very obviously a 9/11 novel but it uses 1974 and the Vietnam War. It creates space for the reader's imagination, and the reader can go in whatever way she wants to, whatever way he wants to, to reinterpret these things. It's sort of a guided morality, if you will. It's like saying: "Oh, I'm not being moral, but here's the world and here's the photograph. Why don't you come into the photograph and then you take whatever it is, you wander around behind it?" Is that legitimate or not? I suppose it is. It has to be, in fact. And in many ways I think of myself as a photographer. You're obviously taking the photograph in the present, right? You're influenced by the present moment, and then you're looking back, right? And your lens goes into the past. I mean, the future doesn't really interest me, because obviously, it's not even here yet.

Maudet: You're not a proleptic writer.

McCann: I'm not. This whole notion of projecting myself forward doesn't really interest me. I'm interested in having the lens that's in the present focused back upon the past because whoever we are now is whoever we have been before. So when we say: "Well, I'll have a look at that back there," it's talking about now, it's talking about the "then" as well. Although *TransAtlantic* goes all the way up to 2011, mostly it takes place in 1845 when Frederick Douglass goes to Ireland, and then 1919, when the flight goes from Canada to Ireland, and then in 1998, when the peace process is up in the North. The peace process is fifteen years old now so that's a good time to start thinking about it and looking at it. I don't know why it is. I mean, some books are good when they're raw and they're right on the edge, but in general I feel that you need that little telescope or periscope back into the past.

Maudet: Rupture in your production is also spatial, I think, because you deal with uprooting, displacement, migration, and with characters who are outcasts, as we said. So, it's quite logically cultural as well. You are often initially unfamiliar with the places you decide to set at the core of your stories, which accounts for the accurate researches that you make. You dig into archives, you spend time in libraries. And even when you do know these places I have the feeling that you aim at making your task as a writer even more complex, because you focus on places the topography of which is less known to you. Indeed, when you write about New York, a place that you obviously know very well, you mainly write about its tunnels or the sky above it. When you write about Ireland, you write about Northern Ireland, or the west of Ireland where I don't think you have lived.

McCann: Well, I lived there for a very short while. I lived in Castlebar, in County Mayo, for a little while when I was seventeen, for six months. But in the North of Ireland I didn't live. What you're saying is true. I've never written about Dublin, ever. Well, in one short story in *Fishing the Sloe-Black River* actually, but that's not a big deal, it was just glancing. I did write about Dublin in *TransAtlantic* though. I don't know what that means but for twenty-five years of writing I generally stayed away from where I had grown up. Is this my own form of interior displacement in order to make myself sort of uncomfortable? I mean, the thing about it is, when I first came over here in New York and sat down to write a book I realized pretty quickly that I had very little to write about. Well, essentially, I had to, I suppose, displace myself. I had to come away and then I had to go out on the road again. So

I went on bicycle. I was going somewhere new every single day for about a year and a half. Some days I'd stay like a week or two weeks but more or less every single day for a year and a half I was sleeping in a new place. And that was a form of continual displacement. Now I know what I was doing: I was gathering stories. But up until that point I didn't have these stories to tell, or I did maybe, but I just couldn't recognize them. I mean, I grew up relatively middle-class. My father was a journalist in Dublin, which was a really hard-drinking, hard-living game, but he didn't involve himself in that. He left home at seven in the morning, came home at four in the afternoon; he wrote his books at home. Anyway a fairly well-behaved, well-mannered sort of life. So when I came away I realized that I had little to write about. I suppose, it's a form of wounding yourself. You know what truck drivers do to keep themselves awake?

Maudet: No, I don't.

McCann: Sometimes they strike matches and they smell the sulfur. Some of them keep razor blades in their hands and they cut their hands. Or, you know the way when you fall asleep, when you try and drive, and you pinch yourself like this? For me that's kind of what the emigrant does. He continually pinches himself because he is away. You remind yourself of your home, whereas if you're home you don't have to pinch yourself. If you're home, you sleep. So, to me, it was a continual form of moving on. That's also what fiction is for me. It is a way, a manner, and a means to continually pinching myself awake. Because I have this ordinary life. Look, oh fine, I live in the Upper East Side, I am a block from the park, but I really want to live a little bit of a crazy life too.

Maudet: By proxy.

McCann: Most of my crazy life is done by proxy, exactly, in that little room inside, and I enjoy that.

Maudet: Well, I'd now like to discuss the style of your writing, if you don't mind. You said you admire Zola[11] and, indeed, it seems that the realist streak runs through your works. Yet, you also resort to magic realism—I have "Cathal's Lake" in mind—a genre typical of postmodern literature. And some of your texts look to me like they have also been influenced by the modernist current—I cannot but think of Claire in *Let the Great World Spin* as a contemporary version of Mrs. Dalloway. Would you be able to tell me to what extent you have been affected by any of these currents?

McCann: I think that we get our voices from the voices of everyone, and I don't know what it is I write. I don't know if I want to know what it is that I write. If I'm forced into a corner, if I'm sitting beside someone on a plane and they ask me what I do, I say: "Well, I'm a writer." And if they say: "What do you write about?" or they say things like: "What is your book about?" I say: "That's about three-hundred-and-fifty pages." But if they really force me into describing what my work is, I say: "Well, it's serious fiction." Then if we have to go further, I say: "It's poetic realism." And it's not magic realism, though I'm very fond of magic realism.

I do now think that I have to further that term because I'm interested in these ideas of hope and cynicism. Obama talked about the audacity of hope. I'm also interested in the audacity of despair, and what it means to be cynical and what it means then also to be an optimist. Ultimately I am an optimist, but I'm very well aware that calling yourself an optimist exposes you to all the slings and arrows of outrageous hatred because it can seem so sentimental to be an optimist. But it seems me to be the best possible optimist you have to be a really, really good cynic first. So we have to get down to the heart of the realism, right down the dark. I would like to be able to take the very best cynic around and sit with her or sit with him in a room and be able to battle them as hard as humanly possible and be just as cynical as they are and then say: "Okay, are we finished?" And then they might say: "Yeah, we're finished. We're exhausted." And I'd say: "No! That's so uninteresting!"

Cynicism is completely uninteresting to me, and I just think it's a failure of the imagination to be just completely bereft and cynical. It's much more interesting to be as cynical as they are, and then just vault away and go somewhere else. And that's the only good optimist because if you're an optimist and you're not prepared to battle, really hard, then you're finished. Cynicism is just too easy. Optimism is much more difficult.

Maudet: In your works despair may be overwhelming, and the way you deal with the body is sometimes very grim, especially in the way of presenting aging—*Songdogs* is quite striking in this respect. Twice in your stories, the tongue is eaten (*This Side of Brightness* and *Songdogs*). The bodies of dead soldiers in *Dancer* end up becoming providential material to make roads; they are also altered by the violence of dance. Brigid, in "Sisters," tears out her nails. What is at stake in this treatment of the body? Why is it often reduced to its most debasing qualities?

McCann: Well, I don't know! I don't know is the simple and honest answer. But, if you take the body of Nureyev, it hits its pinnacle and then starts to disintegrate. In *Dancer*, it's true that you start out with this image of the bodies being used and then, tanks roll over them. And dance is all about the abuse of the body, but to create some sort of spectacular human form, right? In *This Side of Brightness* Treefrog abuses his body, he scars his hands—let me see . . .

Maudet: In "Sisters," Michael and Sheona get raped, and that's related in an anecdotal sort of way. In *This Side of Brightness*, Angela gets raped. What is a supposedly dramatic scene becomes devoid of any intensity because the narrator doesn't enable the reader to empathize with her. It therefore seems that the reader cannot fully empathize with physically suffering characters but only with those who are morally suffering. We empathize with Claire in *Let the Great World Spin*, who is tormented by her deepest wounds, but we do not empathize with Jigsaw (in the same novel) when he gets murdered: the killing scene is way too gory. His remains—as well as those of Faraday in *This Side of Brightness*—become more of a logistical problem to solve than a moral problem—the question after their deaths boils down to something like "What will we do with the bits of brain here on the pavement or on the subway track?"

McCann: That's very interesting, but I don't know. I'll think about it. But if you become too conscious of it, then you lose [your ability to create]. Somebody said to me once how much I write about maps, that I have maps everywhere. But if he knows, recently I haven't had so many maps. You know why? Because somebody told me I wrote about maps!

Maudet: An obstacle to your creation! I'll stop tormenting you about abused bodies then!

McCann: Oh no! The body is really interesting to me and I wonder why . . . I'm trying to think . . . That's interesting . . . Maybe it stems from a weird Catholic [background]. I don't know . . .

Maudet: Talking about religion, it seems to sometimes add dramatic intensity to your texts. In *Let the Great World Spin*, both Corrigan and the funambulist have been perceived by critics as Christ-like figures. Indeed, Corrigan goes down to "the Tombs." (LGWS, 64) About the prostitutes he's trying to help, he also says: "They just don't know what it is they are doing." (LGWS, 29) He has "shoulder-length hair," (LGWS, 26) "carpenter pants" and "sandals." (LGWS, 41) Yet, the religious references may also endow your works with comedy. Many times, those who embody religion are discredited. The priest is drunk for Dana's wedding in "Stolen Child." (FSBR, 105 and 107) He flirts with a girl behind the counter in *Songdogs*. (S, 92), He acts in an inappropriate way, according to the narrator Kevin in "Hunger Strike." (ET, 112) As for the religious ritual, it is desacralized in *Songdogs*, *This Side of Brightness* and *Let the Great World Spin* where mass and prayers are respectively called "spiritual suppository," (S, 157) "spiritual regurgitation" (TSB, 150) and "the Catholic hit parade." (LGWS, 13) So, let me ask you this question: What is left of the sacred in your work? Do you think that sacredness is still possible in literature nowadays?

McCann: Yes, absolutely I think it's possible. In "Hunger Strike" there is that moment when the Lithuanian couple watch the boy smash up the kayak. Their eyes are large and tender. They understand what's going on. That's sacred, that's Joyce, that's possible.

Maudet: Some sort of epiphany?
McCann: Exactly. And the same at the end of *Let the Great World Spin* where Jaslyn's in bed with Claire. So the sacred is personal, the sacred is never public.

Maudet: Never institutional?
McCann: The sacred never involves an institutionalized religion or even a political movement, or bureaucracy.

Maudet: It's intimate.
McCann: It is. It is a moment of complete, personal intimacy. Even Nureyev rescues himself from me at the very end of *Dancer* when Yulia watches him go down the staircase. He just hops in the air, that's it, and then continues down the staircase. That hop is for me one of the most sacred moments of his life. Because he's saying to her: "I'm still alive. I'm going but I'm still alive. And I lived here. I had this joy." And I think that goes to the heart of what we were talking about: optimism and pessimism. In the face of available evidence, in the face of all the shit that we get thrown at us every single day, this stuff in Boston,[12] this stuff in Iraq, this stuff in Connecticut that I'm up to tomorrow. In the face of all that horrible human evidence, there is still possibility that you can create beauty.

Maudet: You often pay tribute to several Irish authors, and you said many times that you've been influenced by Joyce.[13] As far as I know, you haven't mentioned being influenced by classics of British literature. Yet, it occurs to me that your texts do contain some hints at canons of British literature about roaming. Indeed, I was struck by some parallels between Zoli and Charlotte Brontë's Jane Eyre. Like Jane Eyre, Zoli wanders for three days and she doesn't get to eat. She is rescued by a charitable farmer living in a remote place while Jane Eyre finally reaches a house in the middle of nowhere in the moor. Zoli is cast off her social group because she wanted to reach the highest spheres of society with her poetry the way Jane Eyre wants to reach spheres that she's not supposed to belong to by marrying Rochester. Both pay the price for their pride. Both then try to free themselves from the masculine grasp: that of Swann for Zoli, and that of Rochester for Jane Eyre. Such striking parallels somewhat replace Zoli into the lineage of great heroines, of powerful feminine and independent voices. The Romani poet becomes some sort of heroine and is given some grandeur: the margin is put at the center. Could you comment on this reading of *Zoli* as having its heroine dignified?

McCann: Can I tell you a terrible secret?

Maudet: You haven't read Brontë?

McCann: I haven't. But that's okay, and this goes to the heart of my own argument about criticism. I hate when authors get together and dismiss readings and interpretations of a work of art. The beauty of a work of art is that it can create other works of art. And the beauty of a good thought properly placed is that it makes other thoughts that are even more intelligent around it and deepens the thought, deepens the links and the connections that we have to things that are around. So, I love that! I understand what you're saying. There's something classical in it. There's often people who talk about how there's only seven different types of stories. And *Zoli* is very much a classical story about a woman outcast and then goes on a journey.

Maudet: Now, I would like to quote Michael Cronin who, in what seems to be a rather striking and provocative way, says that unhappy families "are [. . .] a staple of late twentieth-century Irish fiction."[14] Although there is no archetypal family in your texts, their common features are that they are never whole and barely big. Usually the father-figures are flawed entities who have given up their status as heads of family, either because they are dead, absent, afflicted, frustrated, withdrawn or disabled. How would you say that you negotiate with this statement by Cronin, that families cannot be happy in Irish literature?

McCann: You know the famous quote that he is quoting off of, right? The Tolstoy quote: "The unhappy families are . . ." or "happy families are all alike, but unhappy families are . . ." I forget what the actual quote is but it's very famous: "Happy families are all alike and unhappy families . . ."[15] Anyway, it goes to the heart of literary experience in that it was Montaigne, I think, wrote that "happiness writes white."[16] It's so difficult to write about happiness. In this new book, *TransAtlantic*, I take on one of the most difficult things that I have ever done and I write about peace. And writing about peace is much more difficult than waging war. But part of it just goes to the fact that this is literary experience. Irish families can be crucibles of tension, an absolute tension. I have no idea why, given the fact that my mum and dad are still together and they're still alive. I have four brothers and sisters. We are scattered, yes, but it's fine.

Maudet: Maybe it boils down to what we were saying, that you can't write about patterns that you are familiar with?

McCann: I like writing about towards what I want to know. If I wrote about what I knew how boring would it be. So my day today: I woke up early, I got a little bit of work done, I helped my nine-year-old boy because he's got a test, I put some ointment on my fourteen-year-old boy because he had a bicycle crash the other day. We all had breakfast—well, we don't really have breakfast together, we're all running around doing all sorts of things—and then I did a little bit more work. I went to see my doctor friend, we went for a run, we went around the park. I came back here and talked to a few people, did a little more work . . .

Maudet: Many things to talk about you see!

McCann: It's so boring, right? It's so boring! Why would anyone want to write a novel about that? We write towards what we want to know. And I am fascinated by it, and I do know about this terror and this difficulty in the world. I have great empathy for all that difficulty. I think this is the big political thing too, our ability to have empathy for others, especially when we have all the information at our fingertips in a most extraordinary way nowadays that we should be so much more deeply empathetic than what we are. And it's the job of the storyteller, or the poet, or the novelist to deepen our ability for empathy—not to deepen our empathy because that's ridiculous to say so—but to deepen our ability for empathy. And again it's all about allowing: you can't do it yourself but you present the case and you hope that somebody is able to look at it. So when you talk about unhappy families, you can pierce somebody else's unhappiness, but you also have to go towards a moment of joy. I mean, I can basically tell you that in every single story that I've written, I don't think there's anything that didn't approach the darkness. "Cathal's Lake" is the story of a man cursed to dig. He has to dig up the souls of the dead. But at the end, he looks at the fences—he's walking away at the very last line—and says: "Someday that will have to be fixed." In other words, it's reminiscent of the peace process. And this was written before the peace process. "Someday that will have to be fixed." The same for Rudolf Nureyev, coming down the stairs, giving us those little skips, for Claire and Jaslyn, and at the end of *Songdogs* even, when the fish jumps out of the water and it's Conor's mother. He understands it's his mother and she's reincarnated—well, that's the salmon of knowledge. I do think that even in the deepest, unhappiest moments of families and fracture, my stories try to achieve some modicum of grace that comes out of them. The other part of it is, quite frankly, that you want to tell a good story. And a good story has conflict, it has drama and it has at least the possibility of some resolution, not necessarily of happy ending resolution, but a possibility or suggestion that there's going to be some resolution. The last line of *TransAtlantic* is "We have to thank the world for not ending on us." That's what it is: optimism.

Second Interview (June 6, 2014)

Maudet: The movement westward is pre-eminent in your texts: in *Songdogs*, most characters' peregrinations are westward (S, 35, 78 and 140). Six characters emigrate to the west in *Fishing the Sloe-Black River* (Brigid, Sheona, O'Meara, Osobe, Flaherty and Padraig), Zoli "strikes out west" after she is banished (Z, 186) while Nureyev defects to France (*Dancer*). Moreover, both Corrigan brothers (*Let the Great World Spin*) and Lilly Duggan leave Ireland for the United-States (*TransAtlantic*). According to Eoìn Flannery, "the west has always been seen as the trajectory of new prospects and hopes, while the east is more often associated with mystery and the unknown"[17]–this conception of the East conjuring up Said's Orientalism[18] (we can notice a powerful example of the way the East—Asia to be precise—ignites the imagination in "A Basket Full of Wallpaper" by the way). Yet, you said that "America was for a long time a dream place, a Tír na nÓg of the imagination [. . .]."[19] which shows that the West is also the object of fantasy. How do you account for this? Why is the movement westward such a recurring motif in your texts?

McCann: I think there's a few things. There is a "Westward Ho!" sort of feeling to a lot of the work. I think that doesn't just pertain to my work in particular. I think it might pertain to a certain facet of the Irish imagination as well. Tír na nÓg, in Irish mythology, was the land of eternal youth and it was always set to the West. It was never set in the East. And on a personal level, my father used to go to the States to lecture. He'd be going West. And the one instance that I have in my own family of somebody going East is my sister who went to England. I was very close to my sister Siobhan— my older sister—and I always felt that England had robbed her in a certain way. When she came home when I was still quite young, she had an English accent. I remember I was quite upset by all of this, so I think it might be a combination not only of ancient mythology and that idea of the westward journey—the dream of going to a better place, a different place, and becoming a different person—mixed in some of my own personal history. And also the journey that I did myself was a westward journey, so it started on the East coast and ended up in San Francisco. It seems much more optimistic to do so, I don't know why it would feel so, but I would not have liked to have started in San Francisco and finished on the East coast. I can't particularly tell you exactly why; it just feels that way.

Maudet: So as you quickly mentioned, you have been inspired by the Frontier. It seems to explain why several allusions are made to this American motif in your texts. Yet, the transition zone that the Frontier represents has more to do with vertical expansion. It may be downward, with the sandhogs, in *This Side of Brightness*, who look like pioneers digging into unexploited soil, or with Fernando, in *Let the Great World Spin*, who is fascinated with the "virgin territory"—as he calls it—that the underground represents when it comes to artistic expression (LGWS, 174). But it may also be an expansion upward, as demonstrated by the unprecedented artistic performance by the tightrope walker, in *Let the Great World Spin*, who takes the sky of Manhattan as his playground, or the building sites dedicated to erecting skyscrapers in *This Side of Brightness*, so as to inhabit a "virgi[n] space" (TSB, 196). So, focusing on the first part of the question first of all, to what extent would you say American history has defined your prose? And then, why such an interest in the vertical organization of space in *This Side of Brightness* and *Let the Great World Spin*?

McCann: Well, I was endlessly interested in the underground being a sort of Frontier space. These characters who are underground would take their shopping trolleys that they would push through the [tunnels]. But what has happened to that idea of "Westward we go," "Westward Ho!"? It has come in upon itself. That sort of "American Dream" has shrunk and become something dark, something where there's not a lot of space and not a lot of light. So it was definitely interesting for me to think about these men and women who are homeless people as being sort of Frontier's people but in an almost horrific sort of way, inhabiting that sort of darkness. And then, in *Let the Great World Spin*, with Fernando the character who takes the photographs down below, that was really just a way for me to get him from the Bronx down into Wall Street. Sometimes these things become practical issues for a novelist too. You and I have talked before about the notion that Dostoevsky talks about, that to be too acutely conscious is to be diseased. So that when you know what it is that you're going to do, you bring a sort of malady to your work. And I increasingly like the idea that you are an explorer and that you're heading out and you don't know what territory it is that you're going to hit. But often you'll end up in a place that you have to make sense of as you go along. A lot of writers react against the idea of their work being interpreted in that way. I love it actually. I enjoy it very much. I like the expansiveness of the imagination whereby my texts would inform your texts and would inform somebody else's texts. To me that's part of the winding and the gyre, the Yeatsian notion of things meeting one another, which I employ actually in *Let the Great World Spin*, because we take the sixth century Mu'allaqât suspended poems—or the hanging poems—and then take Tennyson and then take *Let the Great World Spin*. These things, they take energy from one another. And we go back down too, it's not always a constant rising up so it becomes a comment on the historical process too.

Maudet: I now would like to pinpoint the way you deal with place in your work, especially in *Songdogs*. The description that you make of the train station (S, 130) is redolent of what French anthropologist Marc Augé has coined "non-places," which are "spaces in which no lasting social relations are established (transit spaces, spaces people pass through), [in which] there are [...] evident social deficits.[20] People are only passengers in and users of non-places,[21] and non-places are also said to be "immense parentheses"[22] in people's daily lives, as they are not vectors of identity. In your foreword to the French version of *The Book of Men*, you have written that stories should enable to re-create a form of communication and to struggle against "one of [today's] biggest failures, the lack of empathy [and] our inability to understand one another."[23] Would you say that what you are seeking to do with the association Narrative 4 is to struggle against a universal form of non-place?

McCann: That's an interesting construction of it. I would say that I'd be seeking to put people in a place, to make the story valuable in that particular place. I am fascinated by this notion of place and the language that it gives to us. And this is a spectacular notion, the idea of non-place, especially when you talk about an Internet age where we exist in a sort of everywhere, and we have to establish a place and a value for ourselves. One hopes that you'll be able to go in and make these stories matter. When your stories matter, your place matters, and there's a value there that I find important. The reason I talk so much about empathy is because I do think that it's our biggest political failure, the failure to understand the other person also means the failure to understand the other's place, their history, their geography and where they come from. If we can step into another body out of this place into somebody else's place, then we're making a human leap that seems to me entirely necessary.

Maudet: It's interesting you mentioned the fact that people need to be affected by what they are reading or experiencing because some scenes in your texts convey excruciating violence and intensity (I'm thinking about the rape of Angela or Faraday's death by electrocution in *This Side of Brightness*, as well as Jigsaw's murder in *Let the Great World Spin*). Yet, the critical readers—although likely to experience the principle of the "willful suspension of disbelief"[24]—should be able to envisage things from hindsight and to see the page as a barrier protecting them from the eventual harm that is done to the characters. You said that "what [you] want people to do is to live in the pulse of the moment"[25] when they read your texts, and this is mostly what happens: they live, they experience your texts, and in the case of the illustrations that we have given, they may be appalled. How can what is supposedly unreal affect the readers so deeply? How is this possible that we should react to a text the fictional aspect of which is unequivocally known to us? Would you say that this happens because people are affected not by the fictitious situation, but by the fictitious situation because it possibly looks like everyday experiences? Do you believe in the fact that the readers can be physically affected by what they are reading?
McCann: Yes. I do think that the readers can be [affected]. You can read about the Holocaust, right, and you can read about the Famine, and you can read about the Iraq War, and you can read about things that are going on and you can be profoundly affected by it. You won't necessarily have the scars, right? You won't have the battle scars, but you can be profoundly affected by it. And in this way, I think there is a sort of non-violence that

goes about in the act of literature. It's inviting people in to understand what the violence is and how violence assaults them for a while. It certainly assaults their brains and possibly assaults their hearts, but when you're finished, you come out of it and you're a changed person. You haven't necessarily experienced the actual violence, but you understand it. So you're making this leap into a form of awareness of what violence is without actually having been hit, shot, kicked, abused, gassed, whatever series of horrific things that can happen to us. And in this way the act of imagination becomes sort of real. It becomes also an act of civil disobedience against this violence that is perpetrated upon us, so that the writer and the reader are in this together. And they whisper to one another: "Come with me, we're going to go somewhere really, really dark." When you come out of this, yes, you will be changed, but you won't necessarily be physically hurt by it, at least. But then, you will perhaps have this empathy towards the other who has gone through this. That's why I said we have to tell these stories over and over and over again. There's not just one story, there's not just one story about the Roma, you have to say it over and over again. There's not just one story about the Holocaust, or about the Irish famine. We have to continually have people experience what it might have been like. Yet some people shy away from that, particularly in contemporary literature. They think that there is a duty to entertain. There is a certain amount of duty to entertain, but there's also a duty to get right in under the skin and make people feel somewhat uncomfortable, you know. I think part of the problem with a lot of contemporary literature is that it steps inside, it closes the curtain, and it says: "I won't hurt you, I'll stroke your ego and I'll make you feel good." And I don't think that serves us too well.

Maudet: And when you said that you want to bring people to the darkest core of life, you may also want to lead them there and laugh with them about this. In *Songdogs,* for example, the death of Michael Lyons's protectors—two Protestant nuns—is recounted in such a succinct way that it sounds quite absurd. Let me remind you: "In the water they might have suddenly looked at one another and remembered the essential fact that neither of them could swim." (S, 7) In *Let the Great World Spin,* comedy looms in the text even when the situation is dramatic. Indeed, Tillie's speech is fraught with terms that are so colloquial that they are sometimes even blasphemous (LGWS, 230) or disrespectful. (LGWS, 277) Besides, Gloria's nodding and approval after each sentence that is uttered by her new friend Marcia, moved when talking about the funambulist that reminds her of her dead son, makes the dialogue sound like an evangelical mass. (LGWS, 98–99) Angela, in *This Side of Brightness*, thinks that the coffin of Faraday, who died in atrocious circumstances, is "stylin'" with its "gold handles." (TSB, 132) You don't hesitate to resort to comedy in the most dramatic situations, and it even seems to be mainly there that you use comic devices. What is the role of comedy here? Is this a way to alleviate the tension and play down the pathos?

McCann: I think that's probably exactly what it is. I'm not afraid of sentiment, but I'm deathly afraid of sentimentality. So as a writer, one of the things that I want to do is go as far as I possibly can. But I'm always conscious that if I go too far, I'll fall off the edge of the cliff. You know [Kurt] Vonnegut had that quote that "we should be continually jumping off of cliffs and developing our wings on the way down," and I think one of the wings that we develop on the way down is the wing of comedy in order to alleviate some of the really darkest aspects of what it is that we have around. In the end, you do have to have a laugh. God is playing a big trick on us, and at a certain stage we have to be able to look at it and say: "Maybe we need to experience it in another way." I suppose for me it is the fear of pushing the sentiment into sentimentality. But I will not refuse the sentiment. I think too many writers are so scared of it that they become dry and they become tired and they become old before their time and not really prepared to go to the edge. I'd rather go to the edge and wear my heart on my sleeve than sit in the corner with all the cynics who don't really want to experience life out loud. But I've never thought of myself as a very funny writer!

Maudet: You are, though!
McCann: Really? That's very funny! Well, I think Tillie is funny. I like Tillie. I'm writing a short story right now that's kind of funny. I hope it's kind of funny anyway! Well, we shall see!

Maudet: You also avoid sentimentality in "From Many One" (*Fishing the Sloe-Black River*). It's a short story that I think is very different from all the others that you have written. It seems to be that it can be perceived as belonging to what has been coined "minimalist realism."[26] To what extent would you say that you have been influenced by this trend or writers such as Richard Ford or Raymond Carver?
McCann: Carver. Carver. And at the time I wrote this story I was at the University of Texas and in fact I was reading Carver at that time. Carver is all over that story. [This story] also deals with a thing that happened to me, because when I was at the University of Texas, I was a bartender and we

used to get a lot of girls coming in with a lot of colored coins. And I said: "What's this story with these colored coins?" And they told me that it was the strippers who used them. But so I just took that little piece. Because you magpie from your life, right? That's what you do, you become a magpie and then you build your nest. The nest itself is a story. In this particular case, it's a very minimal nest. That's an older story, but it's true I like to work in different forms.

Maudet: That's what I like about your work, it's so varied.
McCann: Wait and see the new collection of short stories, they go all over the place!

Maudet: Talking about people who may have influenced you, I would like to focus on those writers whose texts focus on father figures. Father figures have long been a significant focus of Irish writings, often presented as unfaltering authority figures. In your texts, though, the fathers are flawed, and do not fulfill their duty as mentors because they are either dead (*Zoli, This Side of Brightness* and "Hunger Strike"), absent (*Let the Great World Spin*), incapable of bringing up their children ("Stolen Child"), disabled ("Wood") or introverted ("A Basket Full of Wallpaper," "Everything in This Country Must" and *Songdogs*). Therefore, the young protagonists look for new role models to rely on: Zoli and Clarence Nathan see their grandfathers as surrogate fathers, Kevin turns toward the Lithuanian, Dana chooses Padraig, Andrew is fascinated by the Orangemen and Katie by the British soldiers. In that regard, some of your texts seem to have been inspired by the stories of initiation, a profoundly American tradition, James Fenimore Cooper's *The Deerslayer* (1841) having paved the way for these. Later, William Faulkner's "The Bear" (1942), and before that, Ernest Hemingway's "Fathers and Sons" (1933) have also been cornerstones as far as coming-of-age tales are concerned. John Cusatis wrote that you "acknowledged a debt to Hemingway's [. . .] *The Old Man and the Sea*, whose protagonist, Santiago clearly influenced the creation of the old Lithuanian in 'Hunger Strike'"[27]but I haven't been able to find a reference for this assertion. Could you elaborate on this a little? Would you say you owe the writers of growing-up tales a debt?
McCann: Yeah. Well, first of all, yes, I think that I owe—I mean, we all owe—these writers a debt. And recently I had a debate with somebody who should go unnamed, a fairly prominent figure in Irish literature, and he said quite proudly: "I have not read Joyce." So though he hadn't physically read

Joyce I made the argument that he had read Joyce anyway because he'd read anything else that'd been around and because Joyce inhabits so much of what we are and who we are as a nation and also as a literary community. Even if he hadn't physically read him, he had actually read him and had been influenced by him. I think we have to acknowledge the influence of others very much so. And *The Old Man and the Sea* was a book that I read when I was in my late teens and, in fact, my father got sick a couple of years ago and I was at his hospital bed and I read him the book aloud. I thought that was an interesting thing to read *The Old Man and the Sea* to my own father. My father was an enormous influence on me. He wasn't absent. I mean, his own father had been absent. I think much of what I write about is actually about—for me personally, if you'd be looking at my own life—an absent grandfather. I never met my Northern Irish grandfather.

Maudet: In Joyce's stories, though, you did meet your great-grandfather.
McCann: But in Joyce's stories I do meet my great-grandfather, yeah. So I know him as a sort of imaginative figure. He's filled out for me. His body is filled out for me by a literary experience. To come back on both my grandfathers, I met my father's father one time in London, and my mother's father I never met. And so it strikes me now, I mean, I've never talked about this before, but it does strike me now that maybe the absent fathers there is really an acknowledgment of the absent father for my own father. Because my own dad is very, very, very important to me.

Maudet: I've seen that documentary on a French television program called La grande librairie (France 5). It was entitled "Gens de Dublin," and you were with your father in Dublin, and it was quite touching.
McCann: Yeah, he's still alive. I will tell you that the first—I suppose the very first—literary experience I ever had was when I was about eight or nine-years-old. My father had a writing shed to the corner of the house and I would go out there and hear him type, and at the end of about six months he came to me with one of those big rolls of paper we used in the newspapers, cut a sheet about this long and he asked me to read this thing and it turned out to be a book, a children's book, his first children book about soccer called *Goals for Glory*. And what he asked me to do, he said: "Would you read this and tell me what you think?" And basically he was asking me to edit it, which was fantastic. And now it strikes me that I read that thing and I really liked it, and I made notes for him and things like this. I didn't know what I was doing, but that's what he just asked me to do. But a year later—or

maybe a year and a half later—the book came out and I brought it to school, and my teacher in school, Mr. Kells, actually read the book aloud to the rest of my class on Friday afternoons. So for me that must have been a bizarre thing to think that my father went out to the side shed of the house and typed away, you know. For however many months he typed away on that book and then suddenly it was there in my education and in my classroom. So, I suppose that's one of the very first immediate literary experiences that I can recall. And so much of it has to do with my dad, yes, and has to do with him putting Dylan Thomas on the record player when I was a kid, and about him coming back from the United States, and, you know, bringing Kerouac and Ginsberg and that sort of things. However, I read more about women than about men and I write more about mothers, and mothers in relation to their sons. So my mum has an important influence on that too.

Maudet: It's amazing you've just mentioned music because that is the subject of my next question. The references to music are incredibly important in your work, be they made by the names of the singers only, the titles of their songs or even the lyrics of the songs. They pervade your texts. If we keep in mind the fact that some of your characters are unable to express themselves, are such recurring allusions to music only a way to infuse the texts with realistic references, or do you also sometimes use music as a way for your characters to replace words when feelings cannot be voiced?
McCann: Sometimes it would be this thing. I wrote this story called "Step We Gaily On We Go!".

Maudet: "Heel for heel and toe for toe!"
McCann: Yeah! I do sing, but I can't sing, that's my problem! I need a few whiskeys and a few pints of beer before I start to sing! Music has always been enormously important for me. And also [I like] just listening to it as I write, listening to Van Morrison or listening to David Gray, or listening to . . .

Maudet: "Old Buttermilk Sky"?
McCann: Yeah, that again is from my dad, the Hoagy Carmichael stuff, you know, "Old Buttermilk Sky," that was all from my dad.

Maudet: Hoagy Carmichael is mentioned seven times in your work![28]
McCann: No way?! Seven times, really? I'll not be able to do it again!

Maudet: I'm sorry, I might create a block once again!

McCann: No, I love that song. My dad used to go around the house singing it all the time. But I don't know why. I mean, it is a very Irish thing to have the music there, to be connected to music, but also the rhythm of language. You know one writes a story like one writes a song. Van Morrison doesn't go into the studio and suddenly knock off "Madame George," you know. He goes in, he works at it, he finds where the saxophone goes, he finds where the lyrics go and then he starts to shape it.

Maudet: And you did write songs, didn't you?

McCann: Yeah, yeah, yeah. Oh I've written a few songs. I wrote one for *TransAtlantic*, with Clannad, that just came out. I wrote one with Joe Hurley, *Let the Great World Spin*. And then I've written one with Joe Henry.

Maudet: With Lisa Hannigan, right?

McCann: Lisa Hannigan, yeah. It's fun to do that sort of things, I like it. I sort of get outside my writing life.

Maudet: How do you get organized to be able to choose between the time you want to spend on writing a novel or a short story, or a song? How do you cope with everything?

McCann: I have a lot of things going on right now. I'm the President of Narrative 4, which is the story-exchange part that you mentioned earlier. I'm a teacher at Hunter College. I'm writing a collection of short stories. I'm writing a screenplay . . .

Maudet: A screenplay? Remember last year, you told me that poems and plays were genres that you didn't want to dedicate yourself to, because you deemed yourself unskilled for writing them.

McCann: I know but the screenplay is different. Poems and plays I can't do, but a screenplay is slightly different—I'm doing that for *Let the Great World Spin*. But also I'm a soccer coach!

Maudet: Are you?

McCann: Yes, I'm in charge of two football teams, my sons' football teams, so I have to do all that too. I've got a lot of different hats! What is it that Jim Harrison says? He says: "Under the storyteller's hat, there are many different heads, most of them troubled."

Maudet: And a lot of voices in your head!

McCann: Exactly! An awful lot of voices in my head. An awful lot of voices in my head. But they are a form of music too. I mean, that engages with your previous question about finding the music of your characters. For example, when I was working on Tillie, I did a lot of work beforehand to find out what the life of a prostitute might have been like in the 1970s in New York. I looked at photographs, I looked at films, I looked at histories, I looked at sociology texts, I looked to see if I could find any interviews with them in the newspapers, all these sorts of things. I went out with cops, and then I talked to older cops who'd been around, then had to find a whole warehouse full of rap sheets. I've started to build up a composite of this character and if you'd asked me at that stage what the life of a prostitute would have been like, I could tell you. I knew a lot.

Maudet: But you didn't have the voice?

McCann: But I had no voice. So it took me a while and when I found the music of her voice, then it came instantly. So it's all about capturing it.

Maudet: The Greyhound buses quote?

McCann: That's right! "The skinniest dog that I ever saw was on the side of Greyhound Buses" (LGWS, 200), that's what she says. And once she'd said that, then I knew how she spoke. Because sometimes when we know how we speak, then we know how we are. Capturing: that's the hard work.

Maudet: You usually start with a very visual image, right? Is that the way you proceed? In your texts, some scenes are so powerfully visual that their pictorial quality makes us forget their original textual essence. You said to Joseph Lennon: "I very seldom try to wrap an image around an idea. [. . .] I get corralled by an image: it bowls me over and I can't avoid it [. . .]."[29]

McCann: Exactly.

Maudet: Your way of operating can be compared to John McGahern's, who wrote, in "Playing With Words," that "Work often begins with an image, or a rhythm, or a line of dialogue that stays in the mind and will not go away until it's written down."[30] This reminds me of what you said about the way you found a voice for Tillie Henderson, in *Let the Great World Spin*, as we just mentioned, by having her saying: "The skinniest dog I ever seen is the one on the side of the Greyhound buses."[31] I would like to understand the way you craft your texts. When you are composing, do you really never intend to write in order to make your text visual? Is it always the other way round, the image popping up first?

McCann: Generally it's the image that pops up first. I like cinema and I like cinematographers. I like the eye that people have. I actually hate being photographed, but I like taking photographs. And I think that's instructive in a certain way. Most photographers don't like to be photographed. It's very interesting. Nowadays when someone wants to take a photograph of me, I say: "Okay, but only if I can take a photograph of you first." And so it becomes a reciprocal sort of relationship. And they become aware that they're taking something from me. So in terms of writing, I write like a photographer or a cinematographer, but when you go in and create the photograph with words you hope that they have a painterly quality, too. So it's not just being a photographer or a cinematographer; it's also being a painter too. Each of those three visual mediums, which are quite different to one another—one being static, one being moving, one being static and moving and also ridged—have a different topography to them. If you can combine all of those, then I think that you can create a scene. I spend a lot of my time with my eyes closed, isn't that weird? I go like this: I close my eyes and I can see things. And then I start to paint them. I use words to try and paint them. And I don't think I'm going to write about man's inhumanity to his fellow man, but that's what the work might be about. I mean, it's not for me to say what my work is about. I get in there and I try to paint and then others come in and try to interpret.

Maudet: When I first met you, you said that "you write the books that you want to read" and that "you hope not to be bored by your [books] and you hope that it still has the electricity that runs through [them]" [first interview]. And like Umberto Eco or Wolfgang Iser, it seems that you are also interested in the readers' response and that you believe that they must be active in the reading process, as you just mentioned. You said that you believed in "creative reading"[32] and in the fact that "the novel should be left open for interpretation."[33]

McCann: For sure.

Maudet: Do you perceive readers as investigators that you like playing with and manipulating before subtly guiding them towards some form of resolution?

McCann: There is a sort of manipulation that goes on, isn't there? I mean, one would like to think that you're not manipulating, you're just presenting, but of course you're manipulating. It's all crafted, you know, your character is driving the car, and he or she is going to get you somewhere. You present these things, but then you hope that the reader might be more intelligent than you, or that the reader feels the exact same emotion that you feel in creating it, so that they go out into the world and operate in the world. I get a chance to meet a lot of my readers, I travel a lot and generally—99% of the time—I like them. They are really interesting people, they are people who engage, they are people who do social work. So I like to think that I write the sort of story that such people get involved in. One would hope that you could convert the legions of cynics, the legions of people who don't want to do anything. It's part of what an artist's desire is. I meet a lot of filmmakers these days too, and filmmakers have an enormous reach and an enormous span. I'm working with J. J. Abrams, who's going to make *Let the Great World Spin* as a movie when he finishes *Star Wars*.

Maudet: Do you realize that? You come right after *Star Wars*! It's just amazing!
McCann: I know! I know! I know! I know! What's interesting about J. J. is that he's enormously smart, but he's using this medium as a popular medium: he's doing *Star Trek* and *Star Wars* and these sorts of things. He really wants to get into something serious now. That's why we're talking about doing *Let the Great World Spin* and wanting to do it in a pretty serious way.

Maudet: What do you mean "something serious"?
McCann: Yeah well, I shouldn't really say that, but I don't think *Star Wars* is all that serious. I mean, some people do, but I don't really want to be on a space ship for two hours, you know. I'd rather be somewhere else. I'd rather be on the street in the Bronx, looking at the human endeavor and human difficulty. I think a part of J. J. wanted to be in both places. I admire him for his message that he wants to get across.

His last *Star Wars* film was very much an Iraq analogy. I don't know if everybody got it, but it was. So there's a part of me who sometimes thinks I might just be snobby by writing these literary books, but I hope not. I hope not.

I want to create a text that people can walk into and walk out of, if not changed, at least about to change, or wanting to affect someone, or pondering over issues of empathy, issues of belonging. I love it when a book does that to me, rattles my heart. There's not many writers who actually truly do it. Somebody like Michael Ondaatje truly does it, John Berger makes me want to change my life when I read his works. I like that sort of thing. I think that's morally responsible. Should a novelist be morally responsible? I'm not going to tell other novelists to be so, but I have to be so.

Maudet: Yeah, we discussed that last year. Not didactic, though.
McCann: I'm not interested in being didactic. I'm not interested in telling anybody how to live. There's enough politicians telling people how to live. There's enough corporations telling people what to buy, what to think, what to feel, what to experience. But if you can present an experience for people, that is authentic. And this is the other thing actually about my Narrative 4 experience: we get these kids from all over the world together to step into one another's shoes and tell one another stories. It's actually an authentic experience for them in a world where there is not a lot of authentic experiences anymore. We hide behind our iPhones, we hide behind our identities online, we give ourselves new names online, we give ourselves new bodies, all sorts of things online. In Narrative 4, when these kids get together and they step across and look each other in the eye, their brains [light up]. We've done brain studies on stories and storytelling and empathy, and the brain becomes a carnival. It lights up when people sit face to face and tell one another stories. It's a fantastic thing.

Maudet: You know there has recently been an article in a local newspaper[34] in which I read that your book *Dancer* has been studied by high school students this year in Brittany (France), two hours away from here.[35] They have associated literature and arts so as to create the object that, for them, best encompasses the whole story of *Dancer*. That's fantastic, isn't it? So it's a cage, a golden cage, in which the birds are replaced by ballet shoes.
McCann: No way? That's cool! I also know a wonderful Italian architect who started a course whereby you create a structure. You read a book, like *Ulysses*, and then you create a house, or a building of some sort. And the building must reflect the themes and the characters, and you can use all sorts of found items like cardboard boxes, Sellotape, toilet roll—whatever happens to be—and you create a structure based on the novel. These sorts of things give me great hope for the novel.

Maudet: Yeah, I think it's really interesting to turn a book into something else, into another artistic medium and way to communicate. Now, we've understood that you try to convey some specific messages, and I think that the way for you to do that is by resorting to symbolism. You said to me that if you had to define what you write, you would say it is "poetic realism" [first interview]. A perfect illustration of this is that your texts encompass a countless number of explicit comparisons between characters and animals, either evoking common physical features between the two, or identical ways to behave. These animals may be mammals—especially cats (FSBR, 139), hyenas (FSBR, 131), horses (ET, 5; S, 163; and D, 59), rats (S, 162), moles (TSB, 126), mules (TSB, 92), dogs (TSB, 57; and D, 164) or giraffes (LGWS, 217), insects (FSBR, 97–98; D, 37; and LGWS, 94)—especially flies (D, 141 and LGWS, 134), cockroaches (D, 154 and LGWS, 212), caterpillars (ET, 32) and crickets (FSBR, 98)—, fish (D, 73)—especially the trout (S, 135–136) and the eel (S, 10)—, seafood (S, 160), invertebrates (TSB, 14), reptiles—especially snakes (TSB, 37 and 144–145) and chameleons (S, 66–67)—, and birds (FSBR, 9, 11, 96, 97–98, and 110; TSB, 56; D, 182, 257, and 304; LGWS, 212 and 223)—especially seagulls (FSBR, 23 and LGWS, 264), owls (S, 197 and LGWS, 152), eagles (FSBR, 158 and S, 198), chickens (S, 48–49 and 160), crows (S, 32) and wrens (FSBR, 66).

McCann: "Owl faced"! That's from *The Great Gatsby*! That's a specific *Great Gatsby* reference.

Maudet: Right. Your texts being thus fraught with an imagery dealing with animals seem to bear similarities with bestiaries or fables. By depicting your characters like animals, what do you intend to do? Do you seek to inject symbolism into your predominantly realistic prose?

McCann: I don't know. I don't know. I don't know . . . I'd have to think about it. I'd be a liar if I told you that I had an immediate answer. I was in Paris yesterday and somebody asked me: "If you could be a word, what word would you want to be?" And he said: "Tell me immediately what you are!"

Maudet: What was it?
McCann: It was "pigeon"!

Maudet: "Pigeon"! Why? You could have chosen "wren" instead!
McCann: Or "sparrow" or whatever!

Maudet: Yeah! Or "elk," you know!
McCann: Well, "elk" is nice, yeah, yeah, yeah, yeah, yeah! No, but the name Colum means two things: either "dove" or "pigeon."

Maudet: Right.
McCann: I don't want to be a dove. So I said "pigeon." Pigeon is sort of dirty and a little bit cynical around the edges, but it still has flight. But to be a

dove would be so boring. The dove of peace, you know. But it's nice to be associated with the dove of peace. A dove is a pigeon anyway.

Maudet: Yeah, but you once said to me that waging war was far easier than waging peace, so a dove would be great.

McCann: Yeah, I am very interested in the idea of peace and I do think that we have to talk about it more and more and more. And all these assholes who are in charge of our military and so on could do with a lesson in how difficult it is to negotiate peace, much more difficult than it is to wage war. I'm a great admirer, as you know, of Senator George Mitchell, who helped in the peace process in Northern Ireland, though it's a little bit shaky right now.

Maudet: The recent Gerry Adams case would be an example of how the past is still overwhelming and how fragile the situation is.

McCann: Yeah, Gerry Adams, and so on. You have to continually work on this idea of peace. But, to come back to your question, I had no idea that I did so much of the animal imagery, so you're going to make me very conscious now!

Maudet: I'm really sorry. Don't worry, you won't meet me too often, though. I may ask for one interview a year, is that a deal?

McCann: Okay, perfect, perfect!

Maudet: I had this conversation with a colleague of mine, and she told me that it seemed that year after year you had more obviously turned into a pacifist, in your literary texts, interviews and pieces of journalism.

McCann: I don't know if I'm a very good pacifist. She's right, I would love to be a pacifist. I would fight my corner if I had to fight my corner. I would fight it very strongly. I do increasingly gravitate towards this idea of peace. I don't want to become soft. I don't want people to interpret it as being soft. I want it to be seen as something muscular, something tough. There is always a danger when you talk about peace, or love. What's that great line by Nick Cave?[36] Elvis Costello sings it. He says: "What's so funny about peace, love, and understanding?" So what is so funny about it? There's nothing funny about peace, there's nothing funny about love or understanding.

Maudet: You said to me that you're more likely to receive arrows when you're a pacifist.

McCann: Sure, sure, sure, you just get kicked around because people think it's easy enough to do so. But then you have to have the courage of your convictions. And I think the really good pacifist would know what war is, what the act of war is, what people do to each other. It's nothing you avoid, you don't avoid the idea of what war is. It's not that as a good optimist you avoid pessimism, no. You've got to be as dark as the light side or as light as the dark side. That's a weird statement to say, but to be somebody who is going to believe in something, you have to be very capable of understanding what the exact opposite is. If you avoid the opposite, then you're in big trouble.

Maudet: About avoidance then—your last statement is serendipitous—you started writing in the 1990s, a paradoxical period in Irish history and literature. While the social isolation and parental violence inherent in the rural way of life were still the main social reality and the preoccupation of Irish literature, Ireland suddenly had to adapt to the aggressive leap of the Celtic Tiger. In the years following the Celtic Tiger, Irish writers have proven to be reluctant to write about the subsequent drastic socio-economic changes. It is only at the end of the decade that Joseph O'Connor in *The Salesman* (1998) or Colm Tóibin in *The Blackwater Lightship* (1999) alluded to a society forever shattered. Although, as soon as 1994 with "Sisters" (*Fishing the Sloe-Black River*), you did allude to the fact that Dublin had become a modern city, it's only later in *Let the Great World Spin* (with the Jazzlyn section, 341) or in *TransAtlantic* (with Hannah struggling to cope, 276–277) that you came back to a globalized and modernized Ireland. Do you understand why the generation of writers that emerged in the 1990s has tended to stay away from the socio-economic realities of that decade?

McCann: Generally it takes writing about ten years to figure out what's going on. And when you write in the heart of it, you don't necessarily see it. It's like a hand in front of the face. It's all there, but you can't actually see it. You have to hold it at this distance. That's part of it. And part of it is that we were very interested in not being at home. We wanted to go to lots of different places. We wanted to go to Argentina, go to America, go to London, go to Germany, go to France and write about those other places. In many ways, the Irish economy was like a teenage economy. I know we're an ancient culture and so on, but we were like a group of teenagers in the 1990s and the early 2000s, and we had a big party. Everybody was hanging out by the swimming pool and everyone was drinking martinis, and at about five o'clock in the morning, just as the music is really thumping, somebody goes up on the staircase and jumps down off the staircase and hangs out at the chandelier, swings out of the chandelier, and suddenly, the chandelier comes crashing to the ground and then somebody else looks up and says: "Oh oh, the parents are coming!" The parents are coming down the driveway and guess who the parents were? The parents were the German banks, well, the European banks, the Irish banks, whatever, but they were primarily German banks. And the parents are coming home to say: "You naughty little children, look at what you did!" And our economy was fucked, I mean, it was really, really bad. We were railroaded, not only by the banks but by our own politicians who allowed the banks to do that. Irish people had to pay for much of what had happened. Yes, some had been recklessly partying, but others had been those people who had allowed this to occur. This is only coming into focus now. A lot of the work is about this now. A lot of the younger writers are writing about this now, it's great. There's some really good stuff coming out. But we have some distance from it. I don't think I'm going to do too much. I did a little bit in *TransAtlantic* but I'm going to leave that territory for somebody else.

Maudet: My last question will focus on your most recent contribution to—or rather huge part in—the project that is *The Book of Men*. You have recently made your interest in the question of gender in literature quite obvious, by editing and writing in *The Book of Men*, and through your contribution to *Poems that Make Grown Men Cry*. Do you feel that in your work as a whole, you try to capture the essence of what it is to be a man (or a woman when you write from a woman's point of view). And do you feel that you have sometimes been about to verge into stereotypes as far as the representation of gender is concerned?

McCann: I got to tell you—this is the honest to God truth—the only reason that book is called *The Book of Men* is pure practicality because I started the organization Narrative 4 with a number of other people and I was sitting in a pub—in a bar—in New York with the editor of *Esquire*. I said to him: "Listen, man, we've started this new organization, I need some help. I need some publicity. Can you give me some publicity for Narrative 4?" He says: "Yeah, let's think about it. What can we do?" And he says: "By the way, my next issue (of *Esquire*) is called 'How to be a man'" And I said: "Okay, why don't we write about how to be a man?" He says: "Okay, why don't you get some of your writers to write about how to be a man?" I said: "How many do you want?" And we were drinking whiskey, and he said: "A hundred of them." And I said: "Okay!" And actually in the end I did, but we reduced those down to seventy-five. It was purely practical, and in six weeks we pulled this stuff together. That's why some entries are so short and that's why some are so terrible! Some of them are good, some of them are not so good. I was a little bit embarrassed by this notion that we were doing this book called *How to Be a Man*. Not anymore, mind you. The next book will be *How to Be a Woman* and then the next book will be *How to Be a Teen*.

Maudet: What about *How to Be a Toddler*, too?!
McCann: Possibly! That's a good idea! *How to Be Dead* as well! *How to Be Dead with Great Respect to Yourself!* No, but really it was just one of those things. People might think that it was intentional, but it wasn't intentional. In relation to *Poems that Make Grown Men Cry*, a friend of mine was in charge of the anthology. He called me up and said: "Can you give me a piece on *Poems that Make Grown Men Cry*?"

Maudet: It's a beautiful poem, the one you chose by Wendell Berry.
McCann: I love that poem: "In a meeting I see my dead friend.[37] He has, I know, gone long and far."

Maudet: Have you known it for a long time?
McCann: Yeah, and it brings tears to my eyes because it reminds me of my friend Brendan Bourke, who died last year. Can I tell you a story about Brendan? Because this goes to the heart of *Ulysses*. I don't think I've told you this. When I met you, had Brendan died?

Maudet: I think he had been dead for a couple of months.
McCann: Yeah, a couple of months, yeah. It was profoundly affecting for me because he was my best friend. So I went back to Dublin, and we were in the funeral home. I was arranging the funeral with his wife—or his partner—and I was in with the undertakers and so on. I had been getting him to read *Ulysses* for years and years and years. I had said: "Come on, you bastard! Read *Ulysses*, Come on!" And we talked about it and he said: "Yeah, I'm going to read it." But he never did. He listened to bits and pieces of it. His partner came to me when he died and she said: "You'll never guess this, Colum. I was going through his stuff, and two weeks before he died he bought a copy of *Ulysses*." The receipt was in there and everything. So she said to me: "I'm going to put it in his coffin." So she put it in the coffin. It was an open coffin because in Ireland we're doing open coffins, and she put it on his chest. And I said: "Okay then, I'm going to open it." I opened it, and then I had an hour with him, because we were waiting for his family

to come in, and I sat down and I read it to him. I read parts of it. I read the "What is my Nation" part, and then I read the naughty bits, the dirty bits from Molly's soliloquy to give him a bit of a laugh. And then I just sort of left it open on his chest and that was a good way to finish things. But that's how books can affect us and also how friendship can affect us. I think it's a good story.

Notes

1. "Birnbaum vs. Colum McCann," *Morning News,* May 2007, [consulted on August 3, 2010], <http://www.themorningnews.org/archives/birnbaum_v/colum_mccann.php>.

2. "Colum interviewed by Robert Birnbaum: Identity Theory."

3. Colum McCann is actually alluding to Jean-Paul Sartre's *Reflections on the Jewish Question.* In this work, the French theoretician has addressed the question of antisemitism and has advocated the idea that the Jewish people had not managed to find their own voice, so that their culture was conveyed through simplistic and stereotypical representations.

4. Colum McCann, "But Always Meeting Ourselves," *The New York Times,* June 16, 2009, [consulted on July 3, 2009], <http://www.nytimes.com/2009/06/16/opinion/16mccann.html>.

5. Colum McCann, "I Am Here to Live Out Loud," *Colum McCann's Official Website,* date unknown [consulted on September 17, 2009], <http://www.colummccann.com/zola.htm>.

6. Colum McCann insisted on his interest in unheard voices in "Conversation with Sasha Hemon" and in "Colum McCann Interviewed by Declan Meade for *The Stinging Fly* Magazine," *Colum McCann's Official Website,* 2003 [consulted on April 13, 2011], <http://www.colummccann.com/interviews/dancer.htm>.

7. Colum McCann is actually referring to the deadly assault that took place in Sandy Hook elementary school on December 14, 2012 in which twenty children and six educators were killed.

8. For a full version of William Faulkner's speech, see "Banquet Speech," *The Official Web Site of the Nobel Prize,* December 10, 1950, [consulted on 25 April, 2014], <http://www.nobelprize.org/nobel_prizes/literature/laureates/1949/faulkner-speech.htmlhttp://www.nobelprize.org/nobel_prizes/literature/laureates/1949/faulkner-speech.html>.

9. Frank Norris, "The Novel with a Purpose," George Perkins (ed.), *The Theory of the American Novel,* New York and Chicago: Holt, Rinehart et Winston, 1970, p. 241.

10. Richard Ford, "Introduction," Richard Ford (ed.), *The Granta Book of the American Short* Story, London: Penguin Books, 1992, p. xvii-xviii.

11. Colum McCann, "I Am Here to Live Out Loud."

12. This interview took place a few days after the Boston marathon bombings that occurred on April 15, 2013.

13. Colum McCann has already paid tribute to James Joyce in several interviews, namely "Colum interviewed by Robert Birnbaum: Identity Theory," in "Conversation with Sasha Hemon," in "Adventures in the Skin Trade, a Conversation with Michael Ondaatje" (*Colum McCann's Official Website*, May 2008 [consulted on May 20, 2013], <http://www.colummccann.com/interviews.htm>) and in *"Everything in This Country Must,* Interview" (*Colum McCann's Official Website*, date unknown [consulted on September 18, 2009], <http://colummccann.com/interviews/everything.htm>).

14. Michael Cronin, "Inside Out: Time and Place in Northern Ireland," *New Hibernia Review*, volume 13, issue 3, Fall 2009, p.77.

15. Colum McCann is referring to the first line of Leo Tolstoy's *Anna Karenina*: "All happy families are alike; each unhappy family is unhappy in its own way."

16. This quote is not one by Michel de Montaigne but is to be found in Henry de Montherlant's *Don Juan* (1955), the eponymous protagonist of which declares: "Le bonheur écrit à l'encre blanche sur des pages blanches" (*Don Juan, pièce en trois actes*, Paris: Gallimard, 1958, p. 98).

17. Eoìn Flannery, *Colum McCann and the Aesthetics of Redemption*, Dublin: Irish Academic Press, 2011, p. 191.

18. This term was coined by Edward W. Said in 1978 and stemmed from his theorizing the Western propensity to stereotype the East (Palestine Diary, "Edward Said on Orientalism," *Youtube*, October 28, 2012, [consulted on June 17, 2013], <http://www.youtube.com/watch?v=fVC8EYd_Z_g>.

19. James Santel, "Funambulism: An Interview with Colum McCann," *Los Angeles Book Review*, June 12, 2013 [consulted on June 17, 2013]. <http://lareviewofbooks.org/article.php?type=&id=1754&fulltext=1&media=#article-text-cutpoint>

20. "Places and Non-Places: A Conversation with Marc Augé," *Autogrill*, January 26, 2009 [consulted on June 5, 2014], <http://onthemove.autogrill.com/gen/lieux-non-lieux/news/2009–01–26/places-and-non-places-a-conversation-with-marc-auge>.

21. Marc Augé, *Non-places: An Introduction to an Anthropology of Supermodernity*, London and New York: Verso, 1995, p.127–130.

22. Ibid, p. 111.

23. Cf Colum McCann (ed.), *Etre un homme*, Paris: Belfond, 2014, p. 8.

24. An expression used by Samuel Taylor Coleridge in 1817.

25. Charlie Rose, "Irish Author Colum McCann on Novel *TransAtlantic*," *Bloomberg TV*, date unknown [consulted on June 5, 2014],<http://www.bloomberg

.com/video/irish-author-colum-mccann-on-novel-transatlantic-3FzGNN5wSEm
_yECc4Z5Qyg.htm1http://www.bloomberg.com/video/irish-author-colum
-mccann-on-novel-transatlantic-3FzGNN5wSEm_yECc4Z5Qyg.html>.

26. "Minimalist realism is a literary streak that has bloomed with Raymond Carver and Richard Ford, and which stands out by the detachment and distance that its prose conveys, and by its simple sentences and repetitive lexicon. Besides, in this literary vein, dialogues are rare and concise but betray tension and misunderstanding between the characters, as well as communicational failures," in Florian Tréguer, *Lectures de Richard Ford: A Multitude of Sins*, Rennes: Presses Universitaires de Rennes, 2008,p. 60.

27. John Cusatis, *Understanding Colum McCann*, Columbia (South Carolina): University of South Carolina Press, 2011, pp. 105–106.

28. He also mentions Sinatra (*LGWS*, 122); Armstrong (*TSB*, 108 and *LGWS*, 65); Jimi Hendrix and James Brown (*TSB*, 185); Rex Stewart and Nat King Cole (*LGWS*, 122); Mary Lou Williams and Henry Red Allen (*TSB*, 120); Cole Porter (*S*, 114); the Rolling Stones (*S*, 145); Mick Jagger, John Lennon, and Yoko Ono (*D*, 247); Charlie Parker (*D*, 182); Motown (*LGWS*, 46); Al Jolson and Billie Holiday (*S*, 80); Richard Pryor (*LGWS*, 74); Marvin Gaye (*LGWS*, 64); Tommy Makem, the Clancy Brothers, Donovan and Tom Waits (*LGWS*, 59); Stevie Wonder et Kool 'N' the Gang (*TSB*, 227); Miriam Makeba (*T*, 272); The Saw Doctors (*FSBR*, 138); Van Halen (*FSBR*, 97); Edith Piaf (*D*, 171); Elvis Presley's "Heartbreak Hotel" (*S*, 143); Hoagy Carmichael (*T*, 266) and his songs entitled "Ol' Buttermilk Sky" (twice in *S*, 138 and *FSBR*, 70) and "Up a Lazy River" (four times in *FSBR*, 5 and 20; *LGWS*, 339 and 342); U2 and the song "I haven't found what I'm looking for" (*FSBR*, 21); Ray Charles and his hit "Hit the Road, Jack" (*S*, 192); Joan Baez and her notorious "We Shall Overcome" (*T*, 272); the popular foxtrot "Ain't We Got Fun?" (*FSBR*, 66); "Molly Malone" (twice, in *S*, 71 and *FSBR*, 62); A Chusla Mo Chroi (*FSBR*, 66); "Maire's Wedding (*FSBR*, 64); the Spanish ballad "Juanita" (*FSBR*, 71); the nursery rhyme "Elephant Bell" (*S*, 71); *Mary Poppins*'s song "A Spoonful of Sugar" (*FSBR*, 140); and even a gospel tune (*TSB*, 9).

29. Joseph Lennon, "'The First Man to Whistle': Two Interviews with Colum McCann," Susan Cahill and Eóin Flannery (ed.), *This Side of Brightness: Essays on the Fiction of Colum McCann*, Oxford: Peter Lang, 2012, collection *Re-Imagining Ireland*, volume 17, p. 150.

30. John McGahern, *Love of the World: Essays*, London: Faber and Faber, 2009, p. 9.

31. Alec Michod, "The *Rumpus* Interview with Colum McCann," *The Rumpus*, June 4, 2013 [consulted on March 3, 2014], <http://therumpus.net/2013/06 /the-rumpus-interview-with-colum-mccann/>

32. Joseph Lennon, "The First Man to Whistle": Two Interviews with Colum McCann," p. 157, as well as in "*Everything in This Country Must*: Interview," in "Birnbaum vs. Colum McCann" and in "*This Side of Brightness* Interview," Colum

McCann's Official Website, date unknown [consulted on September 18, 2009], <http://www.colummccann.com/interviews/brightness.htm >.

33. Laura McCaffrey, "*Zoli* Interview: Questions & Answers with Laura McCaffrey," *Colum McCann's Official Website*, date unknown [consulted on September 18, 2009], <http://www.colummccann.com/interviews/zoli.htm>.

34. Dominique Hosatte, "Le plaisir de lire passe aussi par l'art," *Ouest France*, May 28, 2014 [consulted on June 2, 2014], <http://www.ouest-france.fr/le-plaisir-de-lire-passe-aussi-par-lart-2583457>.

35. The interview took place in Rennes, Brittany (France).

36. It is Nick Lowe who wrote this song, not Nick Cave.

37. "In a dream I meet my dead friend" is the exact quotation.

Do What Is Most Difficult

Synne Rifbjerg / 2013

Colum McCann was interviewed by Synne Rifbjerg at the 2013 Louisiana Literature festival in the Louisiana Museum of Modern Art, Denmark. Permission for the printed transcription granted by Louisiana Channel, Louisiana Museum of Modern Art, Denmark.

Synne Rifbjer: Why did you write *TransAtlantic*?

Colum McCann: After I wrote *Let the Great World Spin*, I was a little bit terrified. It did well—I was very lucky—and I decided I was going to write a novel. I started writing a novel based on a poem by Wallace Stevens called "Thirteen Ways of Looking at a Blackbird." I was calling the novel *Thirteen Ways of Looking*. It was a contemporary novel, set in New York, about video surveillance, of all things. Now how could I get from video surveillance in New York to Frederick Douglass, African American slave, who goes to Ireland in 1845? I don't know. Except that one writes toward one's obsessions, and I was failing miserably with the other novel. Technically, it was working out quite well; it had a nice structure and all those things, but I just didn't like it. And I think if you're going to spend two, three years with anything, you better like it, or preferably love it.

And always at the back of my mind I had this image of Douglass going to Ireland in 1845, and that year had great resonance for Irish people because that was the year our great famine began, and it lasted all the way until 1850, a terribly savage thing to have occurred on our imaginations and on our physical being and welfare. So here was the image of a great American statesman, still a slave of all things—he hadn't yet bought his freedom—going to Ireland, and I can't shake myself of this thing. I tried to write it, but I couldn't catch it. It took me about a year of working and throwing away until I caught a few sentences, and then I thought, but I hate the idea of the term "the historical novel," not that I hate history and not that I hate the novel, but I hate the way those two words match each other and plunge themselves down into an aspic, a softness; it almost wears a bodice of sorts.

181

What I really wanted to do was to shove that time [1845] right up against the Present. And if I actually shoved anything of the Present up against anything as monumental as an African American slave being in Ireland, it had to be something monumental now.

Rifbjerg: And much of this novel takes place in Ireland. How is the Irish character important to what you are trying to do in *TransAtlantic*?

McCann: Now there were two things that are quite important to the Irish character at this particular point. The rise and fall of our economy, which was curiously called the "Celtic Tiger," whatever that means, is a huge story, and an ongoing story and very important to how we look at ourselves. We were sort of vaguely adolescent about our attitude toward money, and then it all fell down. It was like we had a great big party, like when you're teenagers, and the parents came home, and the chandelier's in the middle of the floor. Well, the parents were the German banks, coming knocking.

The ancient iconography of the Irish imagination has to do with eviction, and so many people have been evicted from their homes and evicted from their sense of themselves, so I wanted to write about that. But also, on the flip side, what I think is the great triumph of contemporary Irish history, and maybe history in general at the end of the twentieth century was the fact that with the aid of a number of people, including Senator George Mitchell, we were able to achieve peace in Northern Ireland. Now it's a tenuous peace, and it's still rocky in lots of different ways, but the fact of the matter is that there is peace there. Now you've seen the riots that were on the TV a month ago. That used to be a daily occurrence in Northern Ireland, but now it's news. And the spectacular news of that it is now news.

Rifbjerg: What connection did you mean to make between Frederick Douglass and George Mitchell?

McCann: I wanted to take those two moments of two great American statesmen moving to Ireland and taking the war out of the machine. Although Frederick Douglass was interested in taking the war out of the moral machine, he dared to talk about abolition, but what Mitchell was doing was taking the literal war out of the machine. In the center I wanted something that bridged those two, and I discovered, or re-remembered, the story about Alcock and Brown, and in 1919 they had gone across from Newfoundland and landed in a bog in Ireland, after taking the capability of war out of the machine called the Vickers Vimy.

So when all those things really came together, I was interested in this notion of fiction and nonfiction. These are nonfiction events, what we classically call nonfiction, but I also wanted these events to belong to what we call the corners of human history. These were the stories of three men, but what about the women who not only suffered it and endured it and created it in many ways? If anything needed to be said about the peace process in Northern Ireland, it has to be said it was the women who wanted it much more than the men did. The women who created it in the 1970s, like Mairead Corrigan [(Northern Ireland) and Betty Williams (Britain)], who won the Nobel Peace Prize, said, "Enough of all this ridiculous slaughter, enough of this butchery. Let's try to come to some kind of accord after thirty years of immediate violence but over seven hundred to eight hundred years of ongoing war."

Rifbjerg: Can I say for those here who have not read the novel, since it's just out, that it is almost impossible for me to understand how you can write such a novel because it's so complex as you can hear when you spell it out like this, but where does it start, with the image of Douglass in Ireland? Is it coming out of your longing to write about Ireland? Is it an image, a word, a sentence, or is it the nature of Douglass?
McCann: It was a picture of Douglass originally and knowing that it had to go right up to the present because I had to make him real and be there now. And there is an African scholar who appears at the end of the novel, coming from Kenya, to make sense of all this. In fact, originally I was going to write from the point of view of that scholar—you should never bring in a new character at the end of a novel, but I do. But I've known him for quite a while.

Most novelists will tell you it's like trying to solve a problem in complex mathematics: you're completely confounded by the fact that you can't do this, but you must do this, because there's a problem there in front of you and it's something which must eventually be solved. And then one day, in various fits and starts, it occurs to you, "Ah, Eureka, and the bath water just rises. Ah, it was so easy! Why didn't I understand it was going to be just that way?" To lay it all out beforehand, I couldn't do that. Part of it is just going on an adventure and finding out where this particular book is going to lead you. The terror of it is that you just don't know where it's going to lead you. And you hope that you're going somewhere at the end.

Rifbjerg: And when I was reading *Let the Great World Spin*, which is also chapters or small short stories, I fell so in love with each story that when it ended I thought, Come on, could we go on here, must I interest myself in new people now that I've fallen in love with these women? So do you ever think of the hardship you're giving the reader of making characters so interesting and likable that the reader wants to stay with them?

McCann: Maybe I don't have stamina. No, I like the idea John Berger talks about: "Never again will a single story be told as the only one."

Rifbjerg: I quoted that!

McCann: It's a beautiful idea. Michael Ondaatje actually quotes it also, I think at the start of *The English Patient* or maybe *In the Skin of the Lion*. But what it's talking about essentially is that [storytelling] is kaleidoscopic, and we must look at it from several different angles. Part of our privilege right now in this internet age is that we can look at things from a number, if not dozens, if not hundreds of different angles.

I remember writing a novel called *Dancer* which is a fictionalization of the life of Rudolf Nureyev, and there are at least a hundred different points of view and different characters in that novel. I was just trying to take all these things and join them together and say there is a coherence here, whether it's one I impose myself, or whether it's one the world imposes, or the reader imposes herself or himself. That's kind of important to me.

But who knows where the novels come from. I have no clue. Maybe I'll get one tonight. Actually I thought of something while I was out swimming this afternoon.

Rifbjerg: Do you write that down? Or do you count on remembering?

McCann: I write a lot of things down in a notebook, but then I never look at the notebook afterwards. It's almost like the physical act of writing it down forces you to remember.

Rifbjerg: I've read somewhere that you write in a cupboard. Why would you do that?

McCann: I'm in the closet, basically. No, I have an office. It's about one-hundred-and-twenty square feet, not too large, but I had a friend come in, who's a brilliant carpenter, and I had him build this beautiful desk; it has moving parts and bookshelves that come out underneath it. But there was a cupboard there, and I said I'm going to put the desk around the cupboard because there would be no way to access the cupboard. And then one day I looked at the cupboard and said, That looks like a good place to sit, and I just slid in there, and now, yes, I write in a cupboard, with my legs out front and the cupboard on each side. My friends come along and write nasty messages on the wall to me, but it's good to sit in there because it concentrates the vision and I have nothing to distract me. Except my kids, slipping notes in under the door, saying, "Let's go."

Rifbjerg: The reason why I mention it is that when you tell about how you've written this book *TransAtlantic* I wouldn't be able to make all these ends meet. When you have Frederick Douglass, do you write the entire Frederick Douglass chapter?
McCann: Yes. Almost the way it appears now in the novel is the way that I wrote it. I am interested in shifting things around, but I do think that every word that comes at any particular point is affected by the words that have gone before it. So it's desperately, desperately important to get the words and the texture of the words right.

So the novel starts out with a plane journey and coming in and you land, or crash-land in Ireland. Then Douglass has sort of crash-landed himself in Ireland and then Mitchell comes along and then the women come along. So there's madness behind it, or there's method behind the madness, or madness behind the method too.

Everybody says you should write what you know, but if I wrote what I knew, it would be infinitely boring. I don't want to read about what I know.

I had the world's very worst thing that can ever happen to a novelist: I had a very happy childhood. My Dad wasn't drunk, my Mother didn't run off with the milkman. She might have wanted to but she didn't.

I used to laugh with Frank McCourt, I'm sure as many of you know, the great Frank McCourt, who I miss dearly the four years he's been gone, I used to laugh with him and say, "You've got all the fuckin' misery in Ireland, and there's none for me. I've had to invent it all." I was there the week he died, and he was writing stuff down on a plastic board. I used to go out with him and we'd have some drinks, with his wife Ellen and my wife Allison. I'd write things on his board because he hadn't full use of his voice. I wrote: "When and where are you going to go dancing now?" because he knew he was going. He was in a wheelchair in a hospice on 92nd Street and Third Avenue, and he took the board and was wheeled out onto the balcony where he took about a half-hour to write down his response, which I still have on my wall. He wrote: "I'll go dancing every Sabbath, and next Sabbath it'll be Upstairs—which was true because he was dead by the next week—and I will go dancing with the Great J.C. and Mary M[agdelene] and the Twelve Hot Boys." And then the last thing

Frank ever wrote, which I think is absolutely beautiful, is: "And in the morning all will be forgiven."

He was one of those writers who wrote absolutely about himself, and he would try to write fiction. He would say, "McCann, how do you do this stuff?" And I would say, "McCourt, how do you do this about yourself?" because there was no right way or wrong way to write anything, whatsoever. There is a false impression that there are rules out there in the whole writing world to be followed. But no, there are no rules whatsoever. The beauty of it is that things just break the rules constantly.

I try to say to my students, "You should not write about what you know because it'll bore the pants off you, or maybe you'll have a novel and a half. But you have to write toward what it is you really want to know." So you explore, and you go places. You go on adventures, and you fail, and you fail, but part of it is the excitement of embarking on something new. It's also about keeping yourself alive, and having a laugh, and not getting too serious about yourself, and exploring some new territory.

Rifbjerg: Do you laugh when you write?
McCann: Laugh when I write? I cry most of the time when I write. No, but I do have a laugh in my life. I had an interview with one of my favorite writers, Michael Ondaatje, and I had to interview him at the New York Public Library. And I said, "What the hell am I going to do? I have to ask him a good question to kick things off. I need to knock him sideways somehow so I can throw him off guard." So we opened up, everybody applauded because he was Michael Ondaatje, and I said, "So are you happy?" And he said, "Do you mean am I happy in life, or in writing?" And I said, "Both."

And from there we launched into the difference it means to be a writer, to be conscious of the act of writing but also to be someone who is alive in the world. And I hate the idea that you have to be a writer as you walk down the street, and you see something, and you immediately have to think, Ooop, that's fodder for my fiction. I think that's wrong. So in my immediate life, my kids will never recognize themselves in my fiction, my mother will never recognize herself in my fiction, except they're all buried there. Part of it is that you go to that weird place of desire to understand something new, and in the end you only ever realize it's only what you've written that you inherently know anyway. But that's part of the joy because you're not recycling all the tired tropes. I don't know if that will change; maybe someday I will write about myself, but really I find it quite boring. I live on the upper east side of New York. I don't even live in Brooklyn, partly for the kids. Or the Bronx. Don DeLillo lives in the Bronx.

But I do not want to write about living on the upper east side; it bores me. I like my life, and I live my life and write there. But I write toward other-ness because I want to prod myself awake and live these other lives. And it's fun to wake up in the morning, look at myself, and say, "Jeez, I don't wanna spend the next twenty-four hours with you. Let me go into my little cup-board and become something else."

And that seems to me to be part of the joy of it. But then, you have to be a realist and you have to say, "Well, the world is a very tough, uncompromis-ing, very often brutal place, and you have to paint it that way, even if that's not what you know yourself in your immediate surroundings.

Rifbjerg: Someone described your prose as full of "radical empathy." I thought that was fantastic.

McCann: That comes from a charity that I'm working with called Narrative 4, which Ian McEwan and others have contributed to. We started this new organization, which is trying to bring kids from all over the world, to come together, not just to tell each other stories, because anybody can tell sto-ries in lots of great storytelling organizations, but to exchange stories, which is different. To step into someone else's shoes you tell my story, and I tell yours, and I give you responsibility for my story and take responsibility for your life in telling this particular story in small groups, kids from Gaza, kids from Belfast, kids from Chicago, kids from Newtown, Connecticut, getting together and walking in somebody else's shoes, because the big problem right now is the failure to be empathetic. We don't really understand what it means to be someone else. That's why good readers come in, that's why good reading is absolutely necessary, and good writing is so absolutely necessary because it's one of the times we get to step very fully into the obsession, the neurosis, the awfulness of being somebody else. But also it is classically a nonviolent way of living, that you can experience somebody else's trauma, but don't come out with a scar at the end of it all. So ultimately, all good sto-rytelling to me is about "radical empathy." And all good reading is about radi-cal empathy because you imagine yourself into the shoes of someone else.

Rifbjerg: I tried to explain to someone what it was like to read your novels, and I would say that there are many terrible things happening, but there is a big heart beating all the time.

McCann: I don't know what it is, but for some reason I write a lot about mothers, and in particular, their sons. In *Let the Great World Spin*, I wrote about a woman called Claire; she lives on Park Avenue. That was interesting for me.

Many years ago, I wrote about the homeless people who lived in the subway tunnels of New York, I stayed with them. I didn't really live with them, but I lived with them on and off for a couple of weeks. Most of my early work was with what you would classically call the dispossessed. And when I wrote the Claire section it was the first time I wrote about a really wealthy person. And I said, "I don't really want to do this, but this woman literally lives around the corner from me, 75th and Park Avenue."

She started to create herself, if you will, or I started to create her, but it felt much more like she created herself. She was really interesting to me, and I liked her. And I didn't resent her wealth because she had what all of us have, which is a real grief at the heart of things. She'd lost her son in Vietnam. It was fun to write her and explore her, and I think she led me in many ways to write the book. My German editor Thomas Uberhoff was instrumental in this in that he said, "I really like this character Claire. Why don't you explore some of that stuff?" And I did.

And that's interesting to me too because when I write something I like to throw it out there and have lots of different people read it. But you have to be pretty tough because some people will say, "This is shite."

My wife is my best reader. She's absolutely fantastic. When she reads something, she'll say, "It's good." Just that.

I'll tell you a really funny story. This one's true. I think it was about twelve years ago, and I had come out with a novel called *Dancer*. I was still struggling and getting by, and very worried about how the book would be received. I was out on Long Island, and I had all these bags with me, and I got on the train and then on the subway—*Dancer* had just come out—and I dropped my book *Dancer*, and I started to put it in my bag. This woman turned to me and said, "What are you doing?" I said to myself, "Jeez, this isn't my book. She has my book, right?" I said, "Well, what do you think of that book?" [McCann shakes his head to indicate No.] She says, "I can't get into it." And I said to myself, "Fuck." She said, "Why?" And I said, "Because my brother read it. He really liked it." That was one dagger.

The second one came about two minutes later, when she got off at 42nd Street, and turned at the door and said to me, "But have you read *The Kite Runner*?" [Laughter] Talk about getting a good dose of humility. But it is sometimes good to have people tell you what they don't like. It's tough. But when a book is out there and published, you don't want someone to come along and say something, but when it's still raw . . .

Rifbjerg: . . . when it's still movable . . .
McCann: Right, when it's still movable, it's a good thing to throw it around and see how people react. They don't always agree.

I remember when John Berger, whom I love, suggested a cut in a novel, which I didn't like, I carried that around with me for a long, long time, terrified that I would disappoint him by leaving it in. I left it in, because I thought it was right, and afterwards he said to me, "You were right to leave that thing in." So you go with your gut. In the end the only person who is responsible for your book is you yourself, and you give it to the readers, and they take it and go elsewhere. But you're the one who is going to have it deal with it, good or bad.

Rifbjerg: Is it always best for you to have characters from real life mixed up with . . . I mean, was Claire someone who lived around the corner?
McCann: Claire is completely invented. The weird thing is that I gave an interview to the *Atlantic Monthly*, and I said to the reporter, "Writing about real people shows a real failure of the imagination." About six months or a year later, I was writing about Rudolf Nureyev.

Rifbjerg: That's why you don't want to say you're never going to write about yourself. Why did you become a writer?
McCann: I became a writer because . . . my Dad was a writer, wrote twenty-seven books and it broke his heart he'd never written fiction. He was a really very successful journalist in Dublin, and grew roses, and wrote about wine—this is not a classic Irish upbringing, is it? Wine and roses? He would go to America and would lecture about roses.

And he got a gold medal from the American Rose Society. But the point of the matter was that he would go to America and be gone for three weeks at a time. We were terribly lonely as kids, we missed my father. When I was twelve or thirteen, he came back with Kerouac and Brautigan and Burroughs and Ferlinghetti—and he would give me these books. I would read them, and that's what made me want to be a writer. I started as a journalist. One never knows why one wants to be a writer. I think that if you know too early that might be a problem—you direct yourself too much towards it.

Rifbjerg: What about the word "forgiven" which you were mentioning in the context of Frank McCourt—or "forgiveness"—because there are a lot of your characters who deal with faith in one way or another.

McCann: I suppose I am obsessed by faith. I talked with a Danish journalist just today about the notion of faith. I'm really sort of scared about talking about all of this because I really don't talk about it much in public, but he made me think about a number of different things about myself, including the fact that I do have faith, but I disguise it in all sorts of ways. Mostly my idea of faith is embedded in the notion of stories. I have a faithfulness and a belief in the idea that our stories are the things that matter. The reason our stories matter is that we are actually valuable, which is a sort of faith in itself. But I'm not talking about Catholic faith, I'm not talking about being Buddhist, about being a Protestant, an Episcopalian, but having faith in the notion that you can tell a story and that your story eventually matters. No matter how old you are or where you come from, or how rich you are or how poor you are—that was a revelation to me, thinking that poor people have more valuable stories than rich people, not necessarily—but stories are the place where our democracy actually occurs. A true democracy, that's not tainted by rules or anything, but good stories, and we all get together because we want to tell good stories.

Rifbjerg: Can you explain this notion of democracy? How can you say that that is where democracy is?

McCann: You know, there's no autocratic thing that says one story is better than the other. There's no Olympics for storytelling, there's no gold medal. I mean, there are awards for good books, and that's all fine and good, but one story that maybe hits somebody really hard, perplexes someone else, so there's no one Great Story. But the fact of the matter is that everybody has a story to tell.

It's a very easy thing to say—everybody has a story to tell—but it's true. I learned this when I was twenty-one. I was on a bicycle trip across the United States, because I had nothing to write about. Then I started meeting all these people. They'd all come to me in these weird towns and campsites down by the river or in the mountains, and they'd always open up with the same thing: "Where are you going?" And I'd say, "Well, I'm going across country on a bicycle," how many punctures I'd had and all that kind of stuff, but eventually, sometimes it would take five minutes, sometimes a half-hour, sometimes it would take even more, but they would begin telling me their own stories. It was as if vicariously they knew they had to give me the story, and I would take it, own it, take it down in my belly, and bring it elsewhere. And it wouldn't have any impact on them at home because I was going down the road, and they had to tell me the story, so I learned lots of things while I was traveling like that.

Part of it was learning how to listen, which is really a pain in the ass right now because the more I travel and the more I speak it's really me who's speaking and I'm not listening as much. I wish I were listening more, to be honest, so I try as much as is possible, outside of this sort of surrounding, to listen to people.

Rifbjerg: But not because you need more stories?
McCann: Well, that's just because it becomes part of the DNA. I don't want to be a magpie and steal someone's story and run away with it. That doesn't interest me whatsoever. In fact, I've only done it once, and I felt really bad about it. In an early short story ["Through the Field" about a Texas juvenile delinquent who killed his lover's husband] I sort of stole somebody's true story, and I always felt really bad about it.

Rifbjerg: What is the difference between making a story you heard into a part of your own fiction and telling . . .
McCann: When you create a fiction of it, that original story will enter it, but creating a fiction also liberates you to make a story bigger and better than the original story. But if you're too faithful to the original story, for me anyway, but maybe not for everybody, it restricts the fictional story, tightens it. It chokes off some of the air.

Rifbjerg: But I suppose it also has to do with the language, everybody has the ability to tell a story better or worse, but not everybody has the language.
McCann: Well, that's good. If we did, then we'd all be writing books. Certain people have an ability to do it. Certain people have an ability to throw a baseball at 105 MPH. Certain people have an ability to do a Brazilian flip over the tops of their heads, and other people have an ability to tell stories.

I don't think the writer is better or worse at telling a story than anybody else. I do hate the privileged position of the artist when he or she gets going and she or he pretends it's all so holy and difficult for them, living up in their ivory tower. That annoys me. Yes, it's difficult, it's not the easiest thing in the world. But lots of things are difficult. You know, driving your ferryboat, driving a taxi, or making that painting [hanging in the interview room].

This is the thing: You should do what is most difficult for you. That's a good rule in storytelling. My friend Nathan Englander, a wonderful novelist, I'm sure you know him, he says, "The inexecutable is all I'm interested in." He just sets himself a course that's pretty tough, and then he comes out the far end.

And you never achieve it, of course. When you're writing this essay at school, this essay or poem, and it's going to be brilliant no matter what, but the work is never as good as what you want it to be. I would say, quite categorically that every book I've written has fallen short of what I wanted it to be. And that's a good thing . . .

Rifbjerg: . . . because that's what makes you go on.

McCann: Yes, because I think of Beckett, who everybody thinks of as a great pessimist. But really he's a very funny writer, and in the end there was something innately optimistic about him saying, "No matter. Try again. Fail again. Fail better." "Can't go on, must go on," you know. I think Beckett was winking at the world, especially when they called him so dark. I think he had a little bit of a smile behind all of that. He was one of the greats.

Making It Up to Tell the Truth: An Interview with Colum McCann

Alison Garden / 2014

From Symbiosis: A Journal of *TransAtlantic* Literary and Cultural Relations. 1 May 2014.
Reprinted with permission.

Alison Garden indicates that she had the great pleasure of interviewing Colum McCann at the Ulysses Pub in New York, sitting exactly halfway between the Irish tricolor and the US flag. She would like to thank the Arts and Humanities Research Council for the funding which made this interview possible and Colum McCann for generosity with his time and thoughts, and allowing her to publish this interview.

Alison Garden: A recent critical companion to your work, Eoin Flannery's *Colum McCann and The Aesthetics of Redemption* (2011), places you within the Irish literary tradition, whereas another, John Cusatis's *Understanding Colum McCann* (2010), considers your fiction as part of a series of books entitled "Understanding Contemporary American Literature." How would you respond to this and how would you position yourself within the literary landscape; do you find national labels enabling or restrictive?

Colum McCann: It's nice to be considered a part of both, and straddle the two. Michael Ondaatje has this thing called the "international mongrels of the world." He's a classic example for me. He was born in Sri Lanka, educated in England, moves to Canada, but writes his first book about a jazz singer in early twentieth century New Orleans. To me that's a perfect collision, and that's the way I see my fiction: not operating within any specific national boundaries. When it comes down to it, when you're finally asked what sort of writer you are—other than just a writer—and you have to put a label on it, I have to be an Irish writer. I come from that tradition. I was born into it. I still plow it. But what interests me is the idea that you might be able to break form and break ideas of national landscape and break borders, and so, for example, write a novel about a Russian ballet dancer and have it operate within the sphere of Irish literature, as I tried to do in *Dancer*. So it can be interpreted in an Irish context, it can be interpreted in a Russian context, it can be interpreted in an American context, or even in the context of being an "international mongrel." So I am quite happy to think that all of these things operate for me: which is kind of greedy in a way!

Garden: No, it's not greedy, not at all. Following on from that then, do you think there is something about being Irish, given Ireland's long history of emigration, that means that your national identity is always already more fluid and transnational?

McCann: I would say so, yes. Yes. I come from a country that has always been leaving in one sense or another. Part of the sadness of the Irish character is the very fact that we have such a relationship with leaving. I'm not sure that the Irish identity is more fluid because of this or if there are other factors too—we're a small nation, we're non-threatening, we fit in easily, we adapt. But we can also be very narrow-minded and try to enforce our identity on other people. Sometimes we become more Irish when we go abroad. This is a little sad, but it's also the emigrant trying to remember. Sometimes I think we emigrate precisely because we want—and need—to remember. Joyce said, in a letter to the English painter Frank Budgen, that he had been so long out of Ireland that he could all at once hear her voice in everything. Also there is the notion that we can be very territorial about our past. But in essence I think we are a fluid people. Certainly I like the idea of being transnational and at the same time cleaving to where I came from. And I think we are held together by our culture. Storytelling is the glue of a scattered people. We need our stories to hold us together.

Garden: You've also mentioned in other interviews that you consider yourself both Irish and a New Yorker. Cities have traditionally been characterized as more cosmopolitan and multicultural; do you think it's easier to associate with a city than a nation?

McCann: Well, with this particular city it's easier because with New York it is such an international landscape. It's one of the few cities in the world where you can land and immediately have an allegiance to New York, you can become a New Yorker almost on your first day. You can't become a Glaswegian on your first day, I don't think, or a Dubliner on your first day. That's part of the fluidity that I suppose I've been looking for, or where I feel comfortable in that fluidity: because this is a transnational place. I have more of a difficulty with the idea of being an American writer. So instead, I say I'm a New Yorker. Again there is a greediness here: I don't want to be labeled American, but I want the benefit of being in New York. "Do I contradict myself? Very well I contradict myself." It's my Whitman moment. "I contain multitudes."

Garden: You're just as perceptive writing about a multi-ethnic Ireland as you are a multi-ethnic US. Is the multiracial, multicultural landscape of your prose an aesthetic effect for you, or a genuine reflection of the world you see around you?
McCann: It is reflective of the world around me, but when it gets put in a literary periscope it becomes a deeper issue because books themselves have their borders, they have their boundaries: they have their first page and they have their last page; they have a beginning and they have an end. Yet one's cultural ideas and one's cultural identity are more fluid than the books. But if the books are written in such a way that they have openness to them; what happens is that they can reflect those cultural ideas. I think that an Irish writer confronting a multi-ethnic New York is also writing about Ireland—even if he or she doesn't mention Ireland once in the text. We are allowing Irish readers to say that our experience of elsewhere is valid too. Our experience of Brooklyn informs our experience of Sherrif Street, Dublin.

Garden: In your new novel, *TransAtlantic* (2013), as with some of your other work, most notably *This Side of Brightness* (1998), you explore the intersections between the Irish (and Irish-American) and African-American communities. In *TransAtlantic*, much is made of Frederick Douglass as "the Black O'Connell," for example, in reference to the important relationship between Douglass and Daniel O'Connell, the campaigner for Irish Catholic Emancipation in the late-eighteenth to mid-nineteenth century. Do you think the two groups share a particular affinity?
McCann: In *TransAtlantic* I take the story of Frederick Douglass arriving in Ireland [at the beginning of the Irish famine in 1845], and then in 2011 there's a character who comes into the story—a Kenyan named David Manyaki. He rescues a house and a letter that have been moving fluidly between these two sides of the Atlantic. So the narrative kind of goes back to a form of Douglass, but it's a confident young Kenyan intellectual who lives in Dublin. I don't know what that means or why it occurred. I suppose I have been exploring the relationship between Irish and African people for

quite a while now. I cannot pinpoint a moment when it occurred to me that this is what I wanted or needed to do. It began when I started writing *This Side of Brightness*. Part of the function of that blurring between the Irish and African-American was purely logical; when I was in the tunnels [underneath New York City], hanging out with the homeless people, the vast majority of them happened to be African-American. If I was going to write an honest novel, it would have to confront some of the African-American experience. So I braided in the Irish experience with the African-American experience through the marriage between two of my characters. So part of that was just because of story and not due to any ideology or intellectual bent that I thought would work. So in a way it was an obsession born out of the practical. But the further I get away from it, the more I realize that I do think that there is this touchstone of common experience there between the two communities. I am aware that you can do that with many cultures. You know, the Irish and the Greeks; the Irish and the Swedes, the Irish and the Colombians. But there is a particular identification between the Black and the Green, if you will. The idea of oppression. The idea of belonging. The idea of staking a claim to a piece of territory. Even if you talk about Northern Ireland and how we organized our civil rights marches, how we organized our civil rights dialogue—the murals of Frederick Douglass in Belfast; murals of Miriam Makeba, Stokely Carmichael, Martin Luther King; they went through the streets of Derry singing "We Shall Overcome": you know, taking inspiration from the American civil rights movement. So there is an identification—whether it is logical or not is another question: one hopes it's not sentimental.

Garden: That was a great answer, thank you. What is it about Eastern and Central Europe that attracts you? Both *Dancer* (2003) and *Zoli* (2006) deal with numerous countries from the region, including the former Soviet Union and Czechoslovakia.

McCann: Well, originally it was just because, again, it was a story that obsessed me. I'm generally corralled by images rather than ideas. So the image that led me to write *Dancer* came from a story told to me by a young man in Dublin. He told me that when he was seven years old, his family got his first TV. At first there was no reception and his father, a drunk, beat the living daylights out of him in frustration. But the next day my friend, Jimmy, plugged the TV into an extension cord and carried it out onto the balcony of the flats. The very first image that came on the TV was Rudolf Nureyev dancing, and he fell in love with him. And I thought, what an

incredible story—about Dublin, about fathers, about culture, about celebrity, and about Rudolf Nureyev. But I also knew that it would never fit into
the larger part of Nureyev's "official" historical biography. It deserved to be
told, but it was too "anonymous" to be part of his official history. Yet I knew
down deep in my bones that fiction operates in those anonymous moments.
Those moments are, in fact, the lifeblood of good stories. I was also aware
that fiction could tell a story as powerfully as non-fiction or "history." Part
of the challenge, for me as a writer, is to find the anonymous moment and
to insert it into the larger historical frame and for it to make sense as part
of this larger historical frame. A fiction writer as an unacknowledged historian, if you will. Making it up to tell the truth.

Garden: That actually leads in very nicely to my next question. You've said
that in your work you try to give voice to the anonymous other, and I was
wondering if you could talk about that further. What is the relationship, for
you, between history and fiction?
McCann: I think you've got to bring it down to the notion that history is
written by the winners—and this is a notion that's been around for a long
time. And also the notion that history is a series of agreed-upon lies; and
that generally history is "agreed-upon" at a higher level than most people,
like you and me, will operate in. So if we bring the history back down to
earth and if we put it in the small house, or the field, or the factory, if we
put history in these places, it becomes a new sort of history. A true history
that wasn't legislated before; it doesn't mean that one history is necessarily better than the other. You can see it is a sort of—and this is interesting
although it's off the top of my head!—a sort of Celtic pattern: you know the
outside circle, then coming slowly, slowly, slowly into the center circle. I
would always find the ordinary person at the very center of that Celtic pattern. I like that idea. The wider circles are written by the politicians and the
corporations and the supposed "winners." They have controlled the story
for a long time. We have to learn to give it back to the proper owners of
history—the ordinary person. I think it's the job, the real job, of the fiction writer—or the poet, or the playwright or the journalist—to go in and
discover the value of that supposedly anonymous life and then insert it into
that larger historical narrative, if you can. To make sense of, and retell, the
story over again. John Berger says, "Never again will a single story be told
as if it were the only one." So for centuries we've told stories as if only one
of them exists, but so many of them exist. There are so many facets. Every
story is many stories. And this goes to the heart of the democratic notion

of storytelling; that storytelling is the purest democracy that we have. With storytelling there need be no regard for borders, no regard for boundaries, no regard for wealth: everyone has a story. You have a story; I have a story; the woman down the street has a story. We all have a need to tell it, a desire to tell it, a compulsion to tell it: we have to tell it. Enter the poet or writer who acknowledges that, and then we can start to reframe the story.

Garden: I think that's a really exciting way of looking at literature. I agree with it a lot; of course, literature can be political and a force for change, but people working in and with literature are often put under pressure to defend it and its role in society. In many ways, it has the ultimate role in society. But moving on. In an interview with Michael Ondaatje, you asked him if he thought content dictated form. Do you?

McCann: Yes. What it all comes down to is language, and language has the power. The way you put the language down on the page will eventually reveal to you the structure of your story and the form of your story. It all comes from the soil of language. And it's also about embracing mystery. Mystery joining things together. Letting the content flow so that it finally finds the right form. The more experimental, or the more open, you're prepared to be with the fact that you don't really always know where you're going to go, or what's truly going on with your own thoughts, the richer your work will be. It's about being open to mystery. Which sounds kind of twee, or new age-y, but I don't think it really is. When it's properly examined, language gives us the vessel that eventually reveals the way the story should be told. That means you have to be open to poetry, you have to be open in all sorts of ways. Having an idea is all well and good—we can all have an idea—but we can't all write *Ulysses*, unfortunately.

Garden: If we think about your use of literary form, your novels are quite unconventionally constructed, and you've also written two collections of short stories. I was wondering about your use of the short story as the form you used to reflect on Northern Ireland in *Everything in This Country Must* (2000). You've mentioned Benedict Kiely's *Proxopera* (1977) and Seamus Deane's *Reading in the Dark* (1996) as being key texts for you in illustrating what life is like, and was like, in the North of Ireland. Obviously Deane's text isn't a collection of short stories, but it reads a little like it could be, consisting of often disconnected episodic fragments. I was curious to see if you consciously used the short story as a means of slotting your own work into that tradition?

McCann: I wrote *Everything in This Country Must* just after having completed *This Side of Brightness*, which had been considered very much an American novel, whether rightly or wrongly. And part of me bristled that people thought I was an American novelist and that I'd left my country behind. Some of the most informative years for me were between the ages of seven and twelve when I spent a lot of time up North on my mother's family farm. So I thought, in order to re-prove my Irishness, I'm going to go back into the heart of the matter and the most overarching national question, for me, at that time was: What is going on in Northern Ireland? Why does this exist? How do we negotiate it? I didn't consciously go with short stories, but I had a few ideas that I wanted to work on. I wrote the story "Everything in This Country Must" first, then I wrote "Hunger Strike," then I went back in and inserted the story "Wood," which has a different political slant to it. I was trying to talk about young people and how their political consciousness gets formed. In fact, in some ways I think it's my favorite little book; partly because it's my orphan book and doesn't always get read. It's also because it goes to the heart of the political question, for me, anyway. Also, the Irish are good at the short story.

Garden: Absolutely. I have a bit of theory I've been working on as short stories as a form of literary anti-colonial protest, because the English realist novel has been so closely associated with imperialism, and I think perhaps this is why the short story has done so remarkably well in Ireland and also in the United States, in the earlier twentieth century at least.
McCann: That's a very interesting notion. I think you're possibly correct here. If you take many of the great Irish novels, you'll see that they're written in numerous voices, or from numerous standpoints, with a narrative generosity, whereas the traditional English novel tends to have that one voice, one tone, one movement. There's nothing wrong with it, but it does have a confidence to it, a touch of Empire about it, if you will; a sort of "I have my story to tell and this is it," and it doesn't waver. A lot of Irish novels tend to be digressive, they tend to spin in different directions and don't have a specific fulcrum along which they progress. I think that ties in with notions of colonialism, the experience of being colonized. It also ties in with language: the Irish language was taken away from us. One of the ways that Joyce thought about it was, "I will take this language that was given to us and I will re-appropriate it and remake it." I'm sure that ties in with your argument.

Garden: Yes, definitely, and I think that's what short story writers were doing with the novel, re-appropriating it and making it work in completely different ways.

McCann: I have this idea that the short story is a universe and a novel is too, except the short story is an imploding universe and distils down to a very tight ball of energy; the novel is an exploding universe, sending out shrapnel in lots of different directions. I miss the short story. I have been writing novels recently. Some of it just comes down to the very vulgar notion that you have to sell books, and novels sell more than collections of short stories do. I have kids to feed. "Children pry up our rotting bodies with cries of 'earn, earn, earn.'" Jim Harrison says that!

Garden: Your treatment of the North of Ireland with *Everything in This Country Must* is actually quite unusual. Joe Cleary has argued in his book, *Literature, Partition and the Nation-State: Culture and Conflict in Ireland, Israel and Palestine* (2002), that the North of Ireland has been dealt with in "hermetically compartmentalized terms" and "not as part of a shared history" that includes both the Republic of Ireland and the UK (77). I think you are very adept at negotiating the relationship between the two Irish states but also gesturing beyond even the borders of Ireland, at an even larger landscape of transnational trauma. I was hoping perhaps you might be able to talk a little about this.

McCann: That's exactly what *TransAtlantic* is about; that is part and parcel of what I wanted to do with my new novel, to pull them together. You have the North and you have the South, and then in the final chapter there's this woman up North who goes to the Republic to try and sell a letter she believes belongs to Frederick Douglass. And so the novel goes to the heart of your question—expanding the border of what is national, crossing it, giving it breath, transcending it, questioning it, and even traumatizing it. To be quite frank, a lot of people didn't think I should write about Northern Ireland. This was after *Everything in This Country Must*. This was bizarre to me, but it's true. I can write a novel about homeless people living in subway tunnels, I can write a novel about a Russian ballet dancer. No problem, but to write about the North? Oh no, no, no. It felt like people were saying to me, you're stepping out of your territory; how dare you? I found this staggering. I mean, it's a hundred miles from Belfast to Dublin, but it's a hell of a lot more from Dublin to New York, it's three thousand six hundred. A lot of things were said to me—"You've no right to go into this territory, leave the North to northerners" was one of them. It was as if I couldn't know it because I didn't live there. But I could know something else, I could know Africa or Alabama, but I should not know the North. "You should leave the North to northerners and the South to the South," was the perception. But it seems to me that the proper process of peace, reconciliation, decency, involves understanding someone else's story, as I was saying earlier, stepping in the shoes of somebody else. In certain ways, I always had to make myself into an outsider to go back in and write about Northern Ireland. If my first book had been about Northern Ireland, it would have been a different thing. Although the final story, "Cathal's Lake," in my first collection of stories, *Fishing the Sloe-Black River* (1994), is about the North. It's one of my favorite stories actually. Thankfully, things have changed recently and the reaction to *TransAtlantic* has been very, very strong, and nobody has said anything to me about overstepping my territory. Maybe that has to do with the peace process itself. Or maybe it's just that our lungs are bigger. We live, finally, in a wider world.

Garden: "Cathal's Lake" is a great story. I know there's some transcultural work going on with it too, which perhaps you could discuss: the layering of a story from the Talmud with a Northern Irish context.
McCann: "Cathal's Lake" is based not on an Irish myth, everyone always thinks of the Irish myth, "The Children of Lir," and even though it is in a certain way, the idea of rebirth through the form of swans, really, it goes back to a Jewish myth of the thirty-six hidden saints, the Lamed Vavniks. In that myth there are thirty-six saints in the world, men—of course, although it should be men and women—humble men, carpenters, farmers, cobblers, and they bear the sorrows of the world. But there's one saint who's lost faith and lost his line of communication with God; and it seems to me that's what Cathal is. Cathal is very much an Irish figure, he's a farmer, but he goes back to this Jewish myth: he is carrying the sorrows of the world, and he has lost his line of communication with God. Nobody needs to know that to read the story, but that's where it came from for me. That was the force through the flower, if you will.

Garden: I think it adds a really interesting element in terms of connecting to a larger transcultural framework of storytelling. I'm not sure if this was intentional or not, but a lot of your stories are, for me, quite evocative of Kafka with their emphasis on the body and trauma as a performative act, particularly hunger and starvation. Is this something that you are consciously aware of? What is it about embodied experience that has such enduring appeal for you as a primary focus in your work?

McCann: Well, the short story "Hunger Strike," from *Everything in This Country Must*, goes right to the heart of Kafka's concerns and work on the body. I wish I could say I was better versed in Kafka than I am. I was, of course, aware of "A Hunger Artist," however. And yes, the body has often been a site of enduring focus for me, especially in *Dancer*. My work spins around the body and how it moves through space. I like the idea that the movement of the body is reflective of the movement of the mind. We become what we are thinking. We move through space, as we move through our imaginations.

Garden: You've noted previously that the Northern Irish writer Benedict Kiely has been a huge influence for you. In your story "Everything in This Country Must," there's an incident where the narrator counts out three bullets. Was this a direct allusion to a similar incident in Kiely's "Bluebell Meadow," where the narrator counts out six bullets?

McCann: No, not consciously, no. I love Kiely. Kiely was very important for me when I was about sixteen, seventeen, and he is still important to me today. He used to hang out with my father. He helped me out when I was in my early twenties and encouraged me with my writing. I would go to his house, and he would appear at the door in his pajamas, at midday, with a bottle of whisky in his hand that he'd have just cracked open, as he'd have finished writing. No matter how late he was up the night before, he was always up at seven in the morning. I think an awful lot of Kiely has seeped into my work, sometimes consciously, sometimes not. I used the three bullets because I wanted the reader to think, first of all that he's shooting at the British Army truck that's leaving, secondly that he's going to shoot himself and then that he's shooting the horse. Just to complicate it at the end. It was a dramatic effect for me.

Garden: I've another specific question about an intertextual allusion. I find the anorexic nun, Brigid, in "Sisters" evocative of the iconic image of the Famine: Bridget O'Donnell and her children. This is just one of many instances in your work where intertextual connections are made to a large range of cultural texts and images. Could you comment on the role of literary influence in your fiction?

McCann: One of the things that I find important is acknowledging this debt to your literary forbears. A lot of writers will claim that these associations to other texts that readers find in their work don't exist, that they're not there. But if they're there for somebody else, it just makes the text richer, so that the literary experience, the critical experience, brings something to the novel that expands it as a work of art. So rather than people thinking that it's wrong or stilted to find some things in the work that weren't intentional, I think it's beautiful. So I'll steal that from you! My line is that we get our voice from the voices of others and even if we haven't read it, it somehow creeps in. I see lots of Irish writers who say things like, "I don't know who Ben Kiely is," and therefore he didn't influence me, which is a sham really, because you're influenced even when you don't realize it. It's like music: you've heard it even if you haven't directly heard it. There's a certain guitar riff that somebody else steals, and it becomes part of the whole fabric of the musical landscape, and you have to acknowledge that you're never there on your own. The idea that you can be sprung from some sort of dry well and somehow have a voice is patently absurd. We are an accumulation of others. Which means that we're also an accumulation of other places. *E pluribus unum.* This is our DNA. We are bound to it.

Garden: I just wanted to go back to an earlier question about your interest in, and use of, the starving body. In *TransAtlantic* you devote lengthy passages to the utter terror and horror of the Famine and its devastating effect. Do you think your earlier works that are not directly about the Famine but include starving bodies, like Brigid in "Sisters" and Corrigan in *Let the Great World Spin*, are also a way of dealing with the traumatic legacy of the Famine?

McCann: It's something that in Ireland we haven't really, truly, properly confronted. Not in the same way that, say, Jewish writers have properly confronted the Holocaust. There's always a vague embarrassment in Ireland about the Famine, as if it's sort of twee somehow; something that's over, and we can forget about it or at least not mention it too much. I think it plays into the narrative of Irish culture in ways we don't even realize, like the Hunger Strikes in the North, for example. If you wanted to shame your landlord, in ancient Ireland, you would go and lie on his doorstep and not eat. It was a form of personal political protest. I think all this inhabits us much more than we will actually acknowledge, which is why *TransAtlantic* tries to pull that stuff out again. Yes, I desperately wanted to write about the Famine. It has ancient echoes for me. In some ways I think that *TransAtlantic* is an alternative history.

Garden: In addition to the bodily trauma that you explore in relation to hunger, you often put your characters through horrendous accidents—car crashes and industrial accidents. There seems to be quite a link between trauma and modernity for you.

McCann: I suppose I do! Hmmm. Part of that has to do with plot and creating a dramatic line that I want for my characters. Is it accidental that it occurs? Obviously not, there's obviously something going on in the back of my mind, but sometimes I don't want to think about it. I use this line from Dostoevsky all the time, that "to be too acutely conscious is a disease"; and if I knew why I did certain things I wouldn't do them again. For example, a few years ago I did an interview where the interviewer mentioned that in my first three or four books I wrote a lot about maps. When I discovered that this was true, I couldn't write about maps again!

Garden: In *Let the Great World Spin* (2009), the year 1974 acts somewhat like a transnational connective tissue. You start off early on with the bomb in Dublin—again, moving the Troubles outside of the North—then you have Philippe Petit's walk between the Twin Towers, and the Vietnam War is an obvious undercurrent too. Petit's walk being used as an allegory for the attacks of 9/11 is interesting in itself. You've talked previously about how you thought about the importance of the words—World, Trade, Center— and it seems to me like you've used all the disparate threads of your novel to weave a very global fabric in response to an event that, it has been widely argued, was dealt with in quite a nationalistic manner. Was this a knowing effort on your part?

McCann: Part of it was an accident that it all took place in 1974. But because everything took place in the same year, you notice the connections, and your mind whirls in exactly the kind of ways that you're talking about. For Ciaran to come out of the bomb in Dublin in 1974 and make his way to the United States and then the legacy of what was happening in Vietnam speaking to what was happening in Iraq in the 2000s, speaks to that tissue that goes between these times and these wars. I think tissue is an important word, because it's not muscle and it's not ligament; it's that other stuff that surrounds them. I was aware of it, yes. I didn't want to become hyper-aware of it. You'll see with *TransAtlantic*, most of these ideas that you're talking about are coming together with *TransAtlantic*. But not in a direct way, because I think it's not interesting to be so direct about it. The reader will discover what their intelligence will allow. For some people the Alcock and Brown section will just be a rattling read about an airplane journey. Others will notice that goes to the heart about peace and decency—and my efforts to "take the war out of the machine."

Garden: I think you can read all of your work as "connective tissues," and this is a vitally important context for your literature. Literary criticism and culture more widely tends to view the world through quite restrictive national paradigms. It's something you yourself have written about; in your introduction to *The Collected Stories of Benedict Kiely* (2002), you said that readers often tend to think of books as having a national identity encoded in their spines and that this wasn't a helpful way of reading literature.
McCann: I think if criticism can embrace itself as a sort of poetry and can rely on some of its own intuition, then it becomes even better. The critic as someone who embraces mystery and contradiction, even in their own arguments. So the criticism can be expansive and generous. So it doesn't focus in and really burn itself down to a particular segment of the page, so that the act of proper critical thinking, if it has an agile relationship to the text, all becomes so much better. It doesn't become polemic or didactic.

Garden: I wanted to ask you actually why the artist has such enduring appeal for you. You frequently explore the experience of artists of various kinds, and yet you never resort to a clichéd representation of the artist as tortured by existential angst.
McCann: It really bothers me when writers propel themselves up on this holy pedestal of "Art" and start rattling on about the difficulty he or she embraces as part of making art. I don't like the idea that the artist is somehow more important than the person who buys the art, or is the subject of that art. If you think about someone like L.S. Lowry, and all his matchstick men, those matchstick men are just as important to the intellectual canvas as Lowry himself. In fact, they endure more. The subject of the art is certainly more interesting than the artist himself. I think that goes back to the idea that you leave your work open; you must leave your work open. That then elevates the position of the "anonymous other." The artist must realize that he or she is not entirely in control. But if you elevate the position of the anonymous, you also elevate the emotional intelligence of the artist, rather than degrading the artist, which gives it a further depth. Am I talking shite? I might be. I'll have to go away and think about it. But I do like the idea that the subject of the art

is as powerful to the creation of it. And that there is more dignity in the work when you don't complain about how hard it is. It should be a joy, even if it is difficult. "The Fascination of What's Difficult" in the Yeatsian way.

Garden: One such prominent artist is the photographer Michael from your early novel *Songdogs* (1995). You've mentioned previously that photography is your favorite art form, but I find that it can be quite problematic—exploitative, even. Susan Sontag famously asserted that it led to individuals establishing a "chronic voyeuristic relation" to the world. How does it fit into your thoughts on art?

McCann: I don't know. I love photography but I will say this: I do not own a camera. I don't believe I should carry a camera around. If I carried a camera around, I would always be taking photographs and I would become hyper-aware of the process. I think it comes back to this notion that you can't let your art intrude on your life in certain ways. You have to go ahead and just live things. But I do think I'm a photographer anyway. I love the idea that you can paint a photograph—which is an absurd notion.

How can you paint a photograph? But that is what I'd like to think of my work as doing: painting a photograph with words. The reader then walks into that photograph, and because you have painted the depth, the experience becomes three-dimensional. I wish I were a photographer, a visual artist, but I'm not. But I try to recreate these things with language.

"In the End, We Write to Say That We Matter": A Conversation with Colum McCann

Earl G. Ingersoll / 2016
Printed with permission.

This email exchange of questions and answers, rather than a face-to-face conversation, was forced upon Colum and me by his need to "escape" from New York and be by himself to "kick start a new novel" and my need to complete work on *Conversations with Colum McCann*. Another writer in the same situation might have begged off to focus on that delicate task of beginning again, but this conversation exists because of Colum's commitment to helping others understand why he writes.

Earl G. Ingersoll: Readers are often curious about where stories come from. The long novella, *Thirteen Ways of Looking*, for example, seems to have come from somewhere else.

Colum McCann: I have to go back a few years here. I remember after writing *TransAtlantic* that I felt fairly exhausted. I had just come off two fairly grueling projects over the course of six years, including *Let the Great World Spin*. I had been running at full throttle, and I knew that I wanted to shake up the journey a little bit. I wanted time to recover. I also wanted the project to be smaller in scope, more local, more intimate. A chance to get my breath back. In other words, I didn't want to step back into something very serious and long-term again. So I thought, ah-ha, short stories. As if that might be easier. Well, guess what? Nothing's easy. But at least short stories—if they fail—fail in a shorter amount of time.

I don't mean to question the power or authenticity of short stories—they are just as powerful as, if not sometimes more powerful than novels—but there's not as much at stake in terms of time or effort. The short story is a sprint, and the novel is a long-haul marathon composed of numerous internal sprints. One is not necessarily *better* than the other, but you're more likely to fail with a novel. Novels are more dangerous. You commit yourself to the idea that you might see two, three, or four years disappear down the rabbit hole. With a collection of stories there will always be a way to pick yourself up and dust yourself off. I like both forms and I don't tend to privilege one over the other.

Ingersoll: I understand that collections of shorter fiction are more difficult to market because many readers don't like to keep beginning a new narrative, with different characters. On the other hand, you started with the collection of shorter fiction called *Fishing the Sloe-Black River.* I don't think I was alone in being blown away by the power of "Through the Field," which Dermot Bolger included in his *Vintage Book of Contemporary Irish Fiction.* Shorter fiction put you on the map of readers' experience with that form.
McCann: Precisely what I love about short stories is the chance to operate in a number of different voices. And that first collection allowed me to enter the map, yes. But it's important to note that before I wrote those stories, I wrote a novel called "Uncle Saccharine" and a non-fiction account of my days in wilderness education called "The Wilderness Llamas." They were both godawful. They are my drawer novels: they will remain forever there. In fact, they should be burned. They failed utterly, but they allowed me a chance to put on some literary muscle. They were written when I was twenty-two, twenty-three.

Ingersoll: Was *Thirteen Ways of Looking* originally going to be a novel?
McCann: Yes. I was actually developing it around the same time that I was developing *TransAtlantic*—don't ask me how, because they are so completely different. But at one stage I had the whole construction down. Thirteen different characters, thirteen different camera angles, thirteen voices, all mathematically interlaced. (The mathematics of fiction has always fascinated me). So I had the point of view of Mendelssohn, the housekeeper Sally James, the waiter, the doorman, Elliot, the detectives, and so on. In fact, the detectives were the breaking point for me. I just couldn't write them. They were stock, they were cliché, they were tight. And frankly the whole thing began to bore the living daylights out of me. I began to hate it. I was painting by numbers. The spontaneity was gone. I wasn't challenging myself. No new territory. And the only voice I liked was Mendelssohn's. So,

after I finished *TransAtlantic*, I went back and rescued his voice and his voice only. And it could have been a novel, I suppose. Certainly some of my publishers wanted it to be, not in America, but elsewhere. But it didn't feel full enough. Nor, to be honest, did it feel good enough. I needed to surround the novella with other stories. That was my duty to my reader. They are symphonic. At least what I intended them to be. I need to be proud of a book. It's my duty to people who are going to read it.

Originally I planned to write thirteen stories but that felt stilted too. I was locking myself in a structural harness. There is nothing I hate more. When I travel—which is what I do when I write fiction—I don't want to go in a tepid tour bus. I want to travel in a wild way. I want it to be raw and surprising. So, in the end, I had to go with my gut feeling . . . and it remained a novella.

But I'm avoiding your question I suppose. I wish I knew, or could properly remember, where the story came from. I do recall reading an essay by my friend Dan Barry in his collection *City Lights* about a murder in a White Castle fast-food joint that was captured on camera, and then reconstructed. There might have been thirteen cameras in that case, I can't recall. But that was the genesis. What might happen if I reconstructed a murder from videotape? But I didn't want to write a murder mystery or a detective story. I'm a snob. I wanted it to be literary. I wanted to explore other notions too—especially what it meant to write poetry. I mean, I'm a failed poet, I suppose. I've always envied the great poets. Always wanted to find the Heaney or the Muldoon within me, but I never could. A part of the story was my examination of this. And it seemed that the Wallace Stevens poem was the perfect way to embark on this sort of exploration.

Ingersoll: When you begin to write, how good are you at predicting that this narrative will be a novel, a novella, or a short story? Is length the only criterion? I ask because Ian McEwan got a Booker for *Amsterdam* and the book-makers were laying odds he'd get a second one for *On Chesil Beach* until there was such an uproar on social media to the effect that this narrative was a "novella" rather than a "novel," even though it was about the length of *Amsterdam*. *On Chesil Beach* lost the race.

McCann: I think this necessity to label is an imaginative failing on the part of the literary world. Mea culpa: I ascribe the failing to myself too. Who cares what form a narrative takes? All it should do is attempt to break your comfortable worldview apart, to bring you somewhere entirely new, to shake you up. This can be done with a six-word story, or a newspaper article, or a sestina, or a thousand-page novel. The only thing that really matters is how the words bump up against each other. It can take any form you like.

Ingersoll: Is it true that you'd written the novella before the horrible assault you went through? During your revising or editing the novella, did you reshape it in light of the assault?

McCann: Yes, I wrote it before that assault in Connecticut. But the key thing is that I edited it afterwards. And yes, I did reshape it while maintaining the essence of the original intention. And it was uncanny really, the fact that I wrote about Mendelssohn's assault in advance of my own. To be honest, my own assault was very serious. I was very lucky. I mean, the doctors said I was fortunate to have avoided brain damage. Mendelssohn dies, of course, but in a way Mendelssohn now lives. This is the beauty of fiction. It's what Joyce talked about—the recreation of life out of life. What a spectacular gift, really—it should knock us to the ground with humility . . . the fact that we can weave something real out of the imaginative realm. Is there anything more humbling than this?

Ingersoll: This collection seems light-years from *Spin* and *TransAtlantic*, a sort of After the Fall, with something like a sense of lost innocence, a beginning again as a writer and as a man who's been forced to see things differently. Does it feel that way to you, or does it feel that way to readers because they know about the assault?

McCann: It doesn't feel that way to me, really. It feels like a natural run-on from the other novels. I don't think I changed my intention as a writer, which is fundamentally to write about grace and beauty in the face of the evidence that this shitty world presents us. My job in these stories is what my job always is—to talk about the violence and the pettiness and the horror and the heartache—and then go beyond that, to peel back the most extreme layer of skin. In so doing we become graceful in our recognition of pain. It finally makes sense to us. I'm not interested in conceding victory to the negative. There is something grander at stake here. And there is something perhaps religious about it too, although I am not a religious man, not in a formal sense anyway. Maybe it's just the proper human instinct towards rescue and meaning. To fight against the barrage of lies and misdirection that constantly assaults us in our everyday lives.

In the end, we write to say that we matter.

As for the assault, well, you know what? When all is said and done, I thumped that motherfucker a lot harder than he ever thumped me. And

I didn't do it in a cowardly way. I didn't crawl up behind him and hit him unawares. No, I told the story. And not only that, but I interpreted the *meaning* of the story. And he—and his wife-beating cowardice—will forever be in the shadow of my words. I thumped him with forgiveness. And afterwards I had the chance to give voice to a lot of people's pain, particularly those women who have not had the chance to have their voices heard before. That was the real challenge. I wanted to speak alongside those women who have been battered through the years. I didn't want to speak *for* them, but *with* them. That's why I wrote about it in the author's note at the end of the book. I had to. It was a real dilemma. I wasn't sure if I should or not. In the end I know, now, that it was the right thing. And even showing the photo of my messed-up face on my website was a huge question mark for me. Should I? Should I not? I'm glad I did. My pain was temporary. His was not.

Ingersoll: As something of a Joycean, I was pleased with the echoes of *Ulysses*. Like Joyce's novel, "Thirteen Ways" is a single-day narrative. Do you recall how Joyce got into your workroom? Or has he always been there?
McCann: I wish I could say that Joyce has always been there. I grew up in an Ireland where people were still a little ashamed of Joyce. Hard to believe nowadays, but there were no Joyce statues in the sixties and seventies, no Joyce industry, no big Bloomsday celebrations. He was the darling of a few, of course, but we were still a conservative country, tied to the Catholic Church. They tore down Eccles Street. They let the Martello towers go to ruin. And despite growing up in a literary household, I wasn't keyed in to Joyce. And I didn't study him in school, either. Not even the short stories. It wasn't until years later—when I went to the University of Texas in my mid-twenties—that I was forced into reading him. I say forced, but really it liberated me. I knew I should have read him but I hadn't. Even on first reading I knew that it was part of my DNA. There are lots of people who make it a badge of honor to say they haven't read Joyce. That's idiotic. Even if you haven't read him, you have. Because he is tangled in the very essence of twentieth-century literature and influenced everything that came after him. His voice is there in all other voices.

Ingersoll: And these gestures toward Joyce are what a reader might expect of a beginning writer, not a writer who has produced such masterpieces as *Let the Great World Spin*, for one.
McCann: You're very kind but I would swap a million *Spin*s for one *Ulysses*. My goal is to truly believe—in fact, *know*—that I haven't written anything of

worth yet. And the "yet" is important here. I want to forever keep failing. I want my last word to be my best one.

Ingersoll: Does this square with what you've said about the nightmare period after a novel has been published and you wake with the high anxiety of "Will I be able to write another novel?" Intensified by your following Joyce in not wanting to do the same novel over again with different names and places, but set yourself new challenges?

McCann: Yes, I'm pretty hard on myself. I like to challenge myself. It's a way of not growing old. The body grows old, the hair falls out, the muscles cramp up, but the soul maintains its fire. Beckett knew that. The vivifying air of always wanting to go one step further. I sometimes get a laugh when I say Beckett was an optimist. I know it sounds absurd, but he was. He grew and grew and grew. The beauty of aging is that we can still continue to pose questions for ourselves. That mental agility. And often we can probe deeper than we used to. What an adventure to go on. The unfinished-ness of it all.

You know what? I have a link with Beckett. My grandmother used to clean his family house when their regular housekeeper was on holiday. My father asked her what Beckett was like and she said he was "a little snot." I love that. Because by the time he got to France he was no longer a little snot, whatsoever. And in the deep end of life he was, I feel, wildly empathetic. He was a realist, of course. And he knew how shitty the world can be. So language became his wall against that simplicity.

Perhaps the greatest wisdom of all is that, finally, we know next to nothing about the world at all. This—as a person who wants to experience so much—exhilarates me. It shows me how expansive the world really is, how elastic our lives can be.

Anyway, yes, every time I finish a novel I'm pretty sure that I'll never be able to do it again. People will find me out. They will recognize the charlatan at work. And so I go deeper and deeper—and try to challenge myself into new territory.

Ingersoll: By the way, I've worked with quite a few interviewed writers and cannot recall any more open in talking about their work and revealing incidents that others writers would be embarrassed to mention in public. I'm thinking about your encounter with the woman who didn't like your novel, I think it was *Let the Great World Spin*.

McCann: Actually it was *Dancer*, yeah. I sat beside this woman on the subway, and I didn't know it, but after a while I realized she was reading *Dancer*, right there, on the 6 train. I didn't tell her who I was, just asked her if she was enjoying it. She said she was having a real hard time getting into it. She asked me if I had read it, and I said, No, but that my brother had, and he loved it. Ah, vanity. And then she asked me, as I got up to get off at my station, if I had read *The Kite Runner?* Now that was a novel I should read, she said. It still makes me laugh.

And, well, let's face it, I'm Irish, I'm a ham. I like the world. I live in two of them: the public me who clowns around and is loud and bellicose and happy (I even sing at parties, for godsake) and the private me who hides away and tries to shape these stories that try to uncover a little secret about the darkness of the world.

I don't even mind getting bad reviews. There was this asshole in England who gave me a hard time about my blurb policy. He said he knew I was a bad writer from my blurbs alone and then he went on to give a very juvenile analysis of *TransAtlantic.* I hope to get to meet him some day. I will buy him a pint. And then I will tell him, straight out, that his was a really badly-written review. Not a bad review, but badly written. I can't wait to see his face. I can see his jowls shuddering from here. Maybe I'm a vindictive bastard, I don't know. But sometimes in order to win you have to lose first.

Ingersoll: Then, there's the amended view of the autobiographical, what seems like a 180-degree turn from your mantra as a teacher/mentor of fiction-writing: Don't write about yourself, write about what you don't know. There's that reference to the Clonkeen Road at the end of "What Time Is It Now, Where You Are?" a sort of in-house wink to those of us who've read your interviews. Could you talk about the autobiographical component in fiction?

McCann: Well, the thing is that I *have* always said you should write about what you don't know. But that is physically and indeed philosophically impossible. One cannot write what one doesn't know. But we must write towards what we *want* to know. And in order to do this we have to fool ourselves into writing what we supposedly don't know. It's a way of unlocking the territory of the subconscious.

Everything I write—especially when I am not writing directly about myself—is about myself. There is no other truth. Every word is autobiographical. That is why we have to attempt to unlock the deep truth.

In many ways *Thirteen Ways* is my most personal book. There are a lot of clues as to who I am, or at least who I appear to be.

I've always believed that in literature we can have as many lives as we want and that it's possible for a different person to occur within myself. I don't want this to sound trite or spacey, because there's something very important on the line here. I believe without fear, or without prejudice, that I can not only understand someone else, but actually become someone else in the act of writing—but only as long as we commit to *honestly* portraying or experiencing those lives. It's not just some funhouse-mirror show where you dial in and become "other." It's about honestly trying to reach the authentic through that which seems, on the surface, inauthentic, or certainly distant. So, to be an urban man and write about a female soldier from Ohio. To be Irish, and write about a Lithuanian-born judge. To be a white man trying to imagine the life of a housekeeper from Tobago.

Most of my work has been built on the premise that I want to be able to express all the currents that flow inside me. To have that agility to reach a state of otherness. In the end, though, every line is autobiographical simply because it has come from me. There is no other explanation. I'm not conducting a literary séance: I am putting the words on the page, and I must take full responsibility for what are, in essence, my words. I have imagined myself elsewhere. But the truth is, I'm not really interested in writing about myself: certainly not the guy who lives on East 86th Street, with three kids, and walks the dog in the morning, god forbid I start writing about that. I suppose there is something weirdly maternal in this desire, to give myself over, unprotected, to the inner workings of my characters. They are not me, but they are me. Sounds like a bad koan, my apologies.

Ingersoll: Having written a book on endings in contemporary fiction, including a chapter on *This Side of Brightness*, I'm impressed with the endings in these stories. The novella "Thirteen Ways of Looking" is in part a "detective story" ending but with a suppressed verdict for the assailant. "What Time" shades off into what seems your own wonder at how narrative elements could be endlessly developed. And there's the tour de force ending of "Sh'khol" where you succeed in convincing the reader that Tomas is gone but bring him back from the dead, almost as though the reader is being drawn into Rebecca's wish-fulfilment, with a finesse which in another writer's hands could have been a Hollywood ending. Similarly, in "Treaty" you seem to be moving Sister Beverly into a revenge-story mode but replace it with her achievement of grace through a mode of reconciliation similar to the events in South Africa after the elimination of apartheid and its horror stories. How conscious are you of ending in these narratives?

McCann: Endings are everything. I worked and worked and worked the ending of "Treaty," for instance. One tries to do it without drawing too much attention. You try to do it with the grace of a dancer—all the elegance showing and none of the pain apparent, but with the very important knowledge that you must go through extreme pain in order to achieve the dance.

Ingersoll: I like your allusion to dance, especially since you said in an earlier interview that even after you wrote *Dancer* you felt you still didn't know anything about dance.
McCann: I learned a lot. That was a three, almost four-year book. I still can't dance, mind you. Two left feet.

Ingersoll: Was "Sh'khol" written after the assault? If so, did the assault make you particularly aware of the vulnerability of your children in the City?
McCann: "Sh'khol" was written before the assault, but again some of it was influenced by the editing process. I worry about my kids all the time. But every parent does.

Ingersoll: And circling back to where we began, "What Time" in part seems your anticipation of an audience member's asking you, "Where do these stories and your others come from?"
McCann: You know, I hate to say this because it sounds so new-agey, but most of the stories are a mystery to me. I don't know where they come from really, and I think I prefer it that way. I have often quoted Dostoyevsky in this respect so forgive me if I am repeating myself: "To be too acutely conscious is to be diseased." What this means essentially is that if you think too much about it, you might lose it, it brings a form of sickness to your work.

Ingersoll: I'm always interested in how writers put together stories in a collection such as this one. You write in your afterword that the novella was written before you became a victim of violence and the last story was written after. Did you deliberately withhold the verdict in Pedro's trial to underscore the point that punitive justice may make the victim's family feel a sense of closure, but Sister Beverly's response of reconciliation, similar to the response of the eight families of the victims of the recent murders in the Charleston church, is an impulse that liberates us from the past?
McCann: Well, as I say, I don't want to be too acutely conscious about this (!), but I think you're right, or at least I hope so. Grace can liberate us from

the past. And herein lies the crux of what I often want to say—I write so that my reader sees. His or her interpretation of the story is always valid. I do not write to lecture or moralize. I write to try to nuance a truth that is already known by the reader.

Of course, there is no one absolute truth. But we are all in this together. I believe in the symphonic intent of literature.

Ingersoll: And one question in closing, what are you surprised by?

McCann: I'm always surprised that I'm here. I'm surprised that I'm answering anyone's questions. I'm surprised that anyone would want to hear my answers. And sometimes I'm surprised by the answers I give . . .

Index

Mahon, Derek, 3, 20
Makeba, Miriam, 61, 196
Mandelstam, Osip, 20, 27
Man on Wire (film), 105
Manyaki, David, 195
Marcus, David, 14
Márquez, Gabriel García, 27
Martello towers, 211
Maudet, Cécile, xii, 145–80
Maxwell, William, 41
McCabe, Eugene, 108, 109; "Christ in the Fields," 108
McCaffrey, Laura, 57–64
McCann, Allison (wife), 17, 27, 39, 52, 85, 94, 101, 185, 188
McCann, Colum: advice to young writers, 21, 90, 95, 186; anecdote of Nureyev on TV, 15–16, 30–31, 146, 196; animals, 172; aversion to stealing stories as a magpie, 191; avoiding excessive consciousness, 135; "The Back Street Kids," 93; being an emigrant, x, 132, 152, 194; being interviewed, ix; bicycle trip and listening to others' stories, ix, 8, 26, 27, 49, 93, 125, 126, 128, 129, 135, 138, 152, 190–91; body movement, 202; book tour, 73; "Cathal's Lake" as favorite story, 7–8, 201; celebrity, 73; "channeling," 97, 103, 105, 168; childhood, 91–92, 185; cinema, 28, 146, 169; creative reading, 67, 117, 145, 169; dance, 97, 215; discarding drafts, 17; early writing, 13–14; editor of *Recorder*, 22; effect on his writing of being a father, 11–12; empathy, xi, 115, 157, 160, 161, 187; endings, 9–10, 215; equality of genres, 15, 93; failing à la Beckett, 4, 21, 27, 28, 33, 95, 110, 143, 192; "fascination of what's difficult," xii, 124, 206; father figures, 164; fear of being unable to write the next novel, 124, 212; fiction/nonfiction, 35, 141–42, 143, 183; fishing, 26, 135–36; frontier, 159–60; getting bad reviews, 213; having an editor, 96; Hennessy Award, 14; history/fiction, 197; home, 136; home office, 98, 184–85; Irishness, x, 69; Irish novel, 54, 100, 199; Irish writer, 28, 193–94, 195; landscape, 28; "mathematics of fiction," 208; maps, 136, 154; "mongrel generation" of writers, 69, 193, 194; Narrative 4, xi, 160, 167, 171, 187; National Book Award, 90, 128, 131; never thought of himself as a humorous writer, 163; New York City, 17–18, 25, 29, 35–36, 39, 89, 100, 194–95; 9/11 novels, 102, 110, 114, 150; not a moralist, 117, 216; not writing about real people, 70, 189; novel as dance, 34; novel as music, 105, 112, 143, 147; "obsessed by faith," 190; optimist/cynic, 136–37, 153; otherness, xi, 53, 104, 127; pacifism, 174–75; photography, 4, 169, 206; pleased his fiction is studied, 108, 171; "poetic realism," 153, 171; poetry, 3–4, 150, 209; pressures on writers, 100, 101; pursuing otherness, 214; readers becoming his story's writers, 9–10, 25, 53, 63, 67, 81, 88, 102, 117, 119, 121, 135, 150, 162, 169, 170, 189, 202, 205, 216; reading drafts aloud, 4, 9; rejection slips, 14; research, xi, 11, 12, 16, 20, 23–24, 31–32, 39, 50, 54, 61, 62, 63, 72, 73, 89, 97, 99, 138, 151; rivers, 26; Romani culture, xi,

51–56, 60, 78, 109, 138, 147, 156; sacred in literature, 155; screenwriting, 10, 15, 67, 68, 97, 133, 167; setting greater challenges in next novel, 212; short story/novel, 200, 207–8; singers, 179n28; "Sisters," 14, 55; social novel, 25, 58; songs, 166–67; story as democracy, 81, 93, 146, 190; storytelling, x, xii, 16, 25, 30, 41, 46, 71, 82, 83, 93, 111, 131, 139, 141, 145, 146, 148, 184, 187, 190, 191, 194, 197–98, 201–2; *Thirteen Ways of Looking* as most personal book, 213; ultimate goal of being read in fifty years, 10–11; violence, 162; welcomes sentiment but fears sentimentality, 163; westward movement, 158; where stories come from, 207, 215; work with juvenile delinquents in Texas, 128–31; writing schedule, 17–18, 99; "writing toward what we want to know," 72, 157, 186, 213

Works: "Breakfast with Enrique," 18; "Cathal's Lake," 8, 21, 152, 158, 201; *Dancer*, x, 15, 30–36, 39–45, 57, 65, 67, 72, 97, 138, 141, 146, 153, 154, 155, 171, 184, 188, 196, 202, 212–13; *Everything in This Country Must*, 4–5, 16, 19–20, 48, 107–9, 198, 199, 200, 202; "Everything in This Country Must," 199, 202; *Fishing the Sloe-Black River*, 3, 7, 11, 14, 51, 70, 95, 103, 151, 201, 208; "Hunger Strike," 16, 115, 133, 138, 199, 200, 202; *Let the Great World Spin*, x, xi, xiii, 84–86, 97, 99, 100, 101, 102–3, 104, 105, 106, 110–22, 124, 133, 134, 135–36, 138, 143, 149, 150, 152, 154, 155, 158, 159, 160, 161, 162,

164, 167, 168, 170, 174, 181, 183, 188, 203, 204, 207, 210, 211, 212; *Songdogs*, 3, 4, 9, 11, 25, 28, 47, 136, 158, 162, 174, 206; *Thirteen Ways of Looking*, x, 181, 207–15; *This Side of Brightness*, x, 4, 5, 6, 9–10, 12, 15, 16, 23–29, 46, 48, 67, 104, 118–19, 126, 138, 154, 163, 195, 196, 199, 214; "Through the Field," 129, 208; *TransAtlantic*, x, 106, 132, 140–44, 148, 151, 157, 158, 174, 181, 185, 195, 200, 201, 203, 204, 207, 208, 209, 213; "Wood," 199; *Zoli*, x, 51–56, 57–63, 65–83, 101, 103–4, 109–11, 113, 138, 146, 156, 158, 164, 196

Unpublished book manuscripts: "Uncle Saccharine," 208; "The Wilderness Llamas," 208

McCann, Isabella (daughter), 97–98, 113

McCann, John Michael (son), 99

McCann, Sally McGonigle (mother), 4, 166

McCann, Sean (father), ix, 13, 15, 26, 152, 165–66, 189; *Goals for Glory*, 13, 165; *The Irish in Love*, 13; *The Wit of Brendan Behan*, 13; *The Wit of Oscar Wilde*, 13

McCarthy, Charlie, 98

McCarthy, Cormac, 27

McCloskey, Molly, 22

McCool, Finn, 7

McCourt, Frank, 8, 64, 185–86, 189; *Angela's Ashes*, 8

McEwan, Ian, 90, 128, 209; *Amsterdam*, 209; *Atonement*, 128; *On Chesil Beach*, 209

McGahern, John, 7, 27, 179n30; "Playing with Words," 168

Meade, Declan, x, 13–22, 30–36

Messud, Claire, 90, 102; *The Emperor's Children*, 102